# transatlantic
# disbelonging

# transatlantic disbelonging

Unruliness, Pleasure, and Play in
Nigerian Diasporic Women's Art

BIMBOLA AKINBOLA

Duke University Press   *Durham and London*   2025

Printed in the United States of America on acid-free paper ∞
Project Editor: Bird Williams
Designed by Courtney Leigh Richardson
Typeset in Garamond Premier Pro by Westchester Publishing Services

Library of Congress Cataloging-in-Publication Data
Names: Akinbola, Bimbola, [date] author.
Title: Transatlantic disbelonging : unruliness, pleasure, and play in
Nigerian diasporic women's art / Bimbola Akinbola.
Description: Durham : Duke University Press, 2025. | Includes
bibliographical references and index.
Identifiers: LCCN 2024057290 (print)
LCCN 2024057291 (ebook)
ISBN 9781478032533 (paperback)
ISBN 9781478029199 (hardcover)
ISBN 9781478061410 (ebook)
Subjects: LCSH: Arts, Nigerian—21st century—Themes, motives. |
Belonging (Social psychology) in art. | Other (Philosophy) in art. |
Women artists.
Classification: LCC NX.6.N5 A42 2025 (print)
LCC NX589.6.N5 (ebook)
DDC 700.82—dc23/eng/20250531
LC record available at https://lccn.loc.gov/2024057290
LC ebook record available at https://lccn.loc.gov/2024057291

Cover art: ruby onyinyechi amanze. *the garden palace and the folly of
innocence*, 2014. 6′8″ x 6′10″. Pencil, ink, pigment, enamel, photo transfers,
spray paint. Courtesy the artist.

To all the mothers and the aunties, past, present, and future.

# Contents

# Preface

When I dream of my mom, we're almost always in her store. Sometimes we're together; more often, I'm anxiously watching the glass door while she runs an errand, eagerly awaiting her return before a customer walks in. In my dreams, her store, Batik Arts, becomes a mix of my own childhood memories and details from one of my favorite photos of her. In the photo, she is standing behind a cluttered glass showcase with a *Forbes* magazine, a card reader, and a small rack holding necklaces and bracelets. On the shelves next to her stands a colorful display of bags: Some are knockoff designer brands while others are handmade African designs. My mom looks young and optimistic, a curator and saleswoman confidently wearing a hot pink, purple, and turquoise shirt tucked into white shorts. Her lips are slightly parted like she's in the middle of talking, which she almost always was.

Batik Arts, which my younger brother and I just called "The Store," was my earliest lesson in diasporic homemaking—the practice of settling and dwelling critical to diasporic community formation—that is at the heart of this book. My parents opened the storefront at 816 East Broadway in 1989, when I was about one year old. While I usually say I was born and raised in Columbia, Missouri, it would be more accurate to say I was born and raised in Batik Arts. According to my mom, she was the one who taught my dad how to batik. Remixing the traditional tie-die and *adire* textile dyeing methods she had learned as a young artist in her hometown of Abeokuta, Nigeria, my mom and dad collaborated to create one-of-a-kind wearable art on Fruit of the Loom T-shirts purchased from the local Walmart. After just over a year selling their designs at craft festivals and consignment shops throughout mid-Missouri, they decided to take the leap and open a store of their own. They were two young artists and recent graduates struggling to find employment, and Batik Arts offered the possibility of financial stability. Using a mix of immersion and direct application methods, their designs reflected the bold color combinations of the 1980s and 1990s and featured eye-catching geometric shapes and zigzags. They were all finished with the same looping signature: "Akinbola."

As the store steadily grew, it eventually relocated to a larger location at 1025 East Walnut, which consisted of a storefront, an office space, and a large studio in the back where my dad ran a nonprofit called Arts for Income—an initiative focused on helping artists gain the skills to earn a living from their art—and it drew all sorts of people to the store. Like the artists showcased in this book, my father was also committed to exploring the relationship between artmaking and reimagining one's life and future. Around this time, my mom began carrying everything—from jewelry made in Central America, South America, and Asia to sculptures and fabrics from all over Africa. The walls were covered with Fang Ngil masks from Gabon, Luba masks from Congo, and mud cloth from Mali. She would purchase many of these goods from her merchant, Bunja, who would visit the store a few times a year, pulling up to the curb in his banged-up white van where they would haggle for hours.

My mom's obituary reads, "Batik Arts was a pillar in downtown Columbia, Missouri for 15 years. The store, which was also briefly a cafe, attracted people from all backgrounds, from bikers to southern hippies, with whom Mrs. Akinbola seamlessly cultivated vibrant friendships." Indeed, the combination of one-of-a-kind wearable art and textiles, jewelry, sculptures from all over the world, and my mom's warm welcome to all who entered set Batik Arts apart from anywhere else in Columbia. The Store primarily attracted three groups of people: (1) counterculture Missourians with a global awareness, (2) people wanting to be somewhere that reminded them of home, and (3) people who wanted to be near other people who didn't quite fit in anywhere else.

If you stopped by my mom's store on any given afternoon, you would find her sitting in a (technically for sale) intricately carved wooden chair, likely eating lunch (Hunan chicken with extra rice) from the Chinese restaurant up the street, or drinking a Coke and chewing Double Bubble. Sometimes her soap operas would be playing on the small staticky TV sitting in the corner. She would make conversation with anyone. She had the gift of gab in a way that could be initially surprising before becoming overwhelming, and then somewhat comforting and amusing. Over the course of her days, she was visited by friends who were sometimes customers and customers who turned into friends.

Though there were many Nigerian uncles and aunties we saw outside of the store—for Nigerian Independence Day, baby christenings, and birthdays—

there was something about the way people gathered at my mom's store that seemed to lack the pretense and performance I witnessed everywhere else. As an adolescent, I was surrounded by messages that my value lay in being a "good Nigerian girl," and I was regularly scolded and quietly shamed for failing in this regard. Good Nigerian girls understood *and* spoke their mother tongue. Good Nigerian girls did well at school, but they didn't do too many extracurriculars so they could stay home and serve their parents. Good Nigerian girls were quiet and responded with "Yes, ma" and "No, ma." Good Nigerian girls cooked rice and stew for their siblings. Good Nigerian girls knelt to greet elders and never received things with their left hand. Good Nigerian girls were to become good Nigerian women who got married and had good Nigerian babies. But at the store, among the eclectic mix of objects and people I encountered day to day, this cultural essentialism and exceptionalism fell away. I was allowed to exist beyond just being a good Nigerian girl, and I was allowed to watch my mother exist beyond simply being a good Nigerian woman.

In that space, my mom was first and foremost an artist. An artist who brought traditional Nigerian textile treatments to T-shirts. An artist who brought people together in unique and unexpected configurations. An artist who curated the new and the old, the American and the international, for consumers who wandered in off the streets of Columbia, Missouri. There wasn't just one way to be at her store. It was just people who liked being there and liked being around my mom. The community was unique to the space, and the relationships were significant and consistent. The store became a place of communing and belonging—where people laughed, gossiped, and decompressed after long days at work. At the store, which became a sanctuary of sorts, you could (for the most part) just be.

At some point in the 1990s, my parents decided to open a café in the front of Batik Arts. The menu featured an eclectic mix of vegetarian Egusi stew, jollof rice, and my dad's "famous to us" chili. The customers loved it. For a time, they would host open mic nights on Thursdays—their first intentional attempt at creating a space for community to gather. In another facet of their diasporic homemaking, they created a new home for themselves and others by blending the foods and sounds they loved from Nigeria with those they had more recently fallen in love with in the States.

It was here at Batik Arts in downtown Columbia where my attraction to "outsiderness" began, surrounded by warm, kindhearted weirdos who validated everything I didn't like about myself simply by being adults who weren't ashamed to be different. The Store's location likely played a huge factor in curating the clientele. In our town of 100,000 people, the downtown was the only real walkable commercial center (with the exception of the indoor mall), and it was connected to our mostly suburban landscape by the passably basic bus system. So downtown became a hub, of sorts, for all kinds of people. My mom's customers were the first queer and trans people I ever encountered. I also met people estranged from their families, neurodivergent folks, and those navigating mental illness, though I didn't know it at the time. They were artists and writers and activists. Many of them were immigrants, and some were undocumented.

At Batik Arts, there was somehow something for everyone who entered. It was this eclectic and kind community who taught me that belonging was available to those on the "outside"—you just had to create it.

At The Store, I, too, learned to create worlds where I belonged—drawing everything under the sun, writing stories, making up dances with the girl whose mom owned an antique store at the corner, and playing pretend with my brother for hours on end. For me, The Store was a world within a world, and it was made possible through the things we made with our hands.

After my mom died, when I googled "Batik Arts" and "Anthonia Akinbola" in "Columbia, MO," I expected to see the many articles and news stories that were written about the space during the fifteen years it was in business. But nothing came up. My/our memory of The Store lives in photographs and yellowed newspaper clippings saved by my dad and, of course, in the hearts and minds of the many people who passed time there.

And this is the nature of home and community: powerful and life-saving but ultimately fleeting.

I first encountered courage and experimentation in diasporic space at my mom's store. This book is dedicated to the outsiders who have created and navigated new worlds of belonging with the same spirit.

# Acknowledgments

I could not have written this book without the overflowing insight, love, and support I received from my expansive community.

I am first and foremost grateful to ruby onyinyechi amanze, Njideka Akuny-ili Crosby, Taiwo Aiyedogbon, Nnedi Okorafor, Wura-Natasha Ogunji, Zina Saro-Wiwa and the countless other incredible Nigerian women artists who inspired this project. I have learned so much from your fearless and unapologetic artmaking.

The first rumblings of this project began during my time as an undergraduate at Macalester College. Thank you to Duchess Harris, Karín Aguilar-San Juan, and Jane Rhodes in the American Studies Department for radically changing my educational trajectory. You introduced me to a discipline that made everything I wanted to do possible. I am also deeply indebted to the Mellon Mays Undergraduate Fellowship Program, which paved the way for me to imagine a life in academia. Peter Rachleff and Joanna Inglot: There are no words for how deeply grateful I am for your mentorship. Thank you for your gentle but stern guidance, for introducing me to artists and activists who changed my thinking, for telling me over and over again that there was a place for my work in the academy. This book exists because you saw the potential in nineteen-year-old me.

I am deeply beholden to my cohort and the colleagues and collaborators I met at the University of Maryland, where this book was born: Ilyas Abukar, Stephanie Akoumany, A. Anthony, Tatiana Benjamin, Darius Bost, Michael Casiano, Jason Ezell, Eve Grice, Doug Ishii, Sine Hwang Jensen, Tiffany King, Jaime Madden, Izetta Autumn Mobley, Ashley Minner, Cristina Jo Pérez, Tony Perry, Merle Rogers, Paul Saiedi, Tony Perry, Michelé Prince-Rizzo, Jessica Kenyatta Walker, Kevin Winstead, Terrance Wooten, Gabriel Peoples, and Kalima Young. It was a joy and a privilege to be a part of such a dynamic and academic community. Tony, Jessica, and Cristina: As I have developed this manuscript, I am particularly indebted to you three. Our writing sessions and conversations have expanded my thinking in unimaginable ways, made me laugh so hard I cried, and reminded me how important this work is. Thank you for sharing your genius, for your feedback on early drafts, for your encouragement, and most importantly, for your friendship. To my advisor Mary Corbin Sies: Thank you for the many times you asked me to articulate why this project mattered. Your dedication to your students and your rigorous advising continues to be an inspiration and a model. To my co-chair Renée Ater: I am so grateful for all you have taught me about the importance of slow, deep looking. It has transformed how I approach all of my work and undoubtedly made the book stronger. To the rest of my committee Psyche Williams-Forson, Michelle V. Rowley and Faedra Carpenter: Thank you for your steady support and for asking the hard questions that radically changed my approach and rejuvenated my scholarly spirit. Your mentorship was invaluable as I developed the earliest iteration of this project.

While in graduate school, laughter-filled reunions with my Mellon family at the Mellon Mays Graduate Student Summer Conferences and other convenings throughout the year got me through the most challenging parts of my early academic training. I am especially grateful to, Kimberly Juanita Brown, Nikki Green, and Uri Mcmillan for your mentorship and guidance.

To those I met through the Dance Exchange—MK Abadoo, John Borstel, Matthew Cumbie, Tyler French, Isaac Gómez, Sam Horning, Elizabeth Johnson, Liz Lerman, Cassie Meador, Silvia Roberts, and so many others: Thank you for being an intellectual and creative home and for showing me what it meant to take the body seriously as a site of theory, history, and possibility. You have each pushed me to grow as an artist and an educator in ways I never could have imagined.

My time at Northwestern, first as a Black Arts Initiative postdoctoral fellow and then as an assistant professor in the Performance Studies Department, has been beyond anything I could have hoped for in an academic appointment. To my colleagues (past and present) in Performance Studies and beyond—Chris Abani, Scottie Akines, Masi Asare, Dotun Ayobade, Lori D. Barcliff Baptista, Moya Bailey, Danielle Bainbridge, Marquis Bey, Melissa Blanco Borelli, Kent Brooks, Antawan Byrd, Gianna Carter, Aymar Jean Christian, Huey Copeland, Thomas DeFrantz, Marcela Fuentes, K. R. Cornett, D. Soyini Madison, Justin Mann, Zoe McDaniel, Patricia Nguyen, Nadine George-Graves, Lakshmi Padmanabhan, Mary Pattillo, Miriam Petty, Natsu Onoda Power, Ariel Rogers, Shayna Silverstein, Elizabeth Son, Nicole Spigner, Nitasha Tamar Sharma,

Krista Thompson, Cristal Truscott, Dina Walters, Ivy Wilson, and Mary Zimmerman and so many others—I am so fortunate to work with such remarkable artists and scholars. Thank you for your kindness, your curiosity, and your tenacity.

E. Patrick Johnson and Ramón Rivera-Servera, thank you for believing in my work, welcoming me with open arms, and advocating on my behalf. Josh Chambers-Letson, you have been such a kind, open, honest, and encouraging guiding light since I arrived at Northwestern. Thank you for making this path less scary and more joyful.

Teaching has offered an incredible opportunity to think through many of the theories and schools of thought that shaped this book. To the students who took my Migration, Exile, and Return, Black Feminist Performance, and Queer|African|Bodies courses: Your authenticity, intellectual courage, and difficult questions kept me on my toes and excited about this work. Thank you.

I would be remiss if I didn't name the brilliant individuals all over the country, who have come to make up my broader intellectual community. Thank you, Lanice Avery, M. Aziz, Marlon Bailey, Maia Butler, Kyrah Daniels, Freda Fair, Mohwanah Fetus, Kareem Khubchandani, Moyo Okediji, Jasmine Mahmoud, Jeffrey McCune, Jennifer Nash, Danielle Roper, Sarah Stefana, Kantara Souffrant, Hilary Tackie, Tara Aisha Willis, and Tsione Wolde-Michael. Your deep wisdom, encouragement, invitations to speak, thoughtful questions, and kindness have nourished me and shaped my understanding of what a life in academia could be in profound ways. And to Kyera Singleton, who has been there since the very beginning, when we became friends on Facebook the summer before our freshman year at Macalester College, I did not know you would stay by my side for the next nearly two decades as we both discovered what it meant to not only survive but center joy while living the life of the mind. I am so grateful to have you as a sister, friend and thought-partner. It has been an absolute gift and blessing to be on this journey with you.

The ACLS/Getty postdoctoral fellowship gave me the time and space to both grieve in the aftermath of my mother's passing and to finish this book. I am so grateful for the four days we spent at the Getty sharing work and imagining new possibilities within the discipline of art history.

This manuscript has benefited from the generous feedback of many reviewers, both anonymous and known, for whom I am deeply grateful. Early chapters appeared in *Text and Performance Quarterly* and *Women Studies Quarterly*; thanks to the editors of these journals and to the anonymous peer reviewers who supported the development of these early drafts. Thank you, Kemi Adeyemi and Hershini Bhana Young, for your invaluable offerings during my book manuscript workshop. Thank you, especially, to the anonymous peer reviewers at Duke University Press. Your collective rigorous engagement with my ideas and your tough questions made the project so much stronger.

To my editor at Duke, Courtney Berger and her team, thank you for believing in this project. Working with you has been an absolute delight. I'm also very grateful to Elena Abbott, Cathy Hannabach and Megan Milks, and Stephanie Ward for your thoughtful developmental editing and copyediting: You kept me writing when I felt the most stuck.

There have been so many people who have kept me afloat in big and small ways while I worked on this book. I love you and appreciate each and every one of you. Thank you for the phone calls, the sweet postcards and care packages, the weekly meditations, the silly memes, the delicious meals, the visits to my city, the late nights out dancing, the cozy living room hangs. Thank for you for loving, supporting, and celebrating me. I absolutely could not have done this without you all.

To Angela, Emily, Jamila, and Kyera, my harpies, who I learned to think and dream with: You make life so much sweeter.

Melissa, thank you for the last twenty years of sisterhood and profound friendship. I am so grateful for your unconditional love and support, for all of the times you copyedited papers and dissertation chapters, and for your podcast-length voice memos. You have kept me sane and grounded during the toughest times.

To my niblings Diana, River, and Freddie: I love being your auntie/titi. Thank you for being a beacon of hope. May you model the work of freedom and never stop dreaming new worlds.

I wish my mom, Anthonia Olusola Akinbola nee Macjob, could have been here to witness this book in its final form. She was my first example of disbelonging in action. I am so grateful to her for modeling what it looked like to make a living as an artist and to truly be in community. Dad, thank you for modeling critical thinking and global citizenship to me from a young age. You were the first one who taught me about the power and possibility of being in diaspora. Bunmi, thank you for being my one and only lifelong partner in diaspora, as well as for understanding the struggle and illuminating its beauty with your laughter. You inspire me.

Elise, your support has kept me grounded, soft, and smiling. Thank you for always seeing me and believing in me. You know, perhaps better than anyone, what this process has demanded and you have held me through it all. Your presence in my life makes everything possible.

# Introduction

DISBELONGING: A STRATEGY FOR
OUR COLLECTIVE SURVIVAL

*Transatlantic Disbelonging: Unruliness, Pleasure, and Play in Nigerian Diasporic Women's Art* foregrounds the work of contemporary artists navigating disparate geographies, allegiances, and identities and examines how they resist popular understandings of what has been deemed proper conduct for women in Nigeria and its diaspora—a process I call "disbelonging." The book asks how the creative work of Nigerian diasporic artists speaks to the ways black diasporic women theorize their subjectivity through the practice of disbelonging. Specifically, I examine how these women embrace and employ anti-respectability, taboo, queerness, and play to reimagine and resist oppressive colonial legacies and expectations pertaining to gender, sexuality, and national belonging in Nigerian and Nigerian-adjacent contexts.

While much of the scholarship on diaspora has focused on the loss of home and yearning for belonging, the creative work of performance and mixed-media artists, filmmakers, and writers such as Wura-Natasha Ogunji, Njideka Akunyili

Crosby, Zina Saro-Wiwa, ruby onyinyechi amanze, and Nnedi Okorafor tells a different story. Each of these women artists, a term I use to encompass the vast array of artistic and creative production they are engaged in, has made significant contributions within the Nigerian diaspora's recent creative industry boom. Their diverse experiences as cultural outsiders, I suggest, have offered them the freedom to create home and define belonging on their own terms. Using visual art, performance and video art, and interviews with the artists as my guides, I consider how their works embrace their own ambivalence toward familial, cultural, and national belonging in Nigeria and its diaspora, as they redefine middle-class Nigerian womanhood. *Transatlantic Disbelonging* argues that for these women artists, their artmaking is an act of homemaking that creates opportunities to unsettle oppressive conceptualizations of community and family and embrace a range of affective tensions.

## Disbelonging

Disbelonging as a practice reminds us that trauma isn't the only story there is to tell about being in dispersal. It instead asks us to consider what is gained for individuals who exist on the margins of their communities? Ogunji, Akunyili Crosby, Saro-Wiwa, amanze, and Okorafor resist neocolonial notions of middle-class respectability or morality by locating themselves in the full, complex pre- and postcolonial social and cultural history of Nigeria. Disbelonging as a concept offers language for thinking through how marginal subjects use their anti-respectable positionalities—as displaced, as "lost," as too hybrid to belong in just one place—as a mode of self-fashioning, which gives them a platform from which to challenge oppressive ideologies and envision new ways of relating. Not only normalizing but also embracing disbelonging as a way to orient oneself within and in relation to community pushes back on the deep-seated belief that the feeling of alienation is equal to cultural obliteration, when in fact alienation can serve as fertile ground for connection and possibility.

The idea of disbelonging has largely been used to describe a range of feelings and experiences antagonistic to belonging. [1] Cultural worker Arielle Julia Brown, for example, describes how site-specific black performance resists the contested narratives of disbelonging that stem from displacement and gentrification.[2] Roberto Bedoya follows this line of thinking in his discussion of the politics of creative placemaking, writing, "If Creative Placemaking activities support the politics of disbelonging through acts of gentrification, racism, real estate speculation, all in the name of neighborhood revitalization, then it betrays the democratic ideal of having an equitable and just civil society."[3] In these examples, disbelonging describes the actions that make places uninhabitable for marginalized communities by intentionally displacing them. Yet, when applying the concept of disbelonging to diaspora, the vast majority of the many articles and essays that use the term *neglect* to explicitly define it. The term is generally used to describe a universally known and externally imposed condition rather than an act or position one might strategically embrace.[4]

In this book, I develop the concept of disbelonging to describe the ambivalent relationship between alienation and belonging. Disbelonging in this project refers to the ways Nigerian women artists use their art to remix, recode, and queer normative and coercive conceptualizations of cultural and national belonging in order to revel in the liberatory potential of their liminal diasporic positionalities. Their works depict visual and literary landscapes where women move freely through time and space, take on hybrid and nonhuman forms, and unapologetically embody contradiction.

*Transatlantic Disbelonging* considers how women artists metabolize and redress narratives of loss and displacement by illuminating the generative potential of disbelonging—space for diasporic subjects to embody complex and often taboo ways of being. In *Territories of the Soul: Queered Belonging in the Black Diaspora*, Nadia Ellis speaks of the productive tension between "a desire to belong and a desire to flee the strictures of ground and community," noting that this tension is often marked by frustration and failure.[5] However, Ellis embraces this failure with ease, noting that in these instances, failure becomes an indication of a utopian reach. I take this failure as a jumping off point. Rather than work toward remedying feelings of alienation stemming from trauma and loss by performing hegemonic belonging or embracing antisocial ways of being, disbelonging is a strategy and viewpoint that interrupts colonial shame. Instead, it embraces anti-respectability as a critical tool in the cultivation of alternate belongings for diasporic subjects, particularly women. As Tavia Nyong'o clarifies, "Redress differs from reparation in that it is not a compensation for a loss—loss is immeasurable—but is rather an articulation of that loss."[6] Disbelonging articulates and embraces diasporic loss by considering how these artists stand firmly within their identities as women connected to the place presently called Nigeria, while refusing to be contained by prescriptive notions of the type of belonging they ought to desire or how they might perform it.

Notably, my use of *disbelonging* is inspired by José Muñoz's theory of disidentification, which describes the ways marginalized queer communities resist the dominant culture's "politics of impossibility" by appropriating and recycling components of that dominant culture in ways that reflect and celebrate their own uniqueness. Muñoz writes, "Disidentification is meant to be descriptive of the survival strategies the minority subject practices in order to negotiate a phobic majoritarian public sphere that continuously elides or punishes the existence of those who do not conform to normative citizenship."[7] My theorization of disbelonging speaks to how the artists I highlight embrace the erotic, privilege experimentation and play, and cultivate queer social bonds in order to tell new stories about what it means to be part of a diaspora, imagine alternative embodiments, and cross psychic borders. This allows them to elude the constraints and rigid expectations of geographic borders, citizenship, and nation.

Disbelonging also builds upon the work of Gayatri Gopinath, who locates the queer female subject as "a crucial point of departure in theorizing diaspora."[8] Gopinath examines queer South Asian diasporic texts that are more interested in remaking "home" from within than in leaving it for a more liberatory place. I extend Gopinath's theorizing to discussions of women in the Nigerian diaspora, exploring performance, video installation, drawing, and literature as sites of diasporic dwelling—a practice in a type of diasporic homemaking. The acts of homemaking and home dismantling are central to the practice of disbelonging, which requires diasporic subjects to engage in an iterative and unruly practice of creating home. Moreover, the alienation stemming from the impossibility of the unruly diasporic subject becomes the fertile ground for new types of belonging.[9] Tina Campt describes diasporic homemaking as "practices that are critical to diasporic formation yet frequently overshadowed by an emphasis on diasporic mobility."[10] Looking to photographic representations of domesticity, Campt argues that these images enact diasporic homemaking by emphasizing settling, dwelling, and rootedness, counteracting studies of diasporic migration that overwhelmingly focus on movement. I expand diasporic homemaking to include the act of creating home *within* the artistic works themselves. In the works I examine, the artists engage in a continuous practice of building and dismantling sites where diasporic belonging is practiced, rather than a point of arrival. This practice troubles the reification of the nation-state and the family, for instance, as the only sites where diasporic subjects create home and find belonging. Instead, it envisions the work of art as a dwelling and gathering place.

On Queerness

In his essay "Africa: Queer: Anthropology," Keguro Macharia critiques the anthropological lens that has framed how African studies has approached queerness, writing: "I could not seem to escape anthropology when I turned to

Africa—obligatory reminder, I am not an Africanist. I could not escape how it mapped place and belonging (tribe, ethnicity, clan, kinship); how it marked temporality and being (savage, primitive, undeveloped, underdeveloped, global south); how it marked African knowledge (proverbs, sayings, indigenous wisdom, elders, sages); how it marked African intimacies (kinship, ritual, initiation); how it marked African encounters with modernity (acculturation, loss, deracination); how it kept shuttling between 'tradition' and 'modernity.' I found—I find—all of this stifling and unimaginative and boring." Here, Macharia names how anthropology's focus on colonial categorizations and binaries has limited our understanding of how these categories have never been stable or separate. Macharia looks to queer theory in order to think through what it means to be estranged from these categories and allow ourselves to explore uncharted waters. As he writes, "We would do well to construct queer theory . . . less as the site of what we communally want than as the want of any communal site. Queer theory is no one's safe harbor for the holidays; it should offer no image of home."[11] I position disbelonging as a particularly queer way of being in community, one that destabilizes the categories named by Macharia. While these categories have been used to flatten how African diasporic communities are described, I instead look to the ways labor, affect, and imagination commingle to create fleeting communal sites of belonging—sites that are continuously reimagined and reinvented.

Gopinath argues that attaching *queer* to *diaspora* attends to the practices and subjectivities that have been invisibilized within conventional diaspora and nationalist imaginaries. She writes: "The concept of a queer South Asian diaspora, then, functions on multiple levels. . . . First, in situating the formation of sexual subjectivity within transnational flows of culture, capital, bodies, desire, and labor. Second, queer diaspora contests the logic that situates the terms 'queer' and 'diaspora' as dependent on the originality of 'heterosexuality' and 'nation.' Finally, it disorganizes the dominant categories within the United States for sexual variance, namely 'gay and lesbian,' and it marks a different economy of desire that escapes legibility within both normative South Asian contexts and homo-normative Euro-American contexts."[12] Here, *queer* refers to a range of dissenting and nonheteronormative practices and desires that may or may not fall within sexual identity categories such as lesbian, gay, or bisexual. In this project, then, I use *queer* to describe the gap between the artists I discuss and the myths surrounding nation and womanhood. To borrow the words of Gopinath, "Queerness here does not so much bravely or heroically refuse the normative, the way it appears to in some narratives of queer subjectivity, as much as it names the impossibility of normativity for racialized subjects marked by histories of violent dispossession."[13] The works of these artists show the ways in which their living, breathing diasporic bodies are perpetually at odds with the rigid systems, categories, and identities designed to hold them captive.

Though I use the words *community* and *home* throughout this book, they are as troubled among these pages as they are in my own lived experience. Miranda Joseph's and Zygmunt Bauman's critiques of community, as well as Carol B. Stack's and Michelle V. Rowley's meditations on home, have contributed to my thinking about the complications and limitations of community and home. Joseph writes, "Community is almost always invoked as an unequivocal good, and indicator of high quality of life, a life of human understanding, caring, selflessness, belonging."[14] And yet this is often not the full story, as communities also require members to make sacrifices in order to make their belonging legible. To this point Bauman writes: "There is a price to be paid for the privilege of 'being in a community'—and it is inoffensive or even invisible only as long as the community stays in the dream. The price is paid in the currency of freedom, variously called 'autonomy,' 'right to self-assertion,' 'right to be yourself.' Whatever you choose, you gain some, you lose some. Missing community means missing security; gaining community if it happens, would soon mean missing freedom."[15]

The idea of home is equally implicated in these logics, as Stack writes: "Home is a hard fact, not just a souvenir of restless memory, and for the people I know who made the journey away and back, home is in a hard land—hard to explain, hard to make a living in, hard to swallow."[16] Rowley similarly asserts that "the idea of 'home' becomes (remains) a place where we have no guarantee of safety, a place where we may at times have to make peace with a sense of feeling unsafe."[17] It is this anticipated denial or loss of the freedom, understanding, and safety associated with home that the artists I discuss work to resist and creatively circumvent.

Numerous stories chronicle the pervasive disappointment felt when descendants of the transatlantic slave trade return to the African continent only to find the same complicated feelings of nonbelonging they experienced in the United States.[18] While the contentiousness of community has been taken up by a number of scholars in Black studies, there is a tension between this knowledge and the romanticization of the type of belonging that is speculated to have been experienced by Africans before colonization and to exist today for those "who never left."[19] In exploring the experience of Nigerian diasporas, this book also asks how these theories are complicated by the work of artists like

Akunyili Crosby, Saro-Wiwa, and amanze who take up questions of community, family, and kin for those born on Nigerian soil.

## Methods

This book has grown from my deep investment in understanding the creative choice-making and methods used by these artists to help them navigate their complex identities as artists and as black diasporic women. The goal is not to evaluate or critique the success or failure of the artists and the works I analyze. Instead, I identify the tools and tactics utilized by these artists for their survival and attend to art as a theory-making practice. *Transatlantic Disbelonging* argues that methodologically foregrounding the cultural production of these artists provides us with a strong framework for mapping, visualizing, rethinking, and redefining diaspora as a series of processes that produce a certain type of subjectivity. Moreover, while I occasionally discuss reception as it relates to the experience of the performers, I am more concerned with the significance of the works of art and performances for the makers.

This book makes four key interventions. First, I foreground the role of visual art, performance art, film, and literature in producing some of the most acutely instructive theorizations of how black women experience and embody diaspora.

Second, this project complicates discussions that reduce diasporic flows within, to, and from the African continent to an antagonistic relationship between the local and the diaspora. The artists discussed in *Transatlantic Disbelonging* highlight how these categories fail to capture the complexity and nuance of Nigerian identity, as I examine how the categories of local and diaspora ideologically and aesthetically shape one another.

Third, I center women in conversations about migration, expatriation, and return, acknowledging that we cannot talk about diaspora and belonging without considering how gender and sexuality shape these experiences. I argue that national belonging for black diasporic women is always contested, and I use disbelonging to think through how diasporic women use outsiderness and the experience of "going against one's culture" as a position from which to aspire toward attaining freedom from nationalist, familial, and cultural expectations and sexual regulation. I don't mean for my use of *freedom* here to imply something uncomplicated or uncontested, particularly for black women. Still, it is a guiding light throughout this book, and the longing for it is reflected in each pencil stroke, gesture, and word. As Joshua Chambers-Letson states,

"Freedom, within liberalism, is an impossibility—a cruel joke or what Lauren Berlant describes as cruel optimism. . . . And, still, freedom is that which we cannot not want."[20]

Lastly, I seek to contribute to African diasporic visual and performance art history by expanding the canon of Nigerian diasporic artists beyond the few, primarily male, artists who are taught in every African art survey.

*Transatlantic Disbelonging* takes an interdisciplinary and multimethods approach to questions of national belonging, desire, and diasporic homemaking as an act of resistance and historical reinterpretation. My conceptual treatment of diaspora, reimagining of belonging, and centering of aesthetic practices has been shaped and energized by scholarly work emerging from African, African diaspora, and Black studies; South Asian studies; American studies; women, gender, and sexuality studies; art history; and performance studies. Here I practice disbelonging by refusing to restrict belonging to any one discipline, instead embracing the many, and at times contradictory, schools of thought that I am indebted to.

I deploy the methods of visual analysis, interviews, and literary analysis to consider the works of art from numerous vantage points, particularly as they relate to their creators and social contexts. My methods of visual analysis are similarly hybrid, combining formal analysis, sociohistorical and cultural contextual analysis, and the words of the artists themselves. My decision to include the intentions of the artists alongside my own readings of their works is inspired by the work of art historians Cherise Smith, Renée Ater, and Margo Machida.[21] Citing the work of Sidonie Smith and Julia Watson, Smith argues that autobiographical writing is a "significant site where women assert and give form to their subjectivities, revise concepts of women's life issues, and make visible formerly invisible topics."[22] She positions the writing of artists as being more than "inextricably linked" to their performances, but performances in and of themselves. Moreover, Ater contends that "one deeply troubling aspect of critical theory's insistence on an unknowable subject is that too often it renders men and women of color invisible in art historical texts and excludes them from the construction of art history."[23]

In a project specifically concerned with how women tell their own stories, I argue that it is methodologically critical to consider the multiple sites where these artists produce meaning about their artmaking practice, including articles, interviews, and personal blog posts. Moreover, arguing that a work of art is "an intentional manifestation of mind," and that the meanings embedded in cross-ethnic and intercultural work are rarely transparent, Machida advocates for scholars of art practicing interpretation as a collaborative act with the artist when possible.[24] Machida's assertion resists notions that when deciphering a work of art "the human subject is unknowable, decentered, and dispersed" and that anyone should be able to fully interpret a successful work of art with no input from the artist.[25] She contends that for racialized subjects doing cross-ethnic and intercultural work, the meanings behind their work are not intended to be deciphered easily, and a full and nuanced understanding comes through collaboration with the artists.

The meanings I draw and extrapolate upon come from a combination of formal analysis and my own observations, as well as the knowledge gathered from my correspondence with several of the artists and their public offerings about their work. Together, they offer a multifaceted perspective of the myriad ways their art speaks to the themes of gendered diasporic experience and belonging. Here I embrace Dwight Conquergood's theory of "co-performative witnessing," inspired by Frederick Douglass, who "instead of reading textual accounts of slavery, recommended a riskier hermeneutics of experience, relocation, copresence, humility and vulnerability."[26] As D. Soyini Madison asserts, "Co-performative witnessing is to live in and spend time in the borderlands of contested identities where you speak 'with' not 'to' others and where your (and their) ethnographic interlocutors are as co-temporal in the report and on stage as they were in the field."[27] Through this project, Ogunji, Akunyili Crosby, Saro-Wiwa, amanze, and Okorafor become collaborators in theorizing diaspora and, as such, are positioned alongside African women scholars and activists as my theoretical interlocutors.

I bring to this project my own experiences and curiosities as a second-generation American of Nigerian descent, an artist, and a scholar who has grappled with the stories I was told about Nigeria and what my belonging in a diasporic context was supposed to look and feel like through my own artmaking and through experiencing the art made by other diasporic artists. My interest in using art also stems from my own scholarly investments in centering the visual as a powerful lens through which to study and theorize the slippery affective and everyday experience of diaspora. In this project, although I am theorizing about ways of seeing and being seen, intimacy, and community, I am also very much writing about seemingly insurmountable loneliness and alienation and what it means to sit with it, work with it, and attempt to transform it.

It feels necessary to name the complicated, and at times transactional, nature of some of my interactions with my interlocutors: interviews in bars, over the phone, via email, and over Zoom in the midst of a pandemic; scheduling mishaps, last minute cancellations, and full-on ghosting. I once met an artist at an art opening for the first time after months of correspondence, and we barely spoke the whole night. And then there's the embarrassment of making a joke that doesn't quite land or sharing an experience that your fellow diasporan cannot relate to at all. These are the affective remains of disbelonging, which creates space for moving beyond and through disappointment, opening the possibility for us to meet on our own terms, rather than merely as ideas. This research has taught me that there is no such thing as a "community of the disbelonged." Rather, there are bids for connection and fleeting moments where these bids are successful.[28] I don't share this to discount the beautiful work that has been written about queer, intimate, and transcendent forms of ethnography that blur the lines between researcher and interlocutor to allow for a new type of radical intimacy. Though this has not necessarily been my experience with all the artists I met while conducting this research, this project has also gifted me many opportunities to be witnessed and to witness others in profound ways. But more importantly, this project is about how art exceeds, magnifies, and multiplies our limited offerings as humans. How it speaks, connects, and throws a life raft when community is hard. When I refer to belonging as "fleeting," I am referring to the spontaneous shared laughter during an interview, or magically making eye contact over Zoom, or emailing back and forth about a performance art idea with one of my interlocutors. These moments say nothing about what has come before or what will come after and, through this project, I have learned that sometimes this is all we can hope for, and maybe that can be enough.

### Notes on My Uses of *Diaspora*

This book calls into question the construction of diasporas and how we understand them and disrupts the ways they have been homogenized, pointing to the deep complexity and range of experiences that exist within these dispersed global communities. Although the artists whom I write about are technically situated within what we call the Nigerian diaspora, their experiences are deeply varied. Moreover, each of these artists uses their art to speak to a wider diasporic community as they consider how their blackness and gender identities shape, inform, and disrupt their lived realities in all the places they attempt to call home. I ask: What about a nation presumes a shared experience, and why do we take this approach when talking about diaspora? What is revealed when we allow the nuance of diaspora to unfold? In *Black Europe and the African Diaspora*, Alexander Weheliye writes: "Diaspora offers pathways that retrace layerings of difference in the aftermath of colonialism and slavery, as well as the effects of other forms of migration and displacement. Thus, diaspora enables the desedimentation of the nation from the 'interior' by taking into account the groups that fail to comply with the reigning definition of the people as a cohesive political subject due to sharing one culture, one race, one language, one religion, and so on, and from the 'exterior' by drawing attention to the movements that cannot be contained by the nation's administrative and ideological borders."[29] Focusing on Nigeria specifically, this project pushes against the falsehood of the Nigerian diaspora as a cohesive political or cultural grouping. I use *diasporic* not as a static signifier, but as a way to describe a particular orientation that looks toward the real and imagined homeland in order to decenter and destabilize the West as the primary locus from which to understand and position oneself.

In "The Uses of Diaspora," Brent Hayes Edwards offers a rich history of how *diaspora* has been used in Black Cultural Studies, beginning with shifts toward internationalism and Pan-Africanism in the 1950s and 1960s.[30] Central in Edwards's genealogy is the work of George Shepperson, credited with being one of the first scholars to consider the limitations of Pan-Africanism and introduce the concept of diaspora into the study of black culture and history. In his essay "African Diaspora: Concept and Context," Shepperson makes a clear distinction between *diaspora* as it has been used to refer to the forced dispersal of Jewish people and "African diaspora," where *diaspora* is used metaphorically. Shepperson argues that while in the Jewish tradition, *galut* implies a forced dispersal, *diaspora* in fact "has always included some form of voluntary exile."[31] Shepperson's emphasis on the metaphorical nature of *diaspora* as it applies to individuals of African descent is key here as it pushes us away from attempting to create a static definition or list of traits to apply to the African diaspora.

Indeed, according to Edwards, diaspora—unlike Pan-Africanism—has the potential to account for the "unavoidable dynamics of difference." Explaining how the meanings and uses of *diaspora* for black scholars have changed between 1970 and 2000, Edwards writes: "Like Pan-Africanism [diaspora] is open to ideological appropriation in a wide variety of political projects, from anticolonial activism to what has long been called 'Black Zionism'—articulations of *diaspora* that collapse the term into versions of nationalism or racial essentialism. Unfortunately, some of the most celebrated work on *diaspora* in the past thirty years has served to undo this complex history of emergence."[32]

Edwards thus addresses how diaspora has often been used to unite black people across the globe, with little consideration for the multitude of ways diaspora has been experienced by black people in different parts of the world. This is particularly relevant when considering the implications that diaspora might have on the African continent.

Edwards also examines the differences between diaspora and the Black Atlantic, arguing that although Paul Gilroy's notion of the Black Atlantic is dependent on the concept of diaspora, Gilroy does not actually define *diaspora*. While this is true, Gilroy's emphasis on the importance of acknowledging creolization, *mestizaje*, and hybridity, or "the processes of cultural mutation and restless (dis) continuity that exceed racial discourse and avoid capture by its agents" has pushed scholarship toward a clearer definition of *diaspora*, as has Stuart Hall's emphasis on "difference" in African diasporic cultural identities.[33] While Hall acknowledges that having a shared past of colonization, slavery, and transportation is significant, he also argues that this does not constitute a common origin, and thus we must pay attention to the particularities of each history.

Hall's conceptualization of difference helps illuminate the importance of analyzing artists who are, at a surface level, part of the same diaspora, but positioned very differently. Details such as how people migrate, when they migrate, why they migrate, if they stay in the host country, and why they choose to return speak magnitudes. For Hall, "The diaspora experience . . . is defined, not by essence or purity, but by the recognition of a necessary heterogeneity and diversity; by a conception of 'identity,' which lives with and through, not despite, difference; by *hybridity*. Diaspora identities are those which are constantly producing and reproducing themselves anew, through transformation and difference."[34] In other words, diaspora is not something that you simply *are*, but rather the process of becoming in the face of difference.

In recent years the label of "New African Diaspora," coined by Isidore Okpewho and Nkiru Nzegwu, has been taken up by scholars of diaspora to specifically identify first- and second-generation African immigrants. Drawing the line between the old and new diaspora, Okpewho writes: "We might begin to understand these relations by characterizing the older diaspora as *precolonial* and the more recent one as *postcolonial*, or by using the demarcation Ali Mazrui has drawn between what he calls the diaspora of enslavement and the diaspora of imperialism."[35]

As the name "New African Diaspora" implies, this framework seems to break from the lineage of diaspora explored by Edwards and Shepperson, and it follows Hall's guidance by tending to the specific differences between the descendants of Africans who were brought to the Americas in bondage and Africans who have migrated as a result of the destruction and "disequilibrium in African societies brought about by the intervention of European colonization."[36] A consideration of these two articulations of *diaspora* allows us to better capture the diverse and nuanced ways imperialism and white supremacy have worked to turn human beings into property while also systemically draining resources from the African continent, decimating the natural environment, and creating a political landscape that has made the continent unrecognizable and unlivable for so many.

While this project does not attempt to conflate the experiences of the descendants of the enslaved and those displaced by colonization, I am interested in how the contentiousness of belonging is presumed to be experienced only by those who were forcefully removed from the continent, and less complicated for immigrants and their descendants due to their "blood ties" to one specific place. Gopinath points out that although slavery and postcolonial displacement are distinct from one another, we must treat them as intimately connected, writing: "Clearly, the traumas and space/time disjunctures precipitated by slavery are distinct from those of indentureship and postcolonial displacement; each of these historical phenomena engenders its own affective ties, traps, and possibilities. At the same time, situating these formations as utterly incommensurate rather than as co-constitutive ignores, in Lisa Lowe's evocative phrase, 'the intimacy of four continents.'"[37]

I seek to name and identify the ways that belonging is not so easily remedied by blood and the meaning we attribute to it, and the ways that colonization and global anti-blackness displace and alienate black people within and from our own homelands, creating a perpetual and existential homelessness, or what Homi K. Bhabha calls "unhomliness," that is mediated only through the creation and embodiment of home.[38] As Frank B. Wilderson III aptly reminds us:

> Lest we think that this force is merely the grammar and ghosts of blacks in the "New" World, that somehow Africans of the twentieth and twenty-first century have an altogether different rebar of ontology, we should note Achille Mbembe's argument that, once Hegel (as a placeholder for all the punishing discourse of the Maafa, or African Holocaust) renders Africa "territorium nullius," "the land of motionless substance and of the blinding, joyful, and tragic disorder of creation," even the African who was not captured was a slave in relation to the rest of the world, his or her freedom from chains and distance from the Middle Passage notwithstanding.[39]

In an effort to capture the heterogeneity and diversity of diaspora, *Transatlantic Disbelonging* contributes to the small but growing body of work on second-generation immigrants and the even smaller field of research focused specifically on how gender and sexuality inform and shape how 1.5- and second-generation African women conceive of and navigate national borders. Two pieces of scholarship on this topic are *Beyond Expectations: Second-Generation Nigerians in the United States and Britain* by Onoso Imoagene and the 2019 special issue titled "Identity and Transnationalism: The New African Diaspora Second Generation in the United States," edited by Kassahun Kebede, in *African and Black Diaspora: An International Journal*. Both consider the contributions of second-generation Africans to both the home and host countries. In *Beyond Expectations*, Imoagene examines the process by which second-generation Nigerians incorporate into United States and British society, and their identity formation processes, via interviews with 150 second-generation adults in Nigeria and Britain. Primarily focusing on how they form multifaceted identities, beyond racialization, she argues that their presence in the black middle class has the potential to change the "largely negative ways black people are viewed and possibly help redefine what it means to be black in both countries."[40] The special issue built on this mission, seeking to contribute to a gap in literature on African immigrants, asserting that, despite its large and growing size, the New African Diaspora's second generation is one of the least studied immigrant groups. The special issue used a variety of case studies to explore what we know about the identity formation of this group and considered new directions in research, primarily focusing on questions of racial identity formation and transnational activities among second-generation African immigrants. In his introduction, Kassahun Kebede—taking a primarily sociological approach—focuses largely on questions about how second-generation African immigrants distinguish themselves from African Americans and serve as bridges between the host and home country. He writes: "The New African Diaspora and their offspring can help revitalize interest in Africa among the historic African diaspora. They may also serve as trans-Atlantic bridge builders, 'as cultural mediators between the continent and its old diaspora, whose communication and knowledge of each other has largely been through the distorted lenses and prejudices of imperialist and racist media.'"[41]

In this quote, Kebede sees a key contribution of the New African Diaspora and their offspring as being one of service to the home country on the continent by serving as bridge builders. Though not explicitly stated, this bridge-building capacity also serves nationalistic purposes by seeking to use the diasporans to bolster the reputation of the home country. It is a collectivist rather than individualistic endeavor, which assumes a certain commitment to sameness and unity, rather than attention to differences or friction, which my theorization of disbelonging centers.

In addition to giving much attention to race and class, the special issue also reflects an overall assumption of strong identification and cultural cohesion among Africans, as conflict and misidentification are discussed as part of conflict between Africans and African Americans. In the words of Kebede, "Thus, the attachment of African immigrants to their distinctive ethnic identities is positive rather than negative; they seek to enrich the American cultural landscape rather than merely avoid a stigma they had no part in historically."[42] While the special issue examines how the New African Diaspora maintains transnational ties through practices such as sending remittances, traveling to visit family, and informal diplomacy, there is no significant discussion of artmaking or creative practice.[43] *Transatlantic Disbelonging* names artmaking as a transnationalist and *anti*nationalist practice for Nigerian diasporic women in particular. In her article "Fitting In and Standing Out: Identity and Transnationalism Among Second-Generation African Immigrants in the United States," Elizabeth Chacko describes transnational activities as "the recreation of the home community through social customs, religious practices, foodways and linguistic traditions."[44] Chacko finds that the parents of 1.5- and second-generation immigrants played a major role in the identity formation of her interlocutors, writing:

> The influence of first-generation parents in identity formation during childhood and adolescence was reiterated by the emerging adults in this study. Most parents stressed the importance of national origin to their children and maintained origin country and so-called African values and norms in the home such as respect for elders, strong family and ethnic ties and a focus on education to improve one's socio-economic standing. Parents buttressed ethno-national identities through frequent exposure to and interaction with co-ethnic peers at informal gatherings and through regular connections with a host of ethnic institutions such as ethnic churches and cultural organizations.[45]

This focus on the importance of African "values and norms," respect for elders, and strong family ties in the identity formation of 1.5- and second-generation immigrants also comes up in *Beyond Expectations*, where Imoagene asked her interlocutors what behaviors they felt defined their Nigerianness, particularly in contrast to African Americans. Multiple respondents focused on obeying their parents' strict rules, respecting elders, and focusing on school. For the women interviewed, there was an emphasis on not being sexually active or ending up pregnant. While Imoagene identifies these behaviors as a type of capital that ultimately benefits second-generation Nigerians, my study uses disbelonging not only to draw attention to the limitations and dangers of this thinking but also to better understand those who choose not to adhere to these norms.

Moreover, in Chacko's study, while of the thirty participants interviewed, twenty-two were female, there is no explicit discussion of how gender impacts the particular ways 1.5-generation and second-generation immigrants are expected to participate in transnational activities. While scholars like Gopinath have written extensively about the place of sex and gender in diasporic identity formation, this is an example of how the role of gender in diasporic negotiations has been underexplored in conversations about 1.5- and second-generation African immigrants.

*Transatlantic Disbelonging* unsettles homogeneous characterizations of national diasporas by highlighting the nuance and complexity of Nigerian identity, considering the ways that Nigerian diasporic identity becomes fluid and porous as it crosses, intersects, and overlaps with other diasporas in Nigeria, Europe, and the United States. Given the size and breadth of the Nigerian diaspora, and the growing body of work on migration, diaspora, and the contributions of first- and second-generation immigrants, surprisingly little scholarship has been produced about subject formation within the Nigerian diaspora. While I refer to the "Nigerian diaspora" throughout this book, by focusing on this diaspora, my goal is to consider how a "micro" study of the African diaspora brings to light the minute negotiations, cultural exchanges, and border crossings that are often overlooked when we conduct large-scale surveys of African diasporic art in order to provide a fuller understanding of black subject formations that are not solely beholden to colonial understandings of place.

It is important to remember that the land called Nigeria and the people called Nigerians did not exist until the twentieth century. As Nigerian historians Toyin Falola and Matthew Heaton write: "Over the course of human history, many different groups of people have migrated into and out of the region that is now known as Nigeria. Many societies and states, and even vast empires, have risen and fallen, none of them having had any direct correlation to the Nigerian state that exists today. . . . The only geophysical boundary of Nigeria is the Atlantic Ocean, which forms the southernmost border of the country."[46] The name "Nigeria" is said to have been suggested by Flora Shaw, the wife of British colonial administrator Frederick Lugard, who oversaw the 1917 unification of the Nigerian northern and southern protectorates.[47]

Significant migration out of Nigeria began in 1960 after the country gained its independence from England. Between 1950 and 1970, colonial ties drew Nigerian elites to England to further their education, but it was also common for those who had emigrated to return and assume jobs with the civil service or within the private sector, as part of the booming oil economy. Starting in 1970 and continuing through the 1980s, growing political tensions increased the number of emigrants, who also began flowing into the United States. Unlike the emigrants of the 1950s and 1960s, these Nigerians stayed abroad longer and some never returned. By 1978, an estimated thirty thousand Nigerian graduates from higher institutions in the United Kingdom were living outside the country, and between 1974 and 1995 Nigerian migration to the United States grew from 670 to 6,818—an increase of over 900 percent.[48] According to the 2020 United States Census, Nigerians were the African immigrant group with the largest presence in the United States, with a population of 493,188.[49] Europe is also home to a significant Nigerian diaspora, with the largest number living in the United Kingdom.[50]

*Transatlantic Disbelonging* primarily focuses on works produced between 2007 and 2013, years that proved foundational in the establishment of Lagos as a global city for contemporary art. I credit curator Bisi Silva as playing a critical role in this transformation for Nigerian diasporic women artists with the 2007 transformation of her Institute of Visual Arts and Culture to the Center for Contemporary Art Lagos, which was her first brick-and-mortar arts space in Nigeria.[51] Other significant advances include the founding of the African Artist Foundation in 2007 and the Lagos Photo Festival in 2010.

It is not lost on me that the ability of the artists I discuss to embrace outsiderness is facilitated by their status as diasporans, regardless of their country of birth. To many, these artists fall under the category of "Afropolitans."[52] Where Anima Adjepong defines the Afropolitan they write, "Afropolitans are the newest generation of African emigrants [with] American accent, European affect, African ethos. This definition, which emphasizes an understanding of Afropolitan-as-identity, also affirms hybridity and seamless movement through different spaces."[53]

The presence of US passports, signaling access to the city centers in the West controlling the international art market, as well as prestigious fellowships like the Fulbright and the Guggenheim, give them a social capital that makes possible what is professionally impossible for most Nigerians. Critiques of Afropolitanism have positioned these individuals as "class privileged Africans who reside outside the continent . . . an elite identity primarily concerned with aesthetics and consumerism—Africa without Africans."[54] Adjepong goes on to explain that while class privilege signals economic capital, like money, for most, for Afropolitan subjects, social and cultural capital—the people you know and the way you're able to carry yourself through space—are the more relevant factors.[55] Driven by middle-class cultural politics and social concerns, what Adjepong calls "Afropolitan projects" work in the service of promoting a type of global citizenship. In their words: "Those who enact Afropolitan projects aim to show that middle-class Africans rightfully belong as cosmopolitan citizens of the world. This political project is enacted through an emphasis on respectability and class with a colonial habitus that simultaneously affirms and rejects the idea that 'West is best.'"[56]

In the context of the artists I discuss in this book, the work of disbelonging becomes a type of Afropolitan project and is most easefully utilized and performed by middle-class subjects with a certain amount of class and social privilege, regardless of their subject positions as queer and/or as women. But disbelonging also violates the rules and expectations of an ideal Afropolitan subject, particularly through its embrace of taboo and disinterest in respectability.

In "The Politics of Exclusion: The Undue Fixation on Western Based African Diaspora Artists," Ghanaian artist Rikki Wemega-Kwawu argues that African artists living in the West have been favored over their counterparts living on the African continent. Blaming Nigerian curator, art historian, and cultural critic Okwui Enwezor, Wemega-Kwawu writes: "Enwezor and his disciples should know that we cannot all go live in the West. Many of us continue to live in Africa by choice. African artists living in Africa are enraged and incensed by Enwezor's African diaspora bias. They see it as a diabolical strategy against them, calculated to undermine their efforts in Africa and hamstring their growth. So instead of working in unison for the common good of Africa, African artists in Africa now see themselves pitched in an unholy confrontation against their counterparts abroad: the local versus the Diaspora."[57]

*Transatlantic Disbelonging* seeks to complicate Wemega-Kwawu's interpretation of the diasporic flows to and from the African continent as an antagonistic relationship between "local artists" and "diaspora artists," instead considering how the categories of "diasporan" and "local" are perpetually in flux and often defined by productive friction that introduces opportunities to build solidarity and encourages collaboration. My interest in "friction" is shaped by Anna Tsing's theorizing of what she defines as "the awkward unequal, unstable, and creative qualities of interconnection across difference."[58] For Tsing, friction describes the interactions that coproduce culture. In her words, "speaking of friction is a reminder of the importance of interaction in defining movement, cultural form, and agency."[59] I am also thinking here of Macharia's discussion of the pressing, rubbing, and "intense longing for intimacy" that defines the experience of diaspora. Theorizing this particular friction as *frottage*, he writes, "I use frottage to suggest diaspora as multiplicity of sense apprehensions, including recognition, disorientation, compassion, pity, disgust, condescension, lust, titillation, arousal and exhaustion."[60] Looking to friction and frottage allows for a more nuanced conversation about how the diasporic artists I write about negotiate power, privilege, and difference, while also navigating a range of intimate collaborations, as they slip between the art world in the West and in Nigeria.

In a hypercapitalistic and increasingly globalized Nigeria, the dual status of these artists also gives them the ability to support and amplify the work of less mobile and resourced artists within Nigeria. This, combined with the power of social media to connect artists around the globe, adds to an increased blurring of the divisions Wemega-Kwawu maps. As Jess Castellote and Tobenna Okwuosa write:

> The easy accessibility of global news and information through the Internet and cable television has expanded the horizons of a significant percentage of contemporary Nigerian artists at home, who now see, on a daily basis, art activities in global art worlds such as New York, London, and Paris. These persons have become more global citizens than citizens of a nation-state, and some of them reflect their new global identity and consciousness in their creative works. With the improved condition and democratization of communication, African artists no longer have to live and work in the West to be seen.[61]

While this does not negate the fact that artists positioned in the West are far more likely to find recognition and success, it is not insignificant that many successful Nigerian artists in the diaspora are shipping their works to Lagos to be part of exhibitions, auctions, and art fairs, a sign of the growing global significance of Lagos's art world.[62] By moving between Nigeria and more "powerful" countries like England and the United States, even setting up art spaces in Lagos and Port Harcourt, each of these artists attempts to reconcile the complexities of being black Nigerian women in decidedly anti-black and sexist art worlds. They are also attempting to find success as artists and create new possibilities for future artists on the continent and elsewhere.

Moreover, even within the elite circle of Nigerian diasporic art world darlings, the most celebrated artists since the 1990s have overwhelmingly been male. As bell hooks asserts, "Patriarchal politics in the realm of the visual frequently ensure that works by powerful men, and that includes men of color, receive more attention and are given greater authority of voice than works by women. While feminist thinkers of all races have made rebellious critical interventions to challenge the art world and art practices, much of their groundbreaking work is used, but not cited, by males."[63] For instance, while artists like Rotimi Fani-Kayode and Yinka Shonibare are celebrated as among the most influential Nigerian artists of our times, their female counterparts—take, for example,

Ndidi Dike and Sokari Douglas Camp—have long gone under-recognized. In light of this history, the explosion of young Nigerian diasporic women finding art world success beginning in the late aughts has played a pivotal role in shifting attitudes and has led to the cultivation of more art spaces featuring their work both in Nigeria and throughout the diaspora.

One potential reason for the under-recognition of Nigerian diasporic women artists is the failure of diaspora studies to address gender. This is most exemplified by the masculinist nature of the discourse of diaspora, which has failed to acknowledge its reification of the experiences of men. In the words of James Clifford, "experiences are always gendered. But there is a tendency for theoretical accounts of diaspora and diaspora cultures to hide this fact, to talk of travel and displacement in unmarked ways, thus normalizing male experiences."[64] This project counters the masculinist tendency to focus solely on movement and also considers the, at times, quiet acts of settling and dwelling, and local and national rootedness. Rather than focus on the places diasporic subjects leave and where they arrive, build roots, and attempt to access citizenship, I am interested in what I call "micro rooting points"—in a performance piece, in a work of art, in a film—where diasporic women find fleeting moments of belonging.

African queer feminist and researcher Rita Nketiah addresses the limiting and oppressive masculinist discourses surrounding African and African diasporic women and girls in her article "Why Respectability Politics Is Failing African Women and Girls."[65] She writes, "Respectability politics kills dreams. It forces us to see ourselves not as free and autonomous beings, but always indebted to someone else, always prioritizing the needs and expectations of someone else, always upholding the 'dignity of the family.'"[66] Naming the proliferation of the ideas that "boys will be boys," that women should police their appearance so as not to attract negative attention, that marriage and children are the most important aspirations women should have, and that it is always a woman's job to serve male elders, Nketiah criticizes the pervasiveness of the patriarchal idea that African women do not have control over their bodies or their futures, and are forever indebted to their families and their culture. She ends the essay asserting, "I am interested in an African feminist vision that moves us away from respectability politics for women and girls. I want us to feel liberated to be our full selves without the demands of 'culture' weighing heavily on us."[67] To Nketiah's point, this project calls into question how the artists I discuss work around these cultural demands toward their own liberation.

I characterize these examples of discipline and control, which are often shielded by the banner of "tradition" or "culture," as examples of what Nancy

Van Dyke calls "hazy trauma," which refers to the trauma that cannot be traced back to any one event, but rather numerous recurrent events, which may even be seen as instructive and beneficial by those in positions of authority.[68] This trauma can also be called "complex trauma," which is prolonged and repeated and occurs "where the victim is in a state of captivity, under the control of the perpetrator."[69] Psychiatrist Judith Herman states, "The psychological impact of subordination to coercive control has many common features, whether it occurs within the public sphere of politics or within the private sphere of sexual and domestic relations."[70] This complex trauma is the direct result of attempting to both survive and resist what Pumla Dineo Gqola calls the "Female Fear Factory," which she defines as "a theatrical and public performance of patriarchal policing of and violence towards women and others cast as female, who are, therefore, considered safe to violate. It requires an audience, and relies on a series of recognisable cues to communicate with those who watch, because patriarchy ensures that we are socialized to recognize these cues in a process of fluency. . . . The Female Fear Factory travels through respectability and through repetition so that we no longer recognise it for what it is, consequently taking it for granted as 'life.'"[71] For Gqola, the Female Fear Factory is a cultural performance of collectivity that comes to be understood as "culture." Ezinne Michaelia Ezepue and Chidera G. Nwafor explore the origins of this trauma by tracing its colonial roots in their article "October 1: Metaphorizing Nigeria's Collective Trauma of Colonization," which uses the 2014 Nollywood film *October 1* to examine the complex trauma of colonization in Nigeria, and argue for decolonization as a form of therapy.[72] Pointing to forceful depositions, exiling, the separation of families, and the destruction of homes and sources of livelihood,[73] the authors contend that "Colonization is traumatic to a nation as abuse is to an individual."[74] Additionally, the formal end of colonization brought new traumas, as Kenyan psychiatrist F. G. Njenga writes:

> In the late fifties and early sixties, with the promise of independence, Africans lived the life of hope that the triple problems of poverty, ignorance and disease would evaporate under the wise leadership of their new rulers. For most Africans, the dream of a new life remained just that—a dream. Following the death of the fathers of African independence, and as African governments fell in rapid succession, the stage was set for the steady decline of law and order, and the wars and internal strife rapidly gave way to increasing poverty, ignorance and disease. As often happens, and as had been the case during the colonial era, it was the most vulnerable, women and children who bore the brunt of those conflicts.[75]

I am particularly compelled by Ezepue and Nwafor's proposition that decolonization is the only way to heal this trauma, given that this project considers the role of artmaking in decolonization struggles. In Lisa Biggs's discussion of "stage healing," a practice of radical storytelling that utilizes black expressive culture to redress and examine interpersonal and institutional harm, she writes "cultivating the ability to narrate one's life and tell your own stories is essential for healing and liberation."[76] Speaking to the relationship between storytelling and decolonization efforts, Hawaiian sovereignty activist Poka Laenui writes in "Processes of Decolonization" that there are five steps to decolonization, including (1) rediscovery and recovery, (2) mourning, (3) dreaming, (4) commitment, and (5) action, which don't necessarily progress linearly and can be experienced simultaneously.[77]

I find both Biggs's and Laenui's frameworks useful when considering the relationship between artmaking, healing, and decolonization as it draws clear distinctions between the aspects of healing and decolonization that happen on the individual level and the aspects that require collective action, without demonizing any act as unimportant or without use. While societies are typically framed as either individualistic *or* collectivist (with the Global South almost always falling into the latter category), disbelonging acknowledges that individualism's prioritization of the intrinsic worth of the individual is, in fact, a key part of collective liberation. That is to say, the pursuits and imaginings of individuals have the power to influence not only the material conditions of the collective as a whole but also, on the interpersonal level, the hopes and aspirations of other individuals in a given society. In this vein, the various acts of disbelonging I outline in this project fall into all five of these phases, but especially the dreaming phase. Laenui argues that "this phase is the most crucial for decolonization. Here is where the full panorama of possibilities are expressed, considered through debate, consultation, and building dreams on further dreams which eventually becomes the flooring for the creation of a new social order."[78] *Transatlantic Disbelonging* moves us beyond a preoccupation with how women artists simply represent the trauma of loss and displacement, and considers the ways willed and unwilled—or reluctant—migration are experienced not only as trauma but also as possibility.

## Chapter Overview

Each of the chapters in *Transatlantic Disbelonging* offers a different example of how disbelonging has been taken up and used by Nigerian diasporic women artists. While this is by no means an exhaustive list of artists doing this work,

I point to the work of these groundbreaking contemporary artists as rich and productive examples for thinking through the many uses and manifestations of disbelonging as a strategy and viewpoint. These artists were early to the scene of experimental Nigerian diasporic art, and they have been at the forefront of many of the shifts that have opened the doors for many more women artists to follow.

Chapter 1 examines the problem of return and belonging in the visual and performance art of Wura-Natasha Ogunji. Looking to Ogunji's mixed-media drawings and video work between 2007 and 2010, as well as her 2012 series *Mo gbo mo branch*, I analyze how Ogunji navigates Lagos as a mixed-race American national. I argue that her refusal to be denied belonging while in Lagos and "crashing the party"—or "going" despite not being explicitly invited—disrupts easy understandings of belonging, citizenship, and cultural ownership. Utilizing visual analysis and interviews with Ogunji, this chapter contends that Ogunji's unruly return embodies and represents how return operates as a state of continuous experimentation, problem solving, (re)imagining, and home-making for black women, not only in Nigeria but across the African diaspora.

In chapters 2 and 3, I shift to a discussion of physical intimacy and the erotic in diasporic women's art. Chapter 2 explores representations of domestic intimacy in the paintings of Njideka Akunyili Crosby. I argue that her works challenge hegemonic discourses about respectable Nigerian womanhood and the responsibility that women have for the transference of cultural heritage. It also positions her partnership as identifiably heterosexual and oriented toward both past and future understandings of family despite its deviation from Nigerian social norms. This chapter resists positioning her interracial relationship as an escape from the burdens placed on her as a Nigerian woman. Instead, I consider how her early paintings are sites of messy contradiction, where her deep love for her husband exists alongside histories of colonialism and her internalized Americentrism, which she acknowledges have also played a role in shaping her desires. In chapter 3, I look at the role of the erotic in the study of Nigerian diasporic women, as illustrated by two of Zina Saro-Wiwa's video works: *Sarogua Mourning* and her 2012–13 documentary project and video installation *Eaten by the Heart*. This chapter argues that Saro-Wiwa's work pushes the viewers past shame and repression to embrace vulnerability. Moreover, it argues that her embrace of the documentary style moves her project beyond the realm of the aesthetic into the creation of fleeting affective diasporic communities that converge in her video art. In this chapter I introduce the idea of "affective diasporic communities"—communities built on emotional sharing and connection—and offer another example of alternative kinship networks in art.

In chapter 4, "Queer Diasporic Girlhood in *The Adventures of Ada the Alien* and *Akata Witch*," I attempt my own worldbuilding, examining the work of visual artist ruby onyinyechi amanze and novelist Nnedi Okorafor. I look at two black girl figures: "ada the Alien"—a reoccurring character in amanze's drawings, inspired by her experiences moving through Nigeria—and "Sunny," a black American-born girl with albinism, living in Nigeria, who is the protagonist in Okorafor's novel *Akata Witch*. I argue that the worlds that ada and Sunny move through and their identities as black girls offer a productive framework for thinking about diasporic outsiderness, disbelonging, and the possibility of creating new worlds to belong to, through the frames of leisure, play, and queer social bonds. This chapter identifies speculative investigations of black girlhood as a site for diasporic black girls and women to reclaim play, creativity, and leisure as valuable and necessary for visioning liberatory futures. While it might seem unexpected to turn to literature in this chapter, including a discussion of young adult diasporic literature in a chapter centered around girlhood allows me to delve into the applicability of disbelonging in alternate mediums and for young people.

In the conclusion, I look to the work of the newest generation of contemporary Nigerian diasporic women creators embracing disbelonging on platforms like Instagram and TikTok, and I explore how the work of Ogunji, Akunyili Crosby, Saro-Wiwa, amanze, and Okorafor has already helped shift the creative landscape. Using a variety of creative mediums, the artists in *Transatlantic Disbelonging* render their own spaces of belonging, which are also sites of pleasure, freedom, play, and discovery. It is through these powerful acts of diasporic homemaking that these women demonstrate the powerful potential of art to craft alternatives to the type of belonging that often feels just out of reach for diasporic subjects. Disbelonging as an analytical lens highlights the many ways citizenship and nation are enacted onto and through the bodies of diasporic women and illuminates the creative methods women makers use to resist erasure and radically reimagine home and community for themselves and future generations.

Disbelonging is a strategy for our collective survival. This book maintains that embracing disbelonging offers opportunities for African diasporic women to acknowledge and act on embodied desires, wants, and messy contradictions. So often, we as African and African-descendant women are taught that cultural belonging is conditional, that even one slip-up may call one's entire identity into question. This looks like Akunyili Crosby struggling with the fear that marrying her husband will render her "not Igbo," or Okorafor's protagonist Sunny being called "akata" by her classmates. The repercussions of this type of relationship to the places that we consider home can be grave. When African diasporic women accept the fact that, in order to receive love, protection, and acceptance, we must present only certain parts of ourselves or internalize the beliefs of governments, schools, and religious institutions, it is too easy to carry this assumption into all of our relationships. It conditions us to accept relationships where care and acceptance are bound by rules, regulations, and policing, and it teaches us that belonging can be experienced only alongside small and large violences targeted at us or others. I argue that we do not have to accept that conditional belonging is all there is. A diasporic sensibility that allows for disbelonging is not only necessary but critical for our survival.

# I

Nostalgic Longing and Unruly Return in the
Art of Wura-Natasha Ogunji

*I've been thinking about this question for a few weeks now: Do we shape the world? And in the context of drawing, I wonder if the mark on the page has reverberations in the world. The question is significant for me in this moment, because for a long time I've held the belief that artists have a responsibility to do more than just reflect something about the world, that there should be a kind of shaping or making, an expansion, a making of theory.* —WURA-NATASHA OGUNJI

*Will I still carry water when I am a dead woman?*

It's Thursday morning and *wahala* is brewing in Yaba.[1] Amid the daily hustle of Lagos life, there is a processional of women wearing orange, fuchsia, and lime ankara rompers, featuring pointed shoulders reminiscent of bird wings. The rompers have hoods that completely cover their faces, with slits so they can breathe. The women are moving slowly. Most of them walk with a golden jerry can full of water attached to each ankle with strips of matching cloth—some have tied the ends of the fabric strips to their wrists instead. The women wear an assortment of sneakers, sandals, and at least one is barefoot. Between the women and the cars on the street are young men in flip-flops and matching headbands holding sticks. They use the sticks to beat away honking cars that get too close. A man passing by shouts in Yoruba, "What are they doing?" The weight of the spray-painted jugs is increasingly evident with each step as the women struggle to maintain balance. Eventually, the friction from the road causes the jugs to leak. By the end of the performance, the women stagger forward deliriously, their jumpsuits soaked with sweat.

The instigator of this scene is Nigerian American performance and visual artist Wura-Natasha Ogunji, and the performance titled *Will I still carry water when I am a dead woman?* was inspired by the daily task of fetching water that she and her female cousins performed during her first visit to Nigeria. The piece posed the questions: "How much is enough? What is the tipping point in a society where people struggle to meet basic needs? When do people have an opportunity to rest, reflect, envision, imagine, and enact another way of being?"[2] With these questions Ogunji points to the ways continuous work can become a barrier to imagination and other practices of freedom for women and girls. D. Soyini Madison describes the cultural and spiritual importance of water in West African and black diasporic belief systems writing, "water is to be revered as it holds all of creation in balance. Water is the perfect element in its power to sustain life, destroy life, and renew life. Water is life in Yoruba tradition and is characterized by the female energy and fecundity of specific orishas."[3] *Will I still carry water when I am a dead woman?* highlighted the essential role of water in sustaining life while also bringing attention to the act of fetching water as one instance of the various forms of invisible labor that women are often expected to undertake. As Madison asserts, "the politics and economics of water are inseparable—in the field and on the stage—from water's mythic proportions within rituals of human survival and within ceremonies of cultural beliefs."[4]

When asked about her experiences performing for audiences in Lagos, Ogunji shares in one interview:

> I have found people in Lagos to be very generous. They ask questions. They respect the performance and the performers. They give a lot. But they also require a lot because you can see crazy things here on a daily basis, in any moment. I *am* very interested in interruptions and disorientation. The fact that we are women occupying public space in unexpected ways

is an immediate interruption. I want people to stop to look because they are seeing something that calls their attention in a particular way—and not in a violent way. A fight can stop traffic. I want to interrupt someone's daily journey with something different.[5]

This chapter examines nostalgic longing and unruly return in Ogunji's visual and performance art. Looking at her mixed-media paintings and video work created between 2007 and 2010, as well as her 2012 series *Mo gbo mo branch*, I examine how Ogunji practices disbelonging via her disruptive and disorienting performances, which allow her to construct her own sites of ever-changing and fleeting belonging. This study is particularly concerned with the tension between the imagined and real experiences of return in Ogunji's work. These include not only her psychic renderings of encountering the continent as she blissfully dances under a pomegranate tree or flies like a bird over the Atlantic Ocean but also her physical experience of landing in Lagos for the first time and being called an *oyinbo* on the street while simultaneously feeling completely at home.[6] My evocation of "unruly" here speaks to the inherently revolutionary potential of disruption and refusal, particularly for black girls and women.[7] It is also informed by the Ugandan tradition of "radical rudeness," which has been utilized as an anticolonial political strategy since the 1940s.[8] Historian Carol Summers contends that rudeness was a "publicly celebrated strategy of insults, scandal mongering, disruption, and disorderliness that broke conventions of colonial friendship, partnership, and mutual benefit."[9] I use *unruly* here to think through Ogunji's desire to disrupt and disorient as a diasporic homemaking practice. This act of creating home via unruliness is an act of disbelonging. A framework of unruly return also points to the ways African diasporic return is always already rendered unruly by its impossibility. In this chapter I ask what Ogunji's strategic use of materials like thread and paper, video, and the live female body tell us about the messy materiality of creating belonging—the objects, tools, and embodiments that make tangible longing and home—for black diasporic women, and what her works collectively reveal about the pleasure and challenges of return and constructing belonging anew?

Though the idea of return to the African continent haunts much of black cultural production, the subject of return has been somewhat undertheorized by Black studies and African diaspora studies. As Malik Gaines writes, "The notion of Africa as a homeland for non-African blacks has worked doubly as a romantic image and a political concept. At once an imagined origin, a site of traumatic subjugation, and a utopian destination, Africa has persistently symbolized both impossibility and invention in diaspora."[10] While this is by no means an exhaustive list, I have found the work of Saidiya Hartman, Kamari Maxine Clarke, Michelle D. Commander, and Michelle Wright to be rich contemporary ruminations on the theme of return in the African diaspora. While Hartman's *Lose Your Mother* maps the impossibility of return for the descendants of enslaved peoples, Clarke's fieldwork with the Òyótúnjí African Village community in South Carolina locates the act of return as not only transnational but also a local process for African Americans based in the United States. Building on this investigation of the role imagination and reinvention play, Commander's *Afro-Atlantic Flight: Speculative Returns and the Black Fantastic* considers the importance of psychic return via what she calls "Afro-Atlantic Speculation" for Black American artists, intellectuals, and travelers. Further arguing for a more expansive understanding of time and space in the study of diaspora, in *Physics of Blackness: Beyond the Middle Passage Epistemology*, Wright pulls from the field of physics and argues that the paradox of return for black subjects requires an engagement with both linear and epiphenomenal time, the latter of which recognizes that one is "manifesting the past in the present moment."[11] As Wright proposes, "Because 'home' is also the origin in a linear space-time epistemology of a collective, it becomes fixed in time, untouched by change, but only theoretically: the continent of Africa, like every other continent, is always changing and never static."[12]

Ogunji is a compelling subject because her relationship to homeland has been necessarily nonlinear and non-static. Born in Saint Louis, Missouri, and raised in Baltimore, Maryland, and Colorado Springs, Colorado, Ogunji, who is biracial, was raised by her white mother and never met her Nigerian father.[13] It was not until 2011—after she received a fellowship from the Dallas Museum of Art, and following her father's death in 2000—that she visited Nigeria and met her father's side of the family for the first time. In many ways, Ogunji's diasporic identity was not a burden or an act of obligation to the homeland but something that she chose and pursued. In many ways this speaks more honestly to the reality of diasporic belonging for all diasporic subjects—not an "authentic" process of going back and seamlessly "fetching" what has been left behind, but an act of at times disruptive making and becoming.[14] In her article, "Yoruba Diasporic Performance: The Case for a Spiritually and Aesthetically Based Diaspora" Omi Osun Joni L. Jones posits that Yoruba cultural identity is "less about a place and a people than it is about a base of knowledge, a set of similar cultural/spiritual experiences and facility with spiritual rites. Authenticity, then might be fruitfully fashioned as what one knows and does, and not where one is from and what one's bloodline may be."[15] This is particularly evident in Ogunji's live performances, where she evokes, reimagines, and embodies elements of Yoruba culture and mythology. Nadine George-Graves echoes this emphasis on *what one does* over simply *where one is from* in her essay, "Diasporic Spidering: Constructing Contemporary Black Identities," where she puts the Akan folktale character Anansi the spider into conversation with the digital language of a web crawler—a program that systemically browses the internet in order to provide up-to-date information and copy URLs. She defines diasporic spidering as, "The multidirectional process by which people of African descent define their lives. The lifelong ontological gathering of information by going out into the world and coming back to the self."[16] Diasporic spidering centers the self and assumes an individual with agency allowing for the intercultural complexities of ethnic identity. George-Graves argues that this new configuration of diaspora also pushes back against the notion of "roots," which connect African diasporic subjects to a distant past and the perceived stability of knowing where one came from. She argues that in actuality, the process of defining oneself is "overwhelming, messy, and intangible. It can be both comprehensive and meaningless, and it focuses on the present and future."[17] With this analogy, George-Graves highlights the ways in which individual searches and acts of gathering are necessarily at the root of diasporic subject formation and homemaking.

According to Ogunji, she always felt a deep connection to her biological father's Nigerian heritage, even as a young girl. In a 2013 interview she shares:

> As a child, I felt this connection but I haven't always been able to articulate it, or know what's happening when I see certain things, or know things without being formally taught them. But I think we all have deep knowledge that we can access and do the *work* of accessing. A lot of the work I make is about bringing that information forward through my body and using the body to ask particular questions. One of the questions I asked before I went to Nigeria was does the homeland long for us, does this place that I've never visited have any desire to connect to me? . . . Through these performances, or through the use of video I really try to answer that question and think about, if I'm my ancestor and I'm trying to get to the Americas, how do I get there? I have to fly there, or walk on water.[18]

In this quote, Ogunji names the tension and contradictions embedded in her own sense of belonging. While she echoes the notion of belonging and return as biological and unexplainable, reflecting on her experiences growing up in a predominately white environment and still possessing certain cultural knowledges, she also speaks to the labor embedded in the act of belonging to a place.

*Dancer (Three birds)*

Ogunji's early drawings are a deeply nostalgic grappling with how one goes about finding home and why. In *The Future of Nostalgia*, cultural theorist Svetlana Boym defines *nostalgia* as a longing for a home that no longer exists or has never existed. She writes, "Nostalgia is a sentiment of loss and displacement, but it is also a romance with one's own fantasy. Nostalgic love can only survive in a long-distance relationship."[19] Weightless in material and ethereal in theme, Ogunji's earliest works appear most concerned with this romance Boym speaks of, and the pleasure that she derives from that fantasy. *Dancer (Three birds)* (figure 1.1) is a mixed-media drawing featuring a woman, seemingly modeled after Ogunji, with knees slightly bent and her arms swinging outward as if she is just about to take flight. The figure is faintly drawn with white pencil or chalk and partially embroidered with bird wings and bird heads emerging from her arms and behind her head, blurring the lines between what we see as woman and what we see as bird. Her tank top and skirt are decorated with embroidered lines and a geometric flower pattern using yellow, white, black, and light blue thread. Above the dancer Ogunji has embroidered a tree branch with hanging pomegranates.

The image is suspended on paper that has been painted a deep red in broad, translucent brushstrokes, which create the illusion of ghostly forms and shapes in the background. Her use of red and its intensity in this painting almost overpower the white outline of the figure's form, while contrasting with the yellow embroidered wings. The red also suggests heat and fury, separating the scene from the earth realm and making the figure appear to exist in a dream realm or be lost in an impassioned frenzy of spiritual connection and creativity via dance. The fact that the figure is identified as a dancer is also significant, as dance has long been considered by many cultures as a way to connect with the spirit realm. Moreover, she dances outside and underneath a tree, evoking ritual practices.

In a 2008 interview, Ogunji describes the pleasure that she derives from her drawing process and how it serves as a conduit through which her ancestors communicate with the present: "Drawing and work on paper is a world that is completely my own. . . . It's me and the materials and I love that sense of solitude and complete independence from the outside world. . . . I feel like a vessel in many ways. . . . It's also about being Nigerian—that's a huge influence on my work. We get messages in dreams and through our bodies. We're connected to our ancestors, we are them, we get messages from them even if we're not in our so-called homeland, the knowledge of that comes through us."[20] Ogunji's

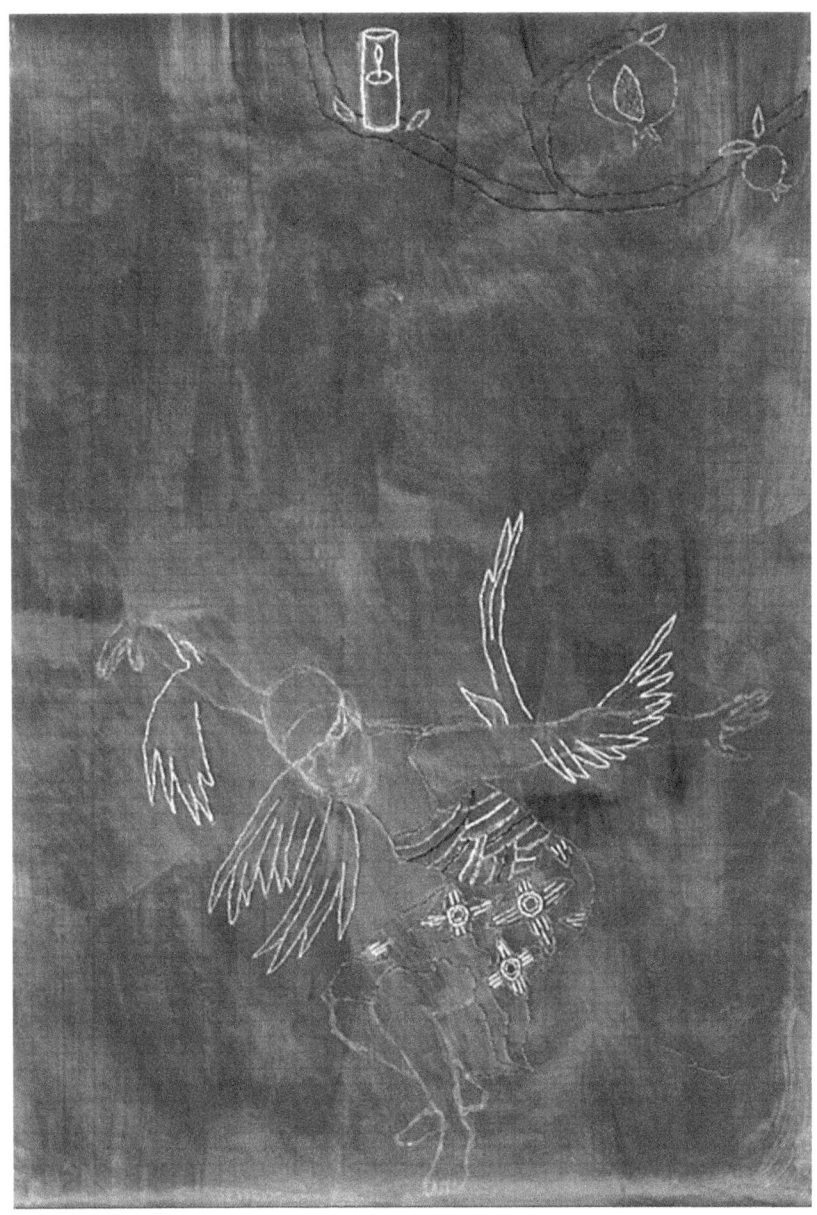

FIG. 1.1 Wura-Natasha Ogunji, *Dancer (Three birds)*, 2007. Thread, acrylic on paper, 2.25 in. × 8 in.

assertion that she is not only connected to her ancestors but *is* them is significant. Embedded in this statement is a disruption of the idea that home and the diasporic subject exist as two separate poles to be brought together. It instead implies that this union always already exists, perhaps imperfectly, within the diasporic subject. She also uses the language of "we" referring to black diasporic women more generally, though her particular connection is to Nigeria. In an interview with Dominican American poet Ana-Maurine Lara, Ogunji also speaks frankly about the relationship between her queer identity, her mixed identity, her spiritual practice, and her creative process:

> Because I'm mixed . . . when people say that there are boundaries and rules and borders, for me, those are always changing and moving and there's nothing that's ever black and white. We're always pulling from many sources and we're a combination of sources and we speak many languages and we change languages all the time even if we think we only speak English and I think that that's totally evident in my work and my combination of materials. . . . That's totally in my work. I see the work as sacred in that way, as profound and there are rituals to how I do the work. Now, I give offerings to the paper. I spit rum on the paper or offer tobacco or draw a symbol that represents one of the Orisa, one of the gods, so that the paper becomes a sacred space, a sacred grove or an altar. . . . I grew up in the West, I grew up in the U.S. so I have a particular way of doing things that's from here, but what else. . . . I think there's something about gayness . . . I don't hesitate to say it. I think that gay people are brilliant, and that we're special. . . . I think that there's a queer way of looking at the world. There's a queer way of writing, there's a queer way of making art and I really think it has to do with drawing from multiple sources that are seemingly not connected, but are very connected and that make a person whole.[21]

Ogunji cites her mixedness, her own diasporic identity, and her gayness as liberating and magical because of the ways in which they require her to pull from multiple sources and influences. Here Ogunji uses the supernatural and mysterious to describe the aspects of her identity that allow her to construct and imagine new ways of being with others through queer worldmaking.

Ogunji also evokes this magic through her incorporation of birds, which are a recurring theme in her thread-on-paper images from this period. In 2006, Ogunji began a daily ritual of stitching in her studio before she began work for the day. During this time she would stitch mythical birds related to the phoenix and Sankofa, sometimes blending features from each.[22] In a blog post

Ogunji describes the daily sewing as a prayer, writing, "It's amazing how the sketches, the prayers, these birds become the work itself—the sketches have a kind of opening and vulnerability to them—they seem to speak so easily about what it is that I'm working toward, their language flows without being self-conscious."[23] Ogunji's use of hand sewing brings to mind the vital role that women have historically played as producers of cultural critique, both inside and outside of the home. Commonly associated with women's work and the decorative arts, the inclusion of threadwork in Ogunji's pieces can easily be seen as resistance to the type of cultural production that has been most valued by the art world and what has been dismissed as craft.

Ogunji has said that the pomegranates in *Dancer (Three birds)* are an offering to Oshun, the Yoruba god of love, intimacy, beauty, wealth, and diplomacy. Her decision to evoke Oshun is significant. Oshun (also known as Osun, Ochún, and Oxum) can be traced across Nigeria, Cuba, Brazil, and the United States and is understood to be the source of life. The mass enslavement of Yoruba people in the late eighteenth and early nineteenth centuries meant that Oshun traditions traveled across the Atlantic and redeveloped in places such as Cuba and Brazil, with Ochún becoming the patron saint of Cuba.[24] Ochún in Cuba is depicted as a mixed-race woman who straddles black and white worlds. Ogunji, in this sense, mirrors Ochún in her constant shape-shifting and straddling of many worlds.

While pomegranates are not native to West Africa, in Western art history pomegranates have symbolized fertility and hope of immortality.[25] Such imagery is fitting for this piece, which explores life cycles, temporal flows, and identity. The tree branch also balances a lit candle, suggesting the presence or welcoming of spirits. One seemingly anachronistic detail is the pair of sunglasses that the figure wears. Sunglasses appear elsewhere in Ogunji's work, where, I suggest, they serve as gateways to Nigeria's bright, hot climate, and a different way of looking at the world: initiating a change in perspective that balances outsider and alien status and offers protection, while also gesturing toward futurity. Ogunji has also said the sunglasses are about representing women as glamorous travelers "enjoying a kind of leisure time that begins with and centers on their desires in all senses of that word."[26]

Although it was not until several years later that Ogunji's work attempted to answer the question: "Does homeland long for us?" her early drawings assume this much. The understanding that she, even as a queer, mixed-race Nigerian American, is both connected to and made of her ancestors is at the center of *Dancer (Three birds)*. The birds represent movement and the longing to travel across time and space in order to experience home in the myriad ways that home is defined for diasporic subjects. *Dancer (Three birds)* is not so much about knowing or representing a static Africa. It is, in fact, quite confident in its not knowing and raises the question: What happens when we give ourselves permission to not only find, but also to create that which we have been told is lost? Through these acts of interpreting, reinterpreting, and imagining, Ogunji connects to homeland in a way that centers her perception and experience.

### *The epic crossing of an Ife head* (2011)

After earning a bachelor's degree in anthropology from Stanford University, Ogunji attended San Jose State University, where she received a master of fine arts in photography. Interested in the absence of people of color in her photography curriculum and the act of recovering these histories, Ogunji began using photography, which allowed her to use her own body to fill in the gaps and invoke the missing people and spirits she sought. Her interest in the photographic archive and embodied knowledges led her to begin creating video works featuring her own body in motion.[27]

Also referred to as artists' video, experimental video, and artists' television, video art was inspired by the technological advances as well as social and political activism of the 1960s in both the United States and Europe. Influenced by Fluxus, performance art, dance, theater, and experimental film, artists were initially attracted to the impermanence and lack of "history or identifiable critical discourse" surrounding the medium, which made the video art form free of the historical burdens and trappings of mediums such as sculpture or painting.[28] Long excluded from fine art discourse, black women especially took advantage of this new accessibility. Prior to 1968, depictions of black people on television and in film were largely fictional and written and/or performed by white individuals. Following social unrest stemming from the Vietnam War and the assassination of key figures like Rev. Dr. Martin Luther King Jr. and John F. Kennedy, there was a new urgent desire among women artists, particularly those spearheading the feminist art movement, to represent themselves and document their work using the video technologies that had become available.[29] Black women filmmakers, writers, directors, and visual artists were especially drawn to the medium, which offered them the opportunity to resist and reframe popular depictions of black womanhood and center the black female body as both "material and metaphor."[30] Referring to the significant representational work these early black women artists did with the video medium, in order to resist the lies that had been created about them, curator Valerie Cassel Oliver argues that a metaphysical exchange took place:

Incredible as it may sound, transcending the fiction to arrive at a place of authenticity lies not only in the ability to absorb the fictional (because truth is often interwoven in fiction) but to do so without being reduced to, or rendered as, fiction. This metaphysical exchange has not only defined the black experience historically but also the struggle toward authenticity. The black body is, after all, a nexus of confounding identities composed of layers upon layers of fiction and the anonymity of unknowingness that resulted from slavery. This unknowingness is only counterbalanced by the residual of lives lived, what can be traced and authenticated, as well as through present day existences.[31]

Ogunji embodies and addresses her own unknowingness and the process of tracing and authenticating her connection to homeland in her video works. She writes, "My creative works investigate physical, historical and psychic connections between Africa and the Americas via the black female body. Performance is central to the narratives and forms of my work. As such, I use my body to understand and experience acts of return and recollection."[32] These new stories and alternative histories are, in her words, "another way of understanding what the narrative is when you are told that there is no narrative."[33] Echoing performance theorist Diana Taylor's assertion that embodied expression has always offered alternative ways of transmitting and understanding the histories of the Americas, Ogunji says in one interview, "In the body there is everything, the history of the world, it is not only the archive of our individual, lived experience. We carry our ancestors in our bodies, their gestures, memories and knowledge. Performance allows us to access this information."[34] These sentiments are also supported by studies showing how trauma is transmitted between generations through DNA.[35]

In her video works *The return* and *Ife head walks on water*, Ogunji uses her body to investigate the "physical, historical, and psychic connections between Africa and the Americas" via her black female body. In a statement about her videos on her website she writes:

I use my body to understand and experience acts of return and recollection. In the performance video *belongings*, for example, concepts of border crossing, migration and immigration emerge as I crawl across the hard earth with water bottles tied to my ankles. I am thinking about the significance, centrality and struggle of the body at a moment when physical belongings are virtually meaningless. With the series *The epic crossings of an Ife head* I investigate homeland and longing. I ask: "Does homeland long for us?" Taking on the persona of the iconic Nigerian Ife head with painted striations on my face I attempt to walk across water and fly across the land, as would an ancestor from Africa seeking her descendants in the Americas. With awkward movement and truncated sounds I move across land, water, and air in an imagined journey across the Atlantic.[36]

By using the video form, Ogunji plays with the notion of documentation and creates a record of her imagined journey.

Ogunji captures the quiet and laborious task of forging diasporic connections and what Hartman calls "recollections of dislocation" in her 2007 video *The return* (figure 1.2), which considers the mechanisms and tools needed to perform the act of return for diasporic subjects. The fifty-second video opens with the camera lingering above a greenish-brown body of water. Simultaneously, we hear rhythmic splashing footsteps and see a shadowy reflection of Ogunji's head in the water, and then her whole body moving toward us.

Her arms swing vigorously, propelling her body forward. Soon her feet appear in the frame, and we see that Ogunji, who is wearing a black skirt with ruffles around the hem, has soles fashioned out of bundles of sticks attached to the bottoms of her feet with red string. We see Ogunji's foot muscles and toes strain to grip the uneven and roughly textured bunch of sticks, making her walking stiff and stunted. At the same time the sloshing and plunking of her feet moving through the water is melodic and soothing, making the sonic experience of *The return* distinctly different from its visuality and creating a multisensorial experience. The video ends with Ogunji simply exiting the frame.

Though the title of the piece, *The return*, gestures toward something finite, as many evocations of "return to homeland" seem to imply, there is a sense that the task of walking is a difficult one for this figure, and we do not see her arrive at her final destination. The makeshift nature of the stick contraptions that make it possible for her to travel on water represents the labor of inventing new ways to perform the act of return, as well as the physically painful and precarious nature of return. In the video, the viewer never sees above Ogunji's waist, speaking to the ways in which Ogunji's work is about the black female body more generally, beyond her singular experience. Ogunji embraces disbelonging and queer worldmaking in *The return* by shifting away from the trope of the "tragic lost diasporan" and instead performing the act of return as creative, experimental, and active. Furthermore, the speed with which she moves is not hurried or anxious, but slow and methodical, indicating mindfulness during the journey.

In the series *The epic crossing of an Ife head* (2011), Ogunji fantasizes about what efforts an Ife head—a traditional bronze sculpture originating in the

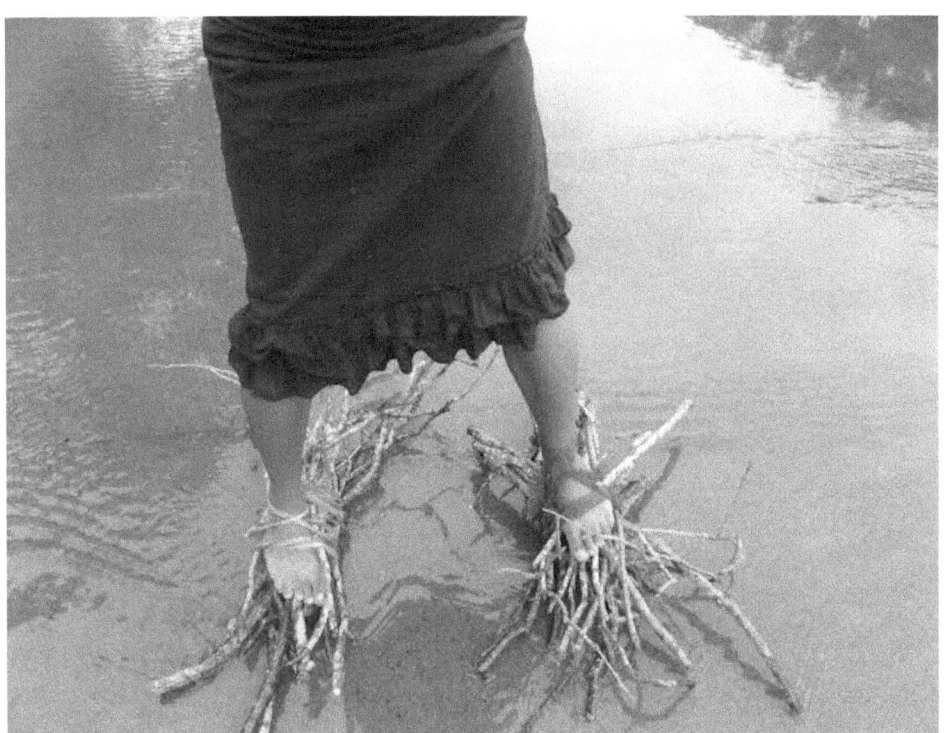

FIG. 1.2 Wura-Natasha Ogunji, still from *The return* (2007). Single-channel digital video, color, sound, fifty seconds.

Nigerian city of Ife—would have to make in order to find her descendants in the Americas. Editing together short clips of herself jumping across land and water, she investigates homeland and longing. Taking on the persona of the Ife head, Ogunji attempts to walk across water and "fly across the land," as she imagines the journey her ancestors from Africa would take in search of their descendants in the Americas. She writes, "My work explores the deep knowledge of the body—both ancestral and cellular—and works to access and make visual the gestures, memories and histories therein."[37] In the nineteen-second *Ife head walks on water* (figure 1.3), Ogunji daubs painted white vertical stripes on her face, evoking the use of kaolin clay in many West African countries as a substance that prepares one to connect to the spirit realm. She choppily jumps across a body of green water, which flows against a gray rock wall shaded by trees, with her arms flailing. Her decision to wear a black skirt and black tank top that reads "100% Negra," Spanish for "100 percent black woman," gestures at diasporic flows and the connection between black women across the diaspora, as well as her own time spent making art in the Dominican Republic

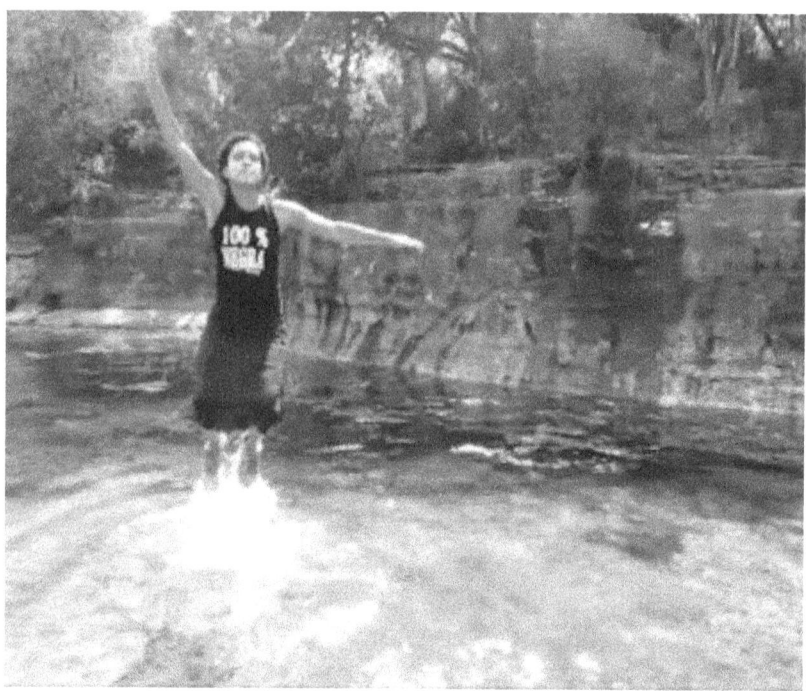

FIG. 1.3 Wura-Natasha Ogunji, still from *Ife head walks on water* (2009). Single-channel digital video, color, sound, nineteen seconds.

and Spain. The shirt, juxtaposed with Ogunji's mixed racial identity, points to the ways her body resists easy understandings of a black community united by sameness. She uses her biracial body to locate the ways in which what Hartman refers to as "the common set of identifications experienced [by black diasporic peoples]" is not fixed but a "fleeting, intermittent, and dispersed network of relations."[38]

In *The epic crossings of an Ife head*, Ogunji uses stop motion filming techniques, originally used to create the illusion of an object moving magically, and glitches as worldmaking strategies. This calls to mind Uri McMillan's theory of "performing objecthood" and Legacy Russell's consideration of glitchiness as a tool used by black women subjects to resist and circumvent hegemonic societal limitations and expectations. McMillan's notion of "performing objecthood" describes instances of black women strategically making themselves objects as a way toward their own agency. He writes: "Wielding their bodies as pliable matter [black women performers] repeatedly become objects, often in the form of simulated beings or what I term 'avatars.' I call this process performing objecthood . . . performing objecthood becomes an adroit method of circumventing prescribed limitations on black women in the public sphere while staging art and alterity in unforeseen places."[39]

By performing as an Ife head, tied to the city of Ife (understood as the spiritual and cultural center of the Yoruba people), Ogunji utilizes experimental methods to imagine her body as not tied to the country of her birth or even her present point in her ancestral lineage. This enables her to "fly" across land and depict the duality of being both herself and her ancestors. This evocation of objecthood also comes across in the video's static-filled soundscape. Russell theorizes "the glitch" and considers its revolutionary potential as disruption for women in digital spaces, arguing for the role of digital practice in "expanding the construction, deconstruction, and representation of the female-identifying corpus."[40] The choppiness of Ogunji's movement combined with the static is intentionally glitchy, allowing her body to simultaneously occupy the position of human and object or avatar as we see her freeze in time. In the words of Russell, "The glitch is the catalyst, not the error. The glitch is the happy accident."[41] *The return* and *The epic crossings of an Ife head* series pose new answers in relation to the problem of return. By decentering the lost diasporan and embodying both the black woman diasporan who builds special contraptions to walk on water and the Ife head who jumps and flies across land and water in search of its ancestors in the Americas, Ogunji's disbelonging and queer worldmaking complicate the Sankofian "go and fetch it" ideology. She does this by depicting the ways that connecting to the homeland is more than a process of retrieving history or community, but requires imagining, creating, and reinvention for the diasporic subject. In doing so, she positions the continent as more than just the unchanging homeland trapped in the past, but as an active agent consistently involved in the formation of her diasporic subjectivity.

Collectively, these pieces are psychic and logistical explorations of what it might look or feel like to time travel across the Atlantic and ruminations on the capacity of the black female body. Ogunji addresses the problems of return by exploring additional possibilities for making connection beyond simply "fetching it." In *Dancer (Three birds)* she demonstrates the spiritual connection to homeland vis-à-vis nostalgia and fantasy, and in *The epic crossings of an Ife head* series, she considers her body's full potential to make contact, using the video form to manipulate and expand the possibilities of her form. Building upon these investigations, her live performance pieces offer the opportunity to interact and engage with themes of belonging and outsiderness in real time within a community of Nigerian and Nigerian diasporic women artists.

*Mo gbo mo branch: Will I still carry water when*
*I am a dead woman?*

In 2012, Ogunji received a Guggenheim Memorial Fellowship and returned to Lagos with the goal of creating a performance series exploring women occupying public space. The series was titled *Mo gbo mo branch* (2013), Yoruba for "I heard and branched myself," referring to the act of party crashing. The performances built upon her investigation of the "physical, historical and psychic connections between Africa and the Americas via the black female body."[42] This refusal to be denied belonging and "crashing the party"—or "going" despite not being explicitly invited—is present throughout Ogunji's creative projects and collaborations in Lagos. In an early blog entry, Ogunji writes, "My cousins love me as if they have always known me. Though people in the street call me oyibo . . . wherever I go, I don't feel like an outsider to this place, or even a stranger."[43] Although it appears that her cousins' love brings comfort, Ogunji has also stated that it was important to her to build her connection with Nigeria on her own terms, causing her to limit her dependence on family members. Moreover, the word *oyibo*, or *oyinbo* in Yoruba, refers to a foreigner. It can be intended derogatorily or used somewhat objectively. By stating that although she is seen as an oyinbo, she does not feel like one, Ogunji calls into question who has the right to assign belonging or insider status, instead privileging her own experience over others' experience of her. Ogunji's statement also calls into question what factors make someone belong in a place if not the approval and acceptance of those who are deemed "native" to that place?

Ogunji created the first iteration of this piece in 2011, during her first visit to Nigeria. It was her first ever live performance piece. Overflowing with feelings, observations, and ideas, and committed to coming to understand Nigeria on her own terms as a queer, mixed-race artist, Ogunji elected to engage the landscape with her body in an effort to better understand what she was experiencing. In the video of the performance, shot by Nigerian performance artist and collaborator Jelili Atiku, Ogunji, who is wearing a black dress and lying on her stomach, pulls herself along a dirt road with two twenty-liter jugs full of water, one yellow and one white, tied to her ankles by bundles of red and light blue string. She propels herself forward with her arms, dragging her legs. In the background, some local adults stand and watch, but they quickly lose interest and disappear, leaving mostly children. People walk past without stopping, and motorcycles zoom by, inches from her head. In her 2007 video *belongings* (figure 1.4), performed and created while she was living in Spain, three years before her first visit to Nigeria, Ogunji also drags herself across dirt- and rock-covered terrain. *Will I still carry water when I am a dead woman?* can perhaps be seen as a sequel, as we imagine that once she exits the frame in *belongings* she continues all the way to Nigeria. *Will I still carry water when I am a dead woman?* also shares an unmistakable similarity to her piece *Sweep* (2011), which Ogunji performed in Abuja, declaring that she wanted the land to remember her presence.[44] In both solo pieces, performed during her first visit to Nigeria, she drags her body across the dirt that covers much of Nigeria, marking the land with her body to ensure that the land has a memory of her presence. Through this act, Ogunji proposes that land, like people, may have its own memory or experience its own longing, which, in turn, may allow it to offer its own queer sense of belonging. Placing Ogunji's performance in conversation with performance artist Pope.L's crawling performances *Eracism*, which explored "the atomization and alienation of being a Black man in white America," performance theorist Hershini Bhana Young argues that, in their performances of crawling, Ogunji and Pope.L "disrupt the putative naturalized feminine position of the prone and notions that the earth is insentient by thinking through pleasure and desire in nonnormative ways."[45] That is to say, the ground offers not only belonging and connection, but also pleasure as earth rubs against skin.

In her modified 2013 performance of *Will I still carry water when I am a dead woman?* (figure 1.5), where this chapter begins, Ogunji, along with six other Nigerian artists (Taiwo Aiyedogbon, ruby onyinyechi amanze, Deola Gold, Odun Orimolade, Mary Oruoghor, and Wana Udobang), took to the busy streets of Yaba near the University of Lagos; they walked two miles from the Centre for Contemporary Art to Ogunji's apartment. Young speculates that "the implicit danger of the performance . . . is part of what prompted the change in her performance from crawling to dragging, from lone woman lying on a dirt road, to a group of masked women moving with each other, while being surrounded by male performers keeping away traffic."[46]

Nigerian art historian Peju Layiwola points out that the matching material used for the costumes in Ogunji's 2013 performance of *Will I still carry water when I am a dead woman?* was reminiscent of "aso ebi," a uniform dress popular among the Yoruba and often worn at events like weddings to show cooperation and solidarity among certain guests.[47] The familiarity of the aso ebi combined with the strangeness of the performance meant that, upon seeing that the women were dragging heavy jugs, many watching the performance responded with fear and confusion, even speculating that the women were being punished.

In *Will I still carry water when I am a dead woman?* Ogunji performs unruly return and disbelonging by pulling from a number of Yoruba customs

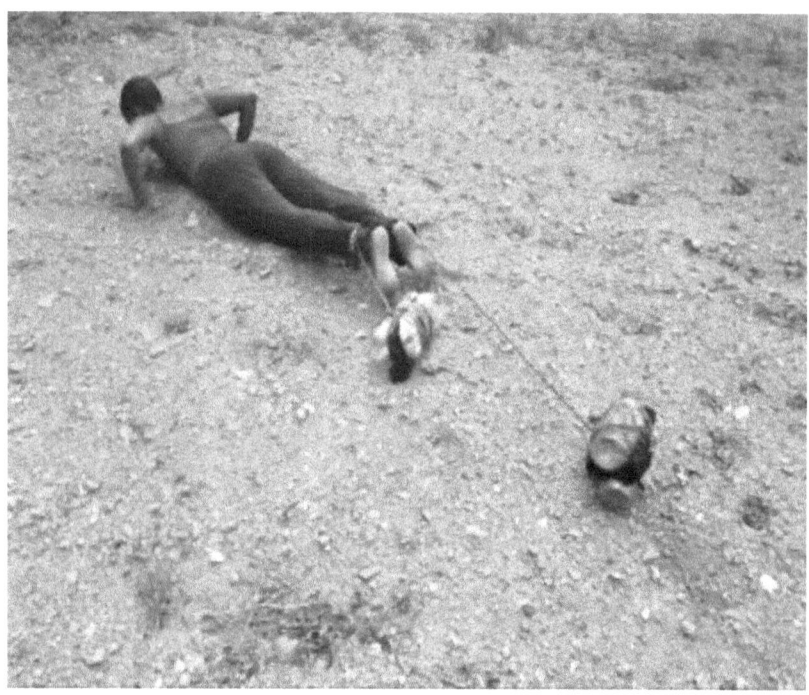

FIG. 1.4 Wura-Natasha Ogunji, still from *belongings* (2007). Single-channel digital video, color, sound, three minutes, fifteen seconds.

and traditions and boldly remixing them. By doing so, she simultaneously cites tradition and breaks social norms in order to say something new and call attention to the hardships faced by women—an example of Muñoz's disidentificatory worldmaking. Muñoz writes that worldmaking practices "transport the performer and the spectator to a vantage point where transformation and politics are imaginable. Worldmaking performances produce these vantage points by slicing into the façade of the real that is the majoritarian public sphere. Disidentificatory performances opt to do more than simply tear down the majoritarian public sphere. They disassemble that sphere of publicity and use its parts to build an alternative reality. Disidentification uses the majoritarian culture as raw material to make a new world."[48]

In *Will I still carry water when I am a dead woman?* Ogunji and her collaborators reimagined the common act of carrying water, performed by women every day, in order to build an alternate reality that felt both familiar and deeply perplexing to those who watched. The performance utilized and reframed familiar Nigerian symbolic rituals, like the egungun masquerade and aso ebi

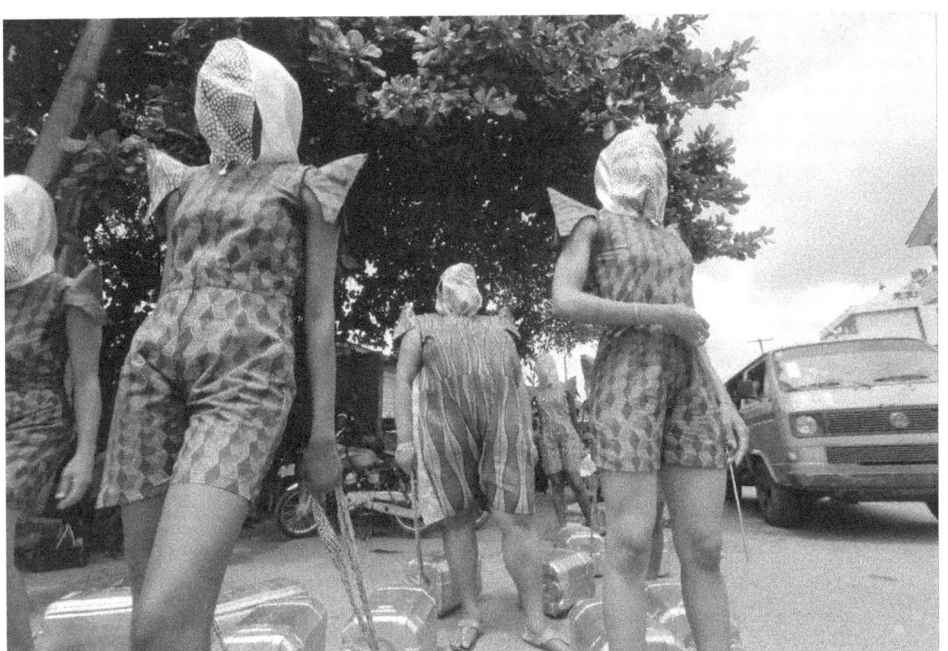

FIG. 1.5 Wura-Natasha Ogunji, *Will I still carry water when I am a dead woman?* (2013). Photo credit: Ema Edosio.

uniform, and used everyday objects as raw material to further emphasize the performers' point, successfully attracting attention.

Fellow performer and poet Wana Udobang wrote about the experience in her personal blog: "When we started, people looked, stared, and some asked what it was we were doing. A gentleman even went as far as dropping a hundred Naira note on my shoulders. We dragged the kegs, leaving trails of water behind. The friction between the plastic and the tarred road had caused for the containers to start to give way. About twenty minutes into our somewhat two-mile journey, people stopped looking, stopped caring, they just went about their business."[49] The man who gave her the one hundred naira note (equivalent to about a dollar at the time of the performance) is significant, as the act of placing money on someone is a sign of witnessing and commending their hard work. His decision to respond to the performance in this way highlights a moment when the cultural customs and rules governing those not involved in the performance collided with the new world created by the women.

The masks used in *Will I still carry water when I am a dead woman?* were designed to mimic those of the Yoruba Egungun masquerade, a ritualized spectacle of performance that occurs in public and private places. In Yoruba culture, the term *egungun* (not capitalized) refers to any masquerade, but when capitalized refers specifically to the Oyo Yoruba practice of honoring ancestors.[50] Moreover, participating in the Egungun masquerade is a status symbol. As Ogunji writes in one blog post about the piece: "Masquerades are quite powerful for both community and performer. The masked dancer is allowed to go anywhere; they are protected. People are not allowed to even touch them. There are men who hold sticks, the cane men (and use them) if you attempt to get too close. 'Will I still carry water when I am a dead woman?' draws from this tradition by allowing women to occupy a sacred and dynamic space within the public environment."[51]

Masquerade performances are used to mark seasonal changes as well as significant community events, such as births, weddings, and funerals. Egunguns are believed to be reincarnated ancestor spirits inhabiting the bodies of the individuals concealed in the masquerade costumes. Egunguns are protected, which allows them to go anywhere. Spoken and unspoken spatial rules that limit the movement of certain individuals according to their gender, class, or age do not apply to the Egungun. John Willis writes that the majority of scholarship on the Yoruba Egungun masquerade "portrays it as a male centered religious-political order and ritual practice used by men to discipline or restrict women." He goes on to argue that this is an oversimplification and mischaracterization perpetuated by nineteenth-century missionaries who did not understand the complex gender dynamics at work in the masquerade.[52] For example, while it is true that men are the only ones allowed to wear the masquerade attire and drum during the performance, the performers of the songs and prayers may be women. Moreover, women can inherit the sacred Egungun mask from family.[53] Scholars like Ulli Beier, Pierre Verger, and Henry Drewal have written about the ritual importance of mothers and motherhood, and Willis focuses on the importance of ritual wives who hold influential and powerful roles within the practice of Egungun.[54] Furthermore, the costumes in *Will I still carry water when I am a dead woman?* were not designed to obscure the women's bodies, like traditional Egungun costumes, but were tailored around their legs, arms, waists, and breasts. The use of masks in the performance simultaneously invited and rejected the gaze, as they allowed the women to see but obscured their faces from the public.

In a city as bustling as Lagos and with a cultural context as expressive as Nigeria, Ogunji's use of quiet in *Will I still carry water when I am a dead woman?* was powerful. In *The Sovereignty of Quiet: Beyond Resistance in Black Culture*, Kevin Quashie argues for the study of quiet in order to see important moments of surrender, dreaming, and waiting in black life: "Quiet is antitheti-cal to how we think about black culture, and by extension, black people."[55] I argue that this is even more the case in Lagos. Ogunji's decision not to use dialogue or music is yet another example of her powerfully disruptive world-making, as she used the absence of speech to reinforce the spiritual essence and otherworldliness of the women performers.

Another key object used in *Will I still carry water when I am a dead woman?* was the jerry can, several of which were repurposed to hold the water that the women pulled. Epitomizing the major role oil has played in Nigeria's history as both a blessing and a curse, jerry cans haunt Lagos's landscape. The jerry can was designed in Germany in the 1930s for military use and was intended to hold up to twenty liters of fuel.[56] In the 1970s (during Nigeria's oil boom), Finnish designer Eero Rislakki created the plastic jerry can.[57] As of 2015, oil in Nigeria accounted for most of the country's export earnings and 70 percent of government revenue.[58] By repurposing the jerry cans, often used to trans-port oil, painting them gold, and including them in the creation of art, Ogunji brought to light the extent to which transnational oil companies and their governmental allies have controlled Nigeria's global interactions and disen-franchised the Nigerian people in order to do so. The jerry cans also represent the precarity and scarcity of water in a country where the tap water is not safe to drink. By requiring them to drag these jerry cans of water, the performance became a microcosm from which the women were able to reflect on their own lived experiences. Udobang writes:

> The experience for me went beyond the test of physical endurance, pain, rebellion or even a loss of self-awareness, but more of a living and breath-ing metaphor. Dragging the heavy containers of water through a public space became a symbolism of the expectations, desires and roles society had placed on women. More interesting is how quickly the observers' curiosity diminishes and the realisation that you have become owner to the burdens that have been placed on you. There is of course the element of selfishness that brews amongst ourselves, you stop waiting because you become consumed with meeting up with the expectations placed on you and getting to the finish line. At the end of the journey, there was no victory parade, no crowd cheering, no homecoming.[59]

For Udobang, the performance became a moment of reckoning: an opportunity for the performers to see the ways in which it is so easy to nor-malize the heavy burdens and expectations placed on women. At the end of the performance, they realize that it does not serve them at all, as attention quickly shifts and the bar is raised yet again. The difficulty of the performance itself highlights the importance of care and support among the women in the group. Ogunji reflected on her own experience in an email to a friend that she later posted on her blog: "i think i mentioned this, but this performance was the first time i felt that i might not be able to do this. i was worried about everyone else. i didn't check my mask's eye holes. i didn't test the weight of the water in my own kegs. i didn't take the time to cut thicker pieces of fabric for myself which i intuitively knew i would need. once we crossed the street i thought, oh fuck, i totally fucked up."[60] Ogunji goes on to describe how the intensity of the act of pulling the water caused her to question the strength of her legs for the first time and how the mask made it hard to breathe, making her wonder if she could finish the performance. What Ogunji describes here is not only the physical discomfort of doing the performance, but also what led to her physical discomfort: her preoccupation with the other women involved. During Art X Lagos 2018, in response to the question: "What are you trying to say about being a woman?" from Senegalese art critic N'Goné Fall, Ogunji responded:

> I'm not trying to say anything about being a woman . . . my thought process is that I first think about the performers. . . . I'm not thinking about the audience when I create the work. So I'm trying to create an experience for the performers and create an experience that is a way for them through their bodies to answer certain questions, and I talk about what my questions are and how those questions land in public space, and they have to be able to connect with them in some way and know that through this experience they're going to be able to expand and figure something out.[61]

Her preoccupation with the comfort and safety of the performers, even at her own expense, demonstrates a feminist ethic of care, characterized by attentiveness, responsiveness, and sympathy, and captures Ogunji in the role of "ritual mother," checking on everyone and making sure that they are comfortable within the performance. In the performance, Ogunji takes on the role women have traditionally played, and in doing so she gestures at the complex gender dynamics that have always been a part of masquerade. She pushes the role of women in masquerade rituals one step further by allowing women to embody the masquerade and making it a site of care and diasporic solidarity. Her worry in the blog post also reveals the ways the care work primarily performed by women often prevents them from caring for themselves and ensuring that their own needs are met.

The *Mo gbo mo branch* performances also brought into question Ogunji's status as an American national claiming a Nigerian identity, and how that might influence her collaborations.

Wemega-Kwawu's interpretation of the diasporic flows to and from the African continent does not account for the type of work that Ogunji is doing, which moves beyond the false "local artists" and "diaspora artists" binary, both realms that Ogunji occupies. Particularly in her two performance pieces *beauty* (2013) (figure 1.6) and *Queens* (2013) (figure 1.7), the line between "local" and "diaspora" is blurred as Ogunji's relationship to her collaborators and the audience is further deepened, complicated, and negotiated.

### Mo gbo mo branch: beauty

The deepening of her relationship with her fellow performers and the contentiousness of space in Nigeria were evident in Ogunji's performance of *beauty*, which she conceived with Nicole Vlado. The piece was inspired by performance artists Marina Abramović and Ulay's piece *Relation in Time* (1977). In the performance, lovers Abramović and Ulay sit quietly with their hair tied together for seventeen hours. Ogunji's adaptation of their work into *beauty* takes up the important and contentious topic of hair for Nigerian women. In their performance, Ogunji and four other artists (Nicole Vlado, ruby onyinyechi amanze, Veronny Odili, Deola Gold) had their hair braided together and stood in the highly congested transportation plaza of Obalende Park, jam-packed with bright yellow buses and street vendors, for four hours.

The individuals who regularly buy and sell in and commute through Obalende Park became part of the performance as both audience members and participants. Footage from the beginning of the actual performance, shot by Nigerian filmmaker Ema Edosio, shows the five performers sitting in a straight line in the middle of Obalende Park as their hair is braided by seven local braiders, who are wearing a mix of Western and traditional clothing. The braiders hold bundles of black synthetic hair, swiftly pulling portions off before quickly incorporating the hair into the braids. The hair is braided in cornrows, which gather at the back of the head.

Once each of the performers is done getting her hair braided, they all stand in a circle, backs facing each other, and the hair braiders connect the braids. The women are in the bright sun, and people move rapidly around them, some seeming not to notice the performance. Their bodies are mostly covered: They wear short sleeves, but their legs are not exposed, as everyday attire for women is generally modest in nature.[62]

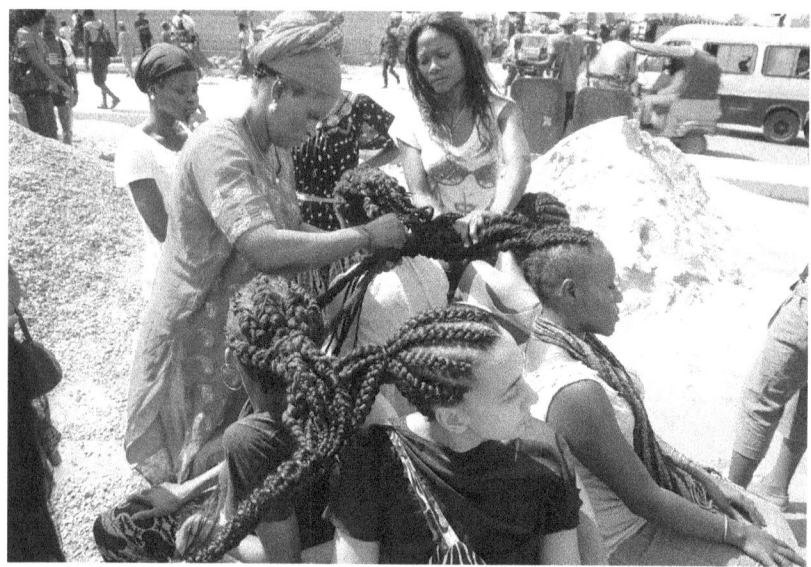

FIG. 1.6  Wura-Natasha Ogunji, *Queens* (2013). Photo credit: Soibifaa Dokubo.

Ogunji shares in her blog: "*beauty* was an incredible experience because we were in the middle of Obalende Motor Park. Hundreds of people passed by during the four hours that we were performing. They were watching us and we were watching them as intently. As performers we all spoke about that experience. We talked about even wanting to film the audience watching us. It's an incredible feeling, to be witnessed in this particular way by strangers and to also be in a position to really take in another person's presence, someone you don't even know."[63]

Ogunji writes vulnerably about the experience of being tied to the other women over the course of the day and the strain of the intense heat on their bodies. Over the course of the day the women bicker, they attempt minor adjustments to ease the pain of their necks, and they rotate the circle so they can change perspectives. *Beauty* also commented on the significance of hair for black women across the diaspora as both a divisive and a unifying phenomenon; the economic importance of hair braiding for African women; the physical toll of the braiding on the bodies of both the braiders and those who get their hair braided; and, more generally, on the burdens that connect women across the diaspora. It spoke to the effectiveness of performance as a way for women to verbally and nonverbally bring attention to their often unseen stress and discomfort. It acknowledged the hardships of the women who spend long hours braiding for relatively low wages, and of their customers, who are required to spend money and withstand tedious hair pulling and sore scalps monthly, or even weekly, to be considered beautiful. *Beauty* challenged notions of "a woman's place" by bringing the private, highly gendered space of the hair-braiding salon to the center of one of the busiest bus parks in Lagos.

The decision of the women to stand in a circle facing out was also intentional, as it offered them each a different perspective on the audience and performance. Layiwola compares them to Esu, the Yoruba trickster god: "Unlike the audience, however, the five fused performers are able to view all sides of the crowd and pull in more experiences. Like Esu, the trickster Yoruba God whose complex nature presents several attributes, the performers are able to see and capture from their various perspectives the comments and reactions of the audience."[64]

Though the women were hot and uncomfortable, the performance also created a site of vulnerability and rest, as they were unable to do anything but stand, connected, for the entire performance.

Ogunji also reflects on her favorite moments of connection with the audience, remembering two seven or eight year old girls in blue-checked school uniforms, "one [who had] her arm wrapped around the shoulder and neck of the other," who stared from about ten feet away, deep in discussion about the performance, and a group of fifteen schoolgirls between the ages of seven and ten who watched for "quite a long time." She proclaims, "they give us energy."[65] Ogunji also writes in her blog about the ways that the presence of two white men temporarily altered the reception of *beauty*. While one of the men was her friend Connor, a Fulbright scholar conducting research in Lagos, the other man was a stranger who began to film the women. Ogunji writes about how their presence led many to believe that the performers were filming a commercial. She also expresses the anger she felt toward the man filming, who she felt did not respect the fact that the piece was not for him, as he asked to interview the women before the piece was even over: "at first i am happy to see more cameras—the archive of all of this is so important. but he doesn't respect the piece itself. he asks to interview me. he is excited. i say, 'at 6 p.m. i will talk to you.' he is up in our faces with his camera . . . at one point he says, 'i don't know about you guys, but i'm having a great time.' no more white people archiving (i did not invite him by the way)."[66] In this moment, we see Ogunji become aware of the not-so-subtle ways the presence of whiteness disrupts the performance space—a space where black women have been intentionally centered. By declaring "no more white people archiving," she makes a statement about the importance of keeping the performance space sacred. Ogunji also shares how her anxieties about the presence of the white men, who were invading the piece with their camera and thus changing its meaning, were interrupted when her friend Connor reported that he overheard one man say in Yoruba, "This is for us," signaling an understanding that Ogunji's art was legible to the Nigerians in the audience.

Yet, rather than overly romanticize the voluntary engagement of the locals in her performances, Ogunji speaks publicly about the exchange of money in *beauty*, bringing to light the ways her worldmaking bumped up against and melted into the buzzing economy that already existed in Obalende Park. For example, Ogunji and Vlado thought that it would have more impact if the braiding of their hair were included in the performance itself (rather than before), but the braiders, upon discovering that they would be braiding in the hot sun (rather than inside their shaded shops), demanded more money, which Ogunji agreed to pay. In addition, before *beauty* began there were individuals wanting to collect money in exchange for allowing the performance to occur. As Ogunji explains, "Space is always regulated in Lagos. A lot of people don't own anything but they will take a space and make it their own and charge for it and regulate it."[67] As Ogunji strategized to figure out how much she should pay the men, a fellow Nigerian performer, Veronny Odili, exclaimed, "No, I wouldn't pay them anything! We are artists. We have a right to be in this place for artistic expression!"[68] At the end of the performance the men returned, this time demanding even more money. The performers, tired and hot, refused to pay and their videographer, Soibifaa Dokubo, entered into a confrontation with the men who were demanding money. In her retelling of the day, Ogunji writes:

> i am furious. crowds gather. more uniformed men emerge. soibifaa, the photographer, isn't taking any of this either. he is taller than all of them. he hands his camera to olu (i think). he is beyond ready. people must express themselves. and there are lines that get crossed . . . it is difficult pulling the guys out of the confrontation. i want us all to be safe. i trust olu and soibifaa. i am also angry because i want them to leave this argument and come drink beer. i trust that the performance will not end badly. we take care of each other. nothing can touch us now.[69]

Ogunji's decision to speak openly about these tense exchanges and record them in her blog is important. She highlights the politics of unruly return and worldmaking, which is not always an act of building a utopia but is sometimes about fighting for the right to challenge the status quo.

I also think that it is notable that, as in Ogunji's 2011 performance of *Will I still carry water when I am a dead woman?*, young children—young girls in particular—had the opportunity to witness *beauty*. *Beauty* was performed between 2:00 and 6:00 p.m., a time children are leaving school, many of them taking transportation from the Obalende Motor Park. Though not the intention of the performers, setting a piece explicitly exploring the themes of gender expectations and the burdens of beauty in a highly trafficked place gave the young women permission to vocalize their thoughts and feelings about many of the expectations the dominant Nigerian culture normalizes for young girls. Perhaps this implicit permission also expanded the possibilities for how the girls could imagine creatively resisting and calling attention to their experiences.

### *Mo gbo mo branch: Queens*

*Queens* took place at the once popular Bar Beach and featured Ogunji and other women artists, as well as bystanders who wanted to participate, sitting on raised platforms wearing towering crowns of Nigerian Aso Oke, hand-loomed cloth made by the Yoruba people.

In a twenty-four-second video from the performance (recorded by Edosio), Ogunji and her friend and collaborator ruby onyinyechi amanze silently sit side by side on raised platforms, which look like wooden coffee tables, facing the sea. Their chairs are wrapped in thick mustard and rust-orange tie-dyed fabric. Ogunji wears a white top and pale yellow pants, while amanze wears black overalls and a navy top, in noticeable but balanced contrast to one another.

Their tall crowns are made of different types of cloth, all in various shades of golden yellow, and sit high on their heads, waving in the sea breeze as the performers tilt their heads forward trying to balance them. The crowns are connected by an additional strip of golden cloth that swings like an umbilical cord between them. This arrangement creates an image similar to Lorna Simpson's 1991 work *Same*, a photograph of the backs of two black women, one shirtless and one in a white shirt, with a long braid connecting their heads.

*Queens* was inspired by amanze, whom Ogunji met in 2012 at the beginning of amanze's Fulbright. The two quickly became friends, connected by the parallels in their separate stories, and began making work together. The text, written by amanze, that inspired *Queens* reads:

> I think about worshiping oneself. Being god-like somehow. I see a throne. Women can't sit on those here. But what if? And a crown. Something about wrapping your hair with one of those traditional, elaborate, crunchy fabric headwraps. But the fabric is super long. Awkwardly long

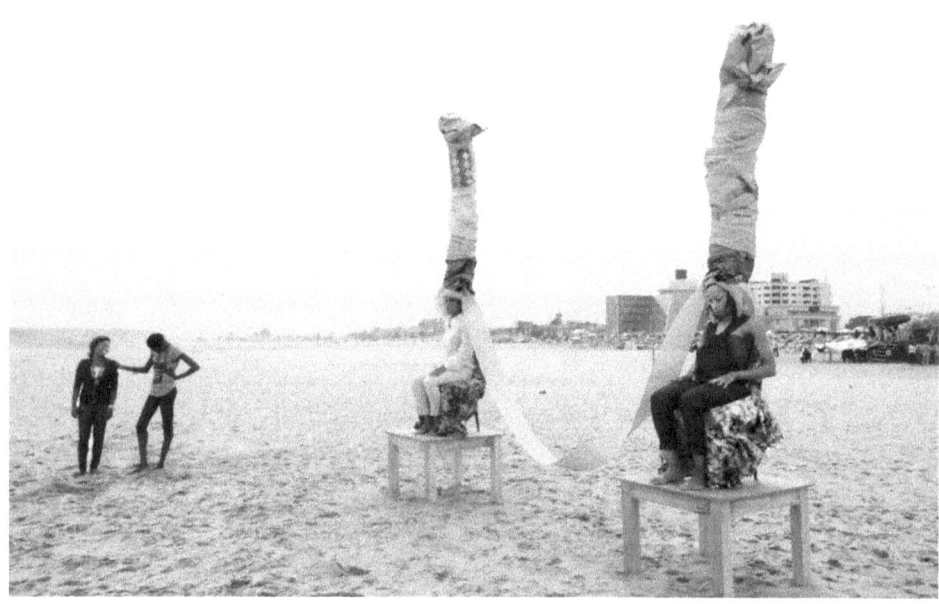

FIG. 1.7  Wura-Natasha Ogunji, *Queens* (2013). Photo credit: Soibifaa Dokubo.

and maybe heavy. And the wrapping takes forever and makes your arms tired. . . . I think about a woman that has a boy inside of her. But I'm not sure how to show that visually. Maybe the wrapping is done by a boy? There is something about a visual balance. Conflict. Duality. The chief eve [*sic*] is part boy. Graceful but choppy. Abrupt. Heavy. Delicate. Women here are all woman. It's all or nothing. Yes and no. Black and white. But what of a diluted woman? A slightly less woman concentration but still capturing the gentleness. The fluidity. The ability to seduce. And to kill.[70]

Amanze's references to the place where choppy meets graceful, where heavy meets delicate, and where seduction meets violence again speak to the many representations of Oshun. Her writing also reflects on dissonance between the complex experience of being a woman and socially accepted notions of womanhood in the Nigerian context. In wearing a crown there is both honor and difficulty due to its weight. In response, she offers the possibility of a "diluted woman" as a challenge to Nigerian society's "all or nothing" understanding of womanhood.

Once a space available to the public, Bar Beach has been appropriated by the city of Lagos and a variety of private investors, who have turned it into Eko Atlantic City—a "hyper-luxury enclave of skyscrapers" built on land reclaimed from the ocean.[71] In 2013, newspapers reported that the project would generate 150,000 jobs and increase tourism to Lagos.[72] According to urban geographer Idowu Ajibade: "The EAC adaptation project is a satellite city located along the Bar Beach shoreline, as an appendage to Victoria Island (VI), one of the most affluent neighbourhoods in Lagos. Its primary goal is to mitigate erosion including storm surges and potential sea level rise. Coastal erosion has long been a problem on the Lagos Bar Beach, occurring at a particularly high rate of 30 m per year. Natural causes are wave tides, littoral drifts, and sediment characteristics, while human causes include harbour activities, beach-sand mining, tourism, shipwrecks, and intensified fisheries activities."[73] The erosion began with the construction of three stone moles between 1908 and 1912 by the British. The moles disrupted the natural flow of the ocean, eroding more than ten kilometers of the Bar Beach shoreline. According to Ajibade's interviews with individuals from Kuramo Beach, which lies next to Bar Beach, many lives have been lost and businesses have suffered due to the increased number and severity of storms. Moreover, in 2012 a fatal surge of the Atlantic Ocean killed sixteen people, mostly women and children, and displaced 1,500 residents in Kuramo. Ajibade writes that the Kuramo interviewees "expressed frustrations and anger over the protection of wealthy Lagosians with a massive seawall vis-à-vis their eviction in response to severe weather events. This dispossession of low-income residents from the beach areas and the appropriation of the common-pool resource for elite estate development have served to deepen social inequality and livelihood vulnerabilities."[74]

In *Queens*, Ogunji created a monument to honor those who had worked and lived at Bar Beach, as well as the lives lost as a result of the Eko Atlantic Project, which she reflects on in her blog: "I have never understood this, the math of people's lives, that you can exchange one thing for another as if they are equal, as if Eko Atlantic is greater than or equal to the dignity of humans, is greater than or equal to homes, is greater than or equal to the efforts of a father who lives on the beach with his family and works hard to send his child to the French school because he knows it will make her life better than his own."[75]

By including the Aso Oke crowns and limiting the participants to women, Ogunji once again channels the power of women to create commentary about social issues and playfully disobey the authority of the state. Urban historian Dolores Hayden argues that "urban landscapes are storehouses for these social memories," referring to both personal memories and connected or social memories: "Even totally bulldozed places can be marked to restore some shared public meaning, a recognition of the experience of spatial conflict or bitterness, or despair."[76]

Unlike *Will I still carry water when I am a dead woman?* and *beauty*, *Queens* was performed in a less-trafficked area, making the piece more about the performers than an audience. The piece created a regal embodiment and peaceful meditation with the ocean for each woman who chose to wear the crown. There were, however, some unexpected attempts at intervention in the performance. In a blog post, Ogunji writes about an encounter with the police:

> There is commotion on the beach. My sister tells me that there is an oga that is higher than the police officers we bribed. He works for Lagos State and wants us to stop performing immediately. From the raised platforms ruby and I stare at each other. The small arguing crowd comes closer. We hear the oga say, "I don't want you to get the impression that I'm a bad man." One of the police officers says it's time to come down. I look at the non-existent watch on my wrist. ruby and I are still staring at each other and now we are laughing. I'm wondering if we will be physically pulled off of the platforms. It's about 5:35 p.m. now. I actually thought we might get kicked out much sooner. We continue laughing while also maintaining our composure. We are *queens* after all. Someone in the crowd says, "They're praying." This brings the arguing to a halt for a moment and buys us time. "Oh, they're praying, well, let them finish praying and then they can come down." More laughter from the *queens*.[77]

In this moment recalled by Ogunji, the performance bumps up against the Lagosian authorities surveilling the area. While the interactions with the police officers and the Lagos State employees were spontaneous, they helped reinforce the intention of the piece and bring to light the ways women taking up public space can be silently disruptive, as well as making a show of the power of women's pleasure and leisure.

The lack of movement in *beauty* and *Queens* become useful tools for visualizing diaspora. In "Performing Stillness: Diaspora and Stasis in Black German Vernacular Photography," Tina Campt asks us to move beyond the binary of movement and immobility to engage stasis. She defines *stasis* as "an effortful equilibrium achieved through a labored balancing of opposing forces and flows. . . . They require us to recognize the forms of muscular tension imaged in them as a performance of stillness that is an active attempt to arrest both physical and affective motion. They require us to read the performance of stillness as an active stilling of motion, albeit one that never attains the complete cessation of movement or motionlessness."[78]

Understanding *beauty* and *Queens* as acts of "stasis" draws attention to the tension the performers held in their necks and shoulders while attached in Obalende Park, their fidgeting fingers as they waited in the sun for four hours, and their slightly nodding chins as they balanced the crowns on their heads at Bar Beach. According to Campt's definition, these are not full moments of stillness, which is not a reality for the diasporic subject, but are representative of "the delicate labor of balancing the multiple forces and flows that constitute diasporic dwelling."[79] Harvey Young also argues for stillness as a key part of Atlantic crossings and the black diaspora in his discussion of the black bodies that were often densely packed, shackled, and transported across the Middle Passage. He writes that these bodies "reveal that stillness, like movement and the body, is an integral and defining part of the Black Diaspora."[80]

The use of external materials to connect the performers in *beauty* and *Queens* sets Ogunji apart from the type of community-based art projects that often occur in Nigeria. I read Ogunji's artmaking practice as distinct from common examples of "community building practices" in which an artist arrives from the United States, leads a "community art project," and concludes with a final creation that is left behind as a reminder of the visitor from abroad. Instead, I suggest a more complex reading of Ogunji's work through attention to her creation and performance of what black performance scholar Xavier Livermon calls "Afrodiasporic Space," which builds upon Avtar Brah's conceptualization of diaspora space as "the intersectionality of diaspora, border, and dis/location as a point of confluence of economic, political, and psychic process."[81] For Livermon, in Afrodiasporic Space, "Africa is a constitutive and continuous site of diaspora. This is not in the service of inclusion or affirmation, although these are not unimportant goals, but for the purposes of rethinking the kinds of interventions African diaspora theory might take, and how practices of solidarity and freedom might be imagined."[82] Afrodiasporic Space describes how the African continent is "as much constructed by discourses of the African diaspora as the diasporic spaces are."[83] Ogunji's *Mo gbo mo branch* performances are an example of the many forms Afrodiasporic Space takes and the endless possibilities for individuals to create it through performance. Her longing and desire to find home in Lagos brought her together with both other artists from the diaspora and local artists, giving her the opportunity to construct a chosen family following her Nigerian father's passing. Their participation also validated Ogunji's observations about a place that she could not completely call home and gave her permission to approach Nigeria as, in the words of Audre

Lorde, "a sister outsider," even suggesting that returnee artists and local artists may have similar things to say. Ogunji confirms this in a blog post where she writes about how, prior to performing *Will I still carry water when I am a dead woman?* she was hyperaware of her position as a Nigerian who had not grown up in Nigeria and wary about how her feelings, ideas, and interest in feminism would play out in the performance and whether they would have relevance for other Nigerians. It was only after she completed the performance that she realized they did. Ogunji's homemaking is a feminist praxis that is invested in an understanding of home that centers women and their desires, particularly in a cultural context where women occupying public space in this manner are out of the ordinary.

Both *beauty* and *Queens* focused on what the women communicated without words, through their actions and simple presence in the given space. Quashie writes: "The quiet subject is a subject who surrenders, a subject whose consciousness is not only shaped by struggle but also by revelry, possibility, the wildness of the inner life. Quiet is not a performance or a withholding; instead, it is an expressiveness that is not necessarily legible, at least not in a world that privileges public expressiveness. Neither is quiet about resistance. It is surrender, a giving into, a falling into self. The outer world cannot be avoided or ignored, but one does not only have to yield to its vagaries. One can be quiet."[84] The performances became meditations for the performers, whom Ogunji asked to be fully present in their bodies for extended periods of time, something that can feel impossible in a city like Lagos that requires one to be constantly thinking, strategizing, and watching one's back, especially as a woman. Through these performance pieces, Ogunji created worlds where she and the women she performed with demanded to be seen in a context of their own creation.

In *Mo gbo mo branch*, Ogunji performs unruly return through her hypervisible engagement with Nigeria as an outsider, woman, and artist. I am struck by the fact that during my research trip to Lagos in 2014, most people I met knew her, speaking to the ways her unruly return has not prevented her from building community with Nigerians and connecting, but has in fact facilitated those connections. In popular discourses of belonging and community, we are not encouraged to think of belonging as something that takes work. In fact, it is shameful to be "trying too hard" to belong or to connect. Ogunji's work brings to light the fact that belonging is continuous work and it is valuable work.

By examining her romantic artistic exploration of her innate connection to Nigeria as existing alongside her experiences of marginality when she began living in Nigeria, I illustrate the ways in which returning to one's homeland necessitates a certain amount of fantasy and idealizing, which can actually help catalyze the material and often-difficult act of creating community and building home. This chapter also highlights the utility of performance art as a medium able to create empowering sites of disbelonging and as a worldmaking practice capable of deconstructing and reconstructing home anew. In each of Ogunji's *Mo gbo mo branch* performances, she manifests a type of worldmaking with her collaborators, which allows her to access feelings of belonging and insert herself into Lagos on her own terms. In one of my email interviews with Ogunji, she writes:

> I first went to Nigeria in 2011. It was amazing. I received a travel grant from the Dallas Museum of Art so my trip was funded by my art. That was really important to me. I went because I wanted to go and I got myself there. After so many years of family saying they would take me, coupled with so many stories about how dangerous it is, I felt so certain about my capacity to make it my own. And my relationship with Nigeria has unfolded in a particular way that is very much influenced and shaped by the fact that I am an artist. I have family—cousins, siblings—but I very much define myself through myself . . . which is quite different from many Nigerians (not better or worse, just different). Part of this is because my father is no longer living so I have had to do some reconstruction of family in the sense of finding people and making connections. And also deciding the tenor of those connections.[85]

In this quote Ogunji emphasizes the fact that her artmaking and desire to go to Nigeria is what got her there, and that fact is important to her. She also highlights the ways that family members born in the homeland, who are so often seen as the facilitators of these types of homecoming trips, are often the largest barriers for 1.5- and second-generation diasporans, with their false promises of returning to the homeland "one day," as well as their own internalized fears and traumas from the homeland. Ogunji's answer to this is to simply trust her ability to make the connection anew. And she does—not through seamlessly conforming to what is already happening, but by engaging in unruly return and embracing her own outsiderness.

# 2

―――――

Ambivalent Interracial Longing in
*I Always Face You, Even When It Seems*
*Otherwise* (2012), *Thread* (2012),
*The Bridge* (2010), and *Re-branding*
*My Love* (2011)

*I feel dismayed by Nigerians' unquestioningly valuing anything Western as superior how-*
*ever, my awareness of this problem does not exempt me from it—indeed, I question whether*
*this mentality played a part in my falling in love with my husband. My art serves as a ve-*
*hicle through which I explore my conflicted allegiance to two separate cultures.* —NJIDEKA
AKUNYILI CROSBY

One snowy afternoon, as I was transcribing the last few minutes of an interview conducted with Njideka Akunyili Crosby in November of 2016, something magical happened. At the time I had been so nervous, that the actual
interview was a blur. But the act of transcribing offers a second chance to be
there, noticing all the small things. The magical moment occurred toward the
end of our conversation. I'd just asked her when she feels most (and least) Nigerian, leading with my own example of cultural triumph and at times failure

as it relates to the Yoruba custom of kneeling to greet elders. It was perhaps the most vulnerable moment for me throughout the whole interview—it touched on my tender spots—but she almost immediately began laughing. She knew exactly what I meant:

> It's kind of annoying, the whole kneeling down [thing], but I'll do it and sometimes I don't do it enough and people complain. But sometimes it irritates me and I don't act well when I'm irritated. For me it more has to do with just the way I think.... I'm very liberal, and it's not because I lived here, I've always been liberal even before I left Nigeria... so when I have discussions, even within my family [and] when I say things that might be too out there for people or when people disagree with me it just irritates me because I feel like I'm always written off very dismissively like, "Oh you don't understand us anymore" or "Oh but you've been gone for too long."

She then exclaimed, "Oh God!... It drives me crazy. Just like how a lot of sexism is [masked as tradition]. And I have tried to have that argument and they're like you don't understand, it's our culture.... It's that kind of stuff that really gets to me. And sometimes I feel like, shoot maybe I'm too different now. You know it's like have I truly just like moved away?"[1] Interestingly, in Igbo culture, it is not customary to bow or prostrate oneself when greeting elders. Regardless, many Igbo individuals feel pressure to perform this act, which is often generalized as "Nigerian culture," especially in the West. In this example, bowing or prostrating becomes a way of performing Nigerian belonging, which Akunyili Crosby experiences as frustrating and unnecessary.[2] I am grateful for this moment of connection over the ways that we, as Nigerian women in the diaspora, "screw up" and alienate not only our family members but ourselves. I'm grateful to learn that, like me, sometimes she wonders if her family is right and she really is too different.

Akunyili Crosby's paintings explore a variety of themes, often all at once: Nigeria's dictatorship, her adjustment from living in her birthplace of Enugu to the megacity of Lagos, Igbo culture, family memories, and her relationship with her husband, Justin, who is white. When Akunyili Crosby reflects on growing up in Enugu, Nigeria, she describes spending her summers in "the village" with her grandmother and living a quiet, simple life. She marks one of the first big shifts in her life as being eleven and going away to boarding school at Queens College in Lagos, where she experienced the outsiderness of being the "Igbo girl with the Igbo accent," an early experience of being in diaspora within Nigeria: "To put it into perspective, I was eleven years old and got sent to boarding school all the way in Lagos, and I only came home like 3 times a year? . . . Even though it was tough for us, I think [my mom] wanted me to experience life somewhere else so Lagos really became my first experience with cosmopolitanism because that was the first place I was living side by side with Muslim people, with Yoruba people, with Hausa people, with Fulani people, with people from all walks of life."[3]

When Akunyili Crosby was in high school, unknown to her, her mother applied for the visa lottery and received it, which allowed her and her siblings to travel and be educated in the United States. Though she originally set out to study medicine, during her first year in the United States, when she planned to study for the SAT and apply to colleges, she began taking classes at the Community College of Philadelphia, including her first oil painting class. When her painting instructor suggested that she and her sister consider Swarthmore College, Akunyili Crosby took the train to visit the school, where she spoke to painting Professor Randal Exon, with whom she would eventually go on to take several classes.[4] She credits Exon with helping her picture, for the first time, what life as an artist might be like, saying, "It's hard to want to do something when you haven't seen someone doing it."[5] Akunyili Crosby eventually went on to attend the Pennsylvania Academy of the Fine Arts, where she refined her childhood practice of drawing and studied with painter Sidney Goodman, and later Yale School of Art, with artists like Peter Halley, whom she credits with inspiring her use of bright colors.[6] Between 2012 and 2018, Akunyili Crosby became one of the most sought-after contemporary African artists. In 2012 she sold out at Art Basel in less than an hour, and in 2016 she was awarded the James Dicke Contemporary Art Prize in Painting from the American Art Museum.[7] She has broken several auction records, with her highest sale being $3 million at Christie's Auction House in London, and in 2017 she was selected as a MacArthur Fellow. She currently lives and works in Los Angeles.[8]

To create the scenes in her works, Akunyili Crosby and her husband pose as themselves as well as stand-ins for the family members she depicts in her paintings. Thus, the worlds in her paintings are created from the conditions of her own alienation—separated from her family and the familiar domestic spaces she grew up in.[9] Her paintings utilize self-representation and the erotic to defiantly linger in the space between longing for homeland and the pleasure of making a home elsewhere. In a 2012 CNN interview, Akunyili Crosby explains: "If I hadn't left Nigeria, I wouldn't be an artist, I would be a doctor. When I told my parents I wanted to be an artist, they couldn't get their heads around why an educated person who went to college in America would want to be an artist. . . . However, there is a new crop of creative Nigerians who are changing this and others will follow. There's a nice energy about the country that's finally coming into its own. I want to be part of that change."[10] By pointing out the fact that she could not have become an artist if she had stayed in Nigeria and yet still identifying with the cultural shift, Akunyili Crosby illustrates the ways in which critical distance from "home" has served as a generative space for her, a space that brings diasporic subjects into more nourishing and fulfilling relationships with the homeland, despite feelings of outsiderness that accompany the act of migration.

Akunyili Crosby has likened the environments she depicts in her paintings to critical theorist Homi K. Bhabha's "third spaces," defined as spaces of hybridity where new forms of cultural meaning blur essentialist notions of identity, and alternative ways of being are imagined. Third spaces encompass contradictory understandings of culture and identity and move us away from exclusionary practices of identification and toward "new signs of identity, and innovative sites of collaboration and contestation."[11] Akunyili Crosby states in one interview:

> I use my art as a way to negotiate my seemingly contradictory loyalties to both my cherished Nigerian culture that is currently eroding and to my white American husband. Most of the Nigerian traditions I experienced growing up are quickly disappearing due to the permeation of Western culture and the ensuing opinion that being "too Nigerian" is uncool. I feel dismayed by Nigerians' unquestioningly valuing anything Western as superior however, my awareness of this problem does not exempt me from it—indeed, I question whether this mentality played a part in my falling in love with my husband. My art serves as a vehicle through which I explore my conflicted allegiance to two separate cultures.[12]

In this quote she reveals her anxiety around what she understands as her problematic affinity for Western culture despite her deep love for Nigeria, even questioning her own romantic relationship with a white American. But it is also within this quote that she locates her work as a vehicle for navigating these tensions. While critics have long favored discussing the themes of hybridity and third spaces in Akunyili Crosby's work, examinations of her work have strategically avoided discussion of her early erotic depictions of herself and her husband. I suspect one reason for this avoidance of the sexual themes in her work has roots in the history of how African sexuality has been discussed and studied.

Global historian Marc Epprecht contends that the study and corresponding stigmatization of African sexuality began with written accounts by Arab

Muslim travelers during the ninth century. According to Epprecht, while scholar Akbar Muhammad found many of these observations to be "respectful meditations upon difference," the travelogues also included claims about the "immense potency and unbridled sexuality" of the Africans that they encountered.[13] Historians speculate that these accounts reached the Portuguese before they arrived on the African coast in the fifteenth century, and by the late eighteenth century, a number of European scholars were writing about African sexuality.[14] Unsurprisingly, these accounts were riddled with racism, inaccurate translations, and exaggeration, and once African scholars began publishing in European languages, they prioritized contesting these descriptions. This dynamic is captured in the work of Jomo Kenyatta, the first known African to be trained as an anthropologist and former prime minister and the first president of Kenya, who wrote *Facing Mount Kenya: The Tribal Life of the Gikuyu* (1938), a monograph about his community, the Gikuyu tribe. In the monograph, Kenyatta denies the existence of nonheterosexual intercourse within the Gikuyu tribe, writing, "Any form of sexual intercourse other than the natural form, between men and women acting in a normal way, is out of the question. It is considered taboo even to have sexual intercourse with a woman in any position except the regular one, face to face."[15] Keguro Macharia argues that "*Facing Mount Kenya* continues an ongoing project to manage the gendered and sexual disruptions occasioned by colonial modernity and experienced by Kenyatta as he navigated the rural—urban spaces of colonized Kenya and the national—diasporic circuits of interwar Europe."[16] Kenyatta's use of words like "natural," "normal," and "regular" embrace the European standard of asserting control via categorization, and by depicting his tribe in a way that would be legible to a European audience and appeal to their moral standards, he attempted (albeit through the colonizers' own lens) to undermine the racist discourse coding African sexuality as deviant and other.

By the 1940s, the study of African sexuality had been abandoned for what were seen as more pressing topics, such as kinship networks and belief systems, and by the 1980s the HIV/AIDS epidemic refocused the study of African sexuality altogether. Though in the past decade there has been an increased amount of scholarship on African sexuality, love, and pleasure, the themes of sexual violence and disease have continued to define African sexuality.[17] Naminata Diabate argues that scholarship and cultural production about the sexuality of West African women disproportionately focuses on reproduction and female circumcision and rarely, if ever, on pleasure. In her dissertation "Genital Power: Female Sexuality in West African Literature and Film," she describes her frustration, upon entering her program in comparative literature at the University of Texas at Austin, with how West African women were continuously depicted in her assigned readings: "I was frustrated with my assigned readings and their images of West African women, continuously caught in the semiotic of cutting (clitoridectomy and infibulation), violation (corrective rape, rape as weapon of war, marital rape), pathology (HIV/AIDS), and over-reproduction, all practices I have come to call the pervasive picture of negative sexualities. To be more specific, an overwhelming number of pre-1990 fictional narratives from West Africa feature a wide spectrum of acts of violence against female bodies. In other words, these imaginings 'restage' or 'perform' the paradigm of victimization of women's lives."[18]

Epprecht's historiography of the evolution of the study of African sexuality illustrates how contemporary African ideas about what constitutes African morality (and perhaps the investment in sexual morality at all) were formed in direct response to European misunderstandings, judgments, and exaggerations of precolonial African love, sex, and intimacy. Primarily invested in countering the inaccurate scholarship produced by European researchers, many Africans, a great number of whom had also converted to Christianity, sought to represent themselves as respectable, moral citizens in the eyes of the colonial elite. In *Fashioning Postfeminisms*, Simidele Dosekun discusses the moral panics that have occurred across the continent about the appearance of new youth fashions, particularly for young women, writing, "A highly gendered trope of 'indecent dressing' is quite alive in contemporary Nigerian public discourse, including to account for sexual harassment and violence against women."[19] These colonial logics of respectability and morality and the desire to, in the words of Nigerian feminist scholar Bibi Bakare-Yusuf, dictate "a pristine Nigerian cultural and moral universe,"[20] have also made public displays of affection taboo in many African communities.[21] As Dosekun highlights, the ramifications are especially dire for women, who may be seen as "loose" or indecent by friends, family, and others in their community.[22] But the high stakes of these decisions also make the realm of sexuality a powerful tool for exploring how women orient to home and community. African studies scholar, Msia Kibona Clark examines how African women MCs address respectability politics, writing, "Female hip hop artists dismantle respectability politics in two ways: through their lyrics and through their aesthetics. Several of the songs in this survey present celebrations of sexuality, expressions of sexual desire, and rejection of passive personas. Twenty-five percent of the songs surveyed address sex, sexuality, love, and relationships. These songs overwhelmingly depict romantic relationships in which women show agency and are not passive participants."[23]

Contributing to the growing body of work about how African diasporic women center sexual empowerment in their creative expression, this chapter looks to Akunyili Crosby's paintings as a site of sexual agency. I argue that she utilizes her body as an archive of photographs and popular culture and an erotic transitional space between Nigeria and the United States, thus simultaneously acknowledging and resisting cultural expectations regarding love and desire, and opening possibilities for alternate forms of belonging. I examine how Akunyili Crosby's erotically charged portraits of herself and her husband—particularly *I Always Face You, Even When It Seems Otherwise* (2012), *The Bridge* (2010), *Rebranding My Love* (2011), and *Thread* (2012)—challenge hegemonic discourses about respectable middle-class Nigerian womanhood and women's responsibility for the transference of cultural heritage, while also seeking to integrate representations of her relationship into a shared visual archive of the Nigerian family. This chapter resists positioning her interracial relationship as an escape from the burdens placed on her as a Nigerian woman, and instead considers how her early paintings become sites of messy dwelling where she boldly acknowledges the ways her deep love for her husband exists alongside histories of colonialism and her internalized love of the West. In these works she takes ownership not only of her desires but also of the ways they have been shaped by colonialism and imperialism.

## *I Always Face You, Even When It Seems Otherwise*

Domestic spaces feature prominently in Akunyili Crosby's paintings, where she combines features from the multiple landscapes she has called home in order to capture her dual allegiances to the United States and Nigeria. She uses paint, charcoal, graphite, and images cut from Nigerian lifestyle magazines and the internet, which she transfers onto paper with acetone so as not to disrupt the smooth surface. In her multimedia paintings, which are vibrant, visually dense, and at times dizzying, viewers are forced to experience the uneasiness of negotiating multiple cultural universes as she explores her own anxiety as a 1.5-generation immigrant drifting away from her home and culture. As Akunyili Crosby captures private moments of love and desire between herself and her husband, she invites viewers to engage with her erotic agency while also grappling with her unease around crossing cultural and racial borders. Gayatri Gopinath argues that within contemporary nationalist and diasporic discourses, home is "a sacrosanct space of purity, tradition, and authenticity, embodied by the figure of the 'woman' who is enshrined at its center."[24] By focusing

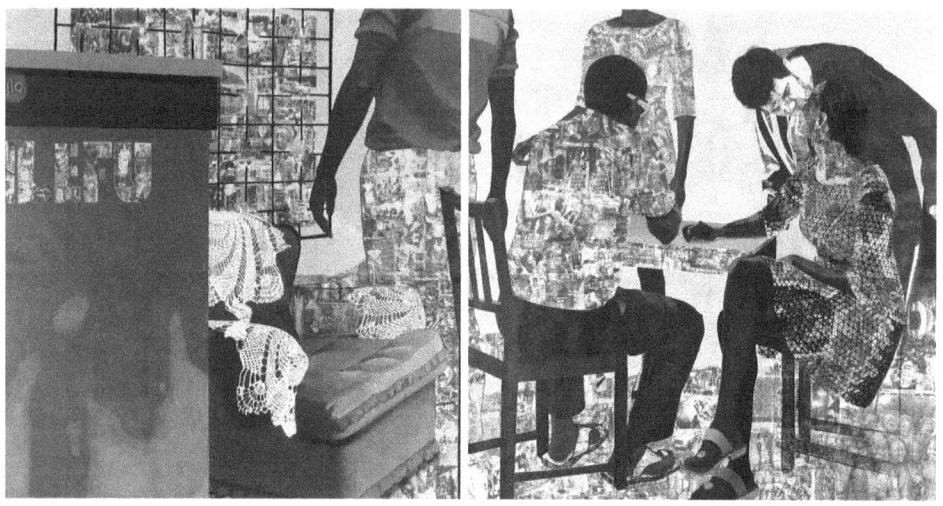

FIG. 2.1 Njideka Akunyili Crosby, *I Always Face You, Even When It Seems Otherwise* (2012). Acrylic, pastel, charcoal, colored pencil, collage, and Xerox transfers on paper (two panels), each panel 6.5 ft. × 6.5 ft.

on domestic spaces created out of her own imaginings and desires, Akunyili Crosby locates the home as a site of contradiction, illustrating the productive tension between conservative traditions and deviance.

The six-and-a-half-foot–by–six-and-a-half-foot *I Always Face You, Even When It Seems Otherwise* (figure 2.1) explores the themes of intimacy, anxiety, cultural loyalty, and outsiderness. The painting, which is split between two panels, positions the viewer on the periphery of the room, perhaps crouching down just out of view. It shows Akunyili Crosby; her husband, Justin; and her siblings gathered around a small orange table with a collaged edge (modeled after the Ikea table in her and her husband's Los Angeles home). The painting features blue and orange in various shades—tangerine, rust, teal, navy, and aqua—creating a sense of cohesion among the sea of collaged photographs of people and artifacts. The photographs fill the window on the left side of the image, the bodies of all of the figures (with the exception of Justin, who wears a long-sleeved navy blue shirt), and even the floor.[25]

The composition in the left panel is obscured by what appears to be the side of a table or desk. Akunyili Crosby has painted a lime green "glo" sticker advertising the popular Nigerian cell phone provider and collaged the last four letters of a word: LEFU, intended to be vague. Behind the desk, there is an empty plush, caramel-colored velvet lounge chair, inspired by her grand-mother's home. Three ornate white lace doilies hang delicately on the back of the chair and the ends of the two armrests (figure 2.2). The placement of the chair, slightly tilted toward the viewer, is inviting, as if beckoning us to sink into its cushions for a better view. In the tiny holes of the doilies are photos of her and her siblings from childhood. In the center of the composition, split between the two panels, is a male figure wearing a red, green, and purple shirt. His deep brown muscular arms hang heavily as he appears to gaze out a window covered with vertical and horizontal black metal bars, a common security measure in Nigerian homes. In the right panel, Akunyili Crosby, who is wearing a yellow and blue dress featuring an intricate fractal design, sits at the table with her sister and brother. Although sitting down, she tilts her head up to kiss Justin, who stands next to the table. The others at the table appear to be looking elsewhere, despite being in such close proximity.

Akunyili Crosby's use of collage in the image tells its own story. On the left side of the window, we see images depicting Igbo cultural history. These include artifacts such as a slender black pot with crisscross details on the outside—the Igbo Ukwu pot, one of the oldest artifacts ever found—masks, traditional masquerades covered in raffia, and photographs of political leaders, including Chukwuemeka Odumegwu Ojukwu, who served as the president of Biafra from 1967 to 1970, and Nnamdi Azikiwe, who fought for Nigeria's independence and was the country's first president. It is a window into Igbo history and culture. In her brother's form, she has collaged photos of her family from the 1980s and 1990s—portraits of little girls in white communion dresses and staged family portraits. The right panel of the painting is primarily filled with photos from popular culture and images from her and her husband's wedding, capturing contemporary Nigeria. Right in the center of her brother's back is an image of Justin in a traditional bright red Igbo cap holding her hand in what appears to be some kind of ceremonial gesture. Details like the white lace doilies, the geometric metal grate over the window, and the "glo" sticker mark the space as distinctly and familiarly Nigerian to anyone who has spent time in the country. In fact, the key detail that differentiates this composition from a traditional Nigerian home scene is the fact that an interracial couple is performing a public act of affection in an intimate space that they share with three other individuals.

The title, *I Always Face You, Even When It Seems Otherwise*, reads like an oath of reassurance intended for her friends and family in Nigeria, and also for Justin. In an interview, Akunyili Crosby explains that the inspiration for

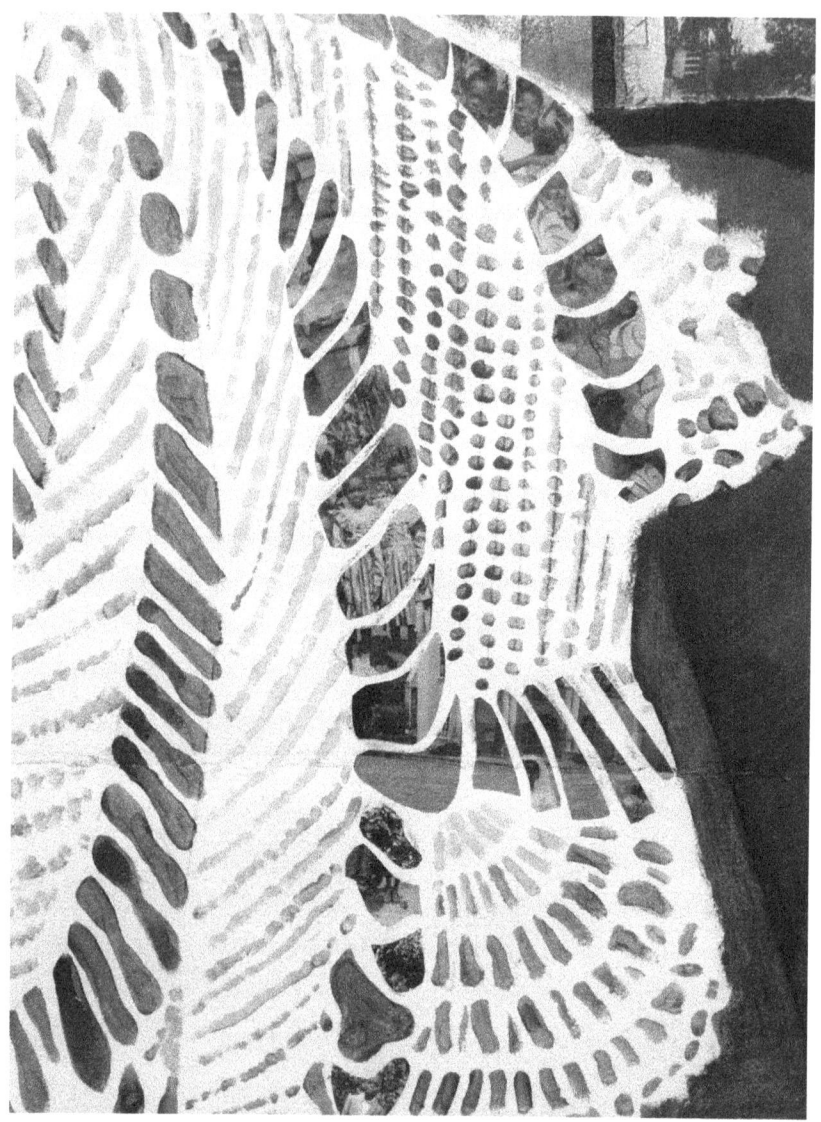

FIG. 2.2 Njideka Akunyili Crosby, *I Always Face You, Even When It Seems Otherwise* (detail) (2012). Acrylic, pastel, charcoal, colored pencil, collage, and Xerox transfers on paper.

the piece came from Chinua Achebe's *No Longer at Ease*.[26] In the story, the main character, an Igbo man, is preparing to study in England. Before he leaves there is a meeting, and he is advised by others in his village not to return with a foreigner because these affairs never last—the foreigners always leave. The wisest man in the village stands up and states that the problem is not that the foreigner will leave but that the foreigner will make the Igbo man turn his back on his kinsmen. Akunyili Crosby elaborates, "That really hit on the anxiety I had felt around my marriage to Justin—this feeling that you will leave us if you marry outside, especially because the culture passes through men. It's as if my children will not be considered Igbo—I'm not really considered part of my extended family/village anymore. It's almost like making the choice to divorce yourself from your culture."[27]

Art historian Tobias Wooford asserts, "A diasporic community is set apart in its present location with its gaze always directed toward the place of homeland."[28] This inability to fully turn away from the homeland is reflected in the positioning of her body: although Akunyili Crosby's head is turned toward her husband, her body faces her family. Moreover, the fractal design on her dress seems to gesture at the ways she is split among multiple places and allegiances. The letters "LEFU" also speak to this anxiety. Akunyili Crosby has said that the letters appear in several Igbo words, one being *efulefu*, which appears in Achebe's *Things Fall Apart* and means "lost one" and, more colloquially, "sell-out" or "traitor." *Efulefu: The Lost One* (2011) is also the name of another of Akunyili Crosby's paintings, which depicts her and Justin in a loving but tentative embrace, her legs awkwardly intertwined with his. In *Efulefu: The Lost One*, their bodies are noticeably more self-conscious than the other figures in the painting, who kick their legs while dancing confidently, but still, she stares intently into his eyes. Although in *Things Fall Apart*, the word *efulefu* describes men, Akunyili Crosby reappropriates the term, creating a Nigerian version of the lost woman who betrays her culture.

This question of how women take on the responsibility of guarding heritage and passing down stories is addressed in the work of feminist scholar Charmaine Crawford, who examines how African-Caribbean women keep Caribbean culture and communities alive abroad while working as foreign domestics. She argues that more pressure may be put on women to preserve their cultural heritage due to their "reproductive role in nurturing and socializing children."[29] While Akunyili Crosby's work interrogates these pressures, what I find most fascinating are the larger implications of her sharing this kiss with Justin. In Nigeria, the colonial logics of respectability and morality discussed earlier have made public displays of affection like this one a distasteful act, even between married couples.

This cultural opinion is reflected on the now-defunct podcast *Waza Africa*, which did an episode on the subject of PDA titled "Public Display of Affection? Not in Africa." In the episode, one man says he frowns upon PDA, explaining, "We know that Africa is known for [having a] good moral standard. So this issue of PDA in Africa is still seen as immorality."[30] In a 2020 article titled "6 Nigerian Women Talk About Overcoming Purity Culture," a twenty-three-year-old woman by the name of Yinka shares, "A lot of the guilt and shame I felt around sex and decency came from following Christianity. I was taught that I needed to be 'pure' until marriage. No sex, no masturbating, you have to 'dress decently.' So, abandoning Christianity has helped me abandon that conditioning. I learnt to understand that wanting sex is completely human and that it doesn't make me dirty or any less of a person."[31]

For Yinka, the shame she experienced was directly tied to Christianity, and leaving the church was what allowed her to destigmatize her relationship to not just sex but pleasure. Another woman, Mo, age twenty-two, explains how even once she believed she had stopped caring about purity culture, it was difficult for her to completely let go. While the emphasis in both examples is on sex, the ambiguous use of "decency" can and often does include how one dresses, behaviors like cursing, and acts such as public kissing.[32]

The question of decency came up during my 2016 phone interview with Akunyili Crosby, who shared that on her and Justin's wedding day, she gave him the "heads up" that they couldn't kiss. In her words, "I was like you better not do anything because we don't do this in Nigeria, and he thought I was being dramatic and was like, 'No we have to kiss! blah blah,' and we did a little quick peck and at the end, everyone was like, 'What were you thinking?'" As she spoke I was reminded that when I watched the VHS of my own parents getting married it struck me as odd that my father gave my mother only a quick kiss on the cheek at the end of the ceremony. Up until my phone conversation with Akunyili Crosby, I had thought that it was because he did not want my mother's lipstick to rub off on him. I shared this with Akunyili Crosby and she laughed, knowingly exclaiming, "You do it on the cheek!"[33]

The interracial element of this encounter in *I Always Face You* adds to the taboo of the kiss, as interracial marriages, particularly between black Nigerians and white foreigners, are understood as rarely occurring in local Nigerian contexts. That is to say that you may travel abroad and marry a foreigner, but you would not bring them back home. This is a somewhat popular Nollywood plotline, where the white Westerner has an impossible time adjusting to life in the village.[34] Moreover, section 26 of the Nigerian constitution grants citizenship through marriage only to foreign-born women marrying men who hold Nigerian citizenship, further emphasizing the lack of power Akunyili Crosby has in a cultural context. Not only does her relationship with Justin threaten her own cultural belonging, but there is no path for her to remedy this through granting him a type of legal belonging.[35] In light of this, Akunyili Crosby's decision to depict a space where this socially taboo act can occur is a rebellious act. In this scene, she has made an intentional decision to allow this kiss to happen without turning her back on her family. She instead invites them to gaze upon her and Justin. The inappropriate nature of this kiss in this distinctly Nigerian context is supported by the body language expressed by the three other figures in the composition, who all seem to be intentionally looking away from the kissing couple at a table so small that it almost demands spatial proximity and eye contact. We see one brother's elbows as he gazes out the window, another stares at the table, and her sister faces straight ahead, directing her attention to the end of the table. It is not unlikely that this type of public kiss would garner this response in a Nigerian context. Anthropologist Arjun Appadurai contends that global labor diasporas involve immense strains on women, as marriages become "the meeting points of historical patterns of socialization and new ideas of proper behavior."[36] While Appadurai speaks specifically of families who migrate together, this can also be the case for female household members who move away but are still accountable to elders in the homeland and responsible for preserving the reputation of the family abroad. In *I Always Face You, Even When It Seems Otherwise*, Akunyili Crosby captures an uncomfortable moment where tradition and her romantic and erotic agency meet, gesturing at the ways in which national allegiances are read onto the bodies of diasporic subjects, particularly women, who carry greater responsibility as cultural reproducers. Akunyili Crosby challenges these hegemonic discourses about respectable middle-class Nigerian womanhood, and the responsibility women have for the transference of cultural heritage, by integrating representations of her relationship into a shared visual archive of the modern Nigerian family.

## *Thread, The Bridge,* and *Re-branding My Love*

*Thread* (figure 2.3) depicts Akunyili Crosby hovering over a white masculine body, assumed to be her husband, whose head is just out of the frame. Her puckered lips just barely touch the small of his back, the silhouette of her breast clearly visible. Her body is densely filled with collage images including photographs of fashionable young black women and movie advertisements. Streaks

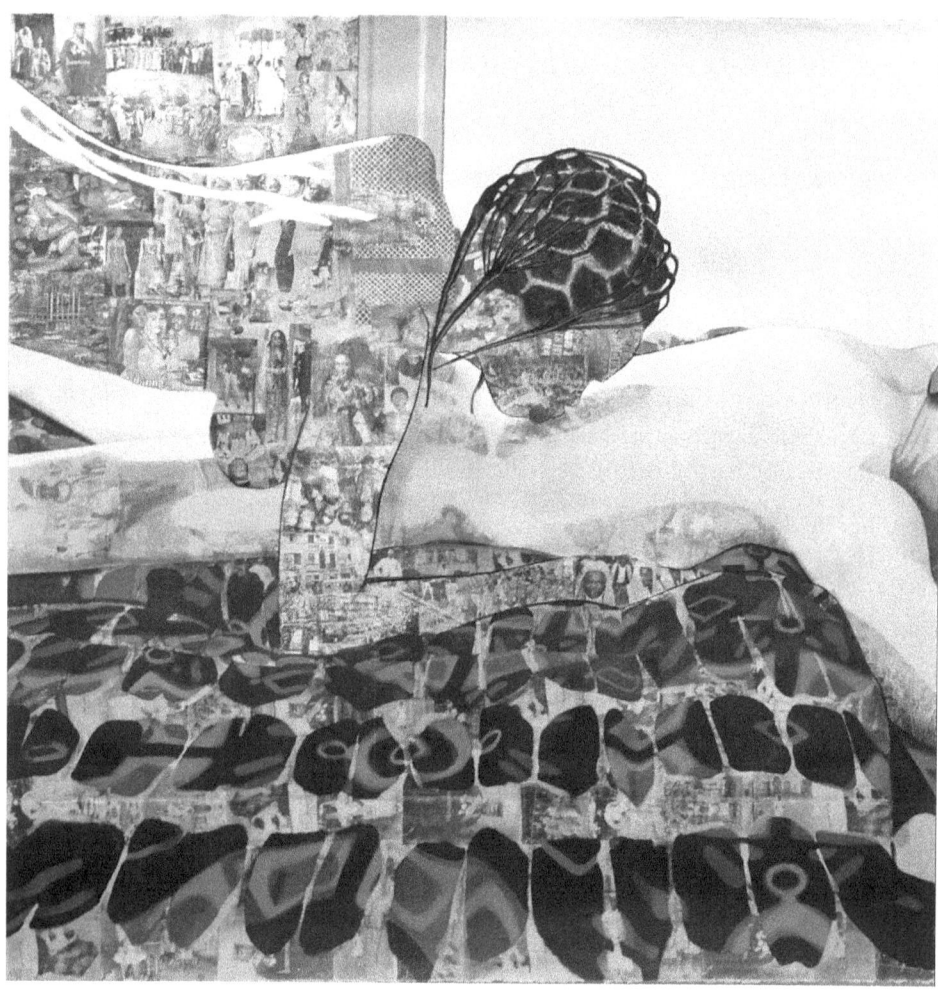

FIG. 2.3 Njideka Akunyili Crosby, *Thread* (2012). Acrylic, charcoal, pastel, colored pencils, and Xerox transfers on paper, 4.33 ft. × 4.33 ft.

of the white canvas are left bare to highlight the muscles in her back, communicating visually that she, too, is naked. The two lie on a vibrant yellow and royal blue patterned comforter, which also has photographs collaged into it, although these images are obscured by the paint. Behind her is a pale green window, with a light brown border, filled with black-and-white colonial-era pictures of Nigerian officials and other elites.

In this image, Akunyili Crosby has collaged family photographs, images from Nigerian lifestyle magazines, advertisements for Nollywood movies, and photos of herself and Justin onto her own skin. The pictures are densely concentrated on her body and appear on his body in the form of shadows, the forms concealed by his skin tone. The hair has been rendered so realistically that it jumps off the surface. The lack of recognizable skin tone or facial details makes her look not quite human, calling to mind Kenyan artist Wangechi Mutu's otherworldly depictions of the female form. Akunyili Crosby's use of collage seems to gesture at her ambivalence about being in an interracial relationship at two points in the painting. Where her lips touch Justin's skin, she has collaged her own painting *The Bridge*, another intimate portrait of the two of them, which I discuss later in this chapter. At the second point of contact, where her right hand snakes underneath his chest, there are images of Nigerian lawyers in white powdered wigs, a relic of colonialism in many African countries and perhaps an allusion to Nigeria's adoration of all things Western and Akunyili Crosby's curiosity about how much of a role her husband's Americanness and whiteness played in her falling in love with him.

The title of the piece, *Thread*, points to a key example of disbelonging that Akunyili Crosby depicts: her hairstyle, which she says she was teased about when she moved from Enugu to Lagos. While a common hairstyle in rural areas, Akunyili Crosby says that the style earned her the name "bush girl" when she arrived in Lagos. "Bush girl" in Nigerian vernacular is a playful name used to tease individuals seen as uncultured. It draws a line between those raised and socialized in rural areas and those with cosmopolitan sensibilities. I read Akunyili Crosby's decision to wear this particular hairstyle in *Thread* as an indication of the ways that she has experienced alienation in Nigeria. By reclaiming the style, which brought her ridicule, she creates an image that speaks to the various ways she is seen as an outsider, even within her own culture.

Akunyili Crosby's treatment of her own cultural, familial, and affective excess, in the form of the collaged shadows she casts on her husband's pale skin, illustrates L. H. Stallings's assertion that "Women's bodies and sexualities are their canvases and creative tools . . . the process of creating out of the body and sexuality is in and of itself evidence of power that exceeds the human."[37] Gopinath writes in her discussion of South Asian nationalism, "Gendered constructions of nationalism are reproduced in the diaspora through the figure of the 'woman' as the boundary marker of ethnic/racial community in the 'host' nation. The woman also bears the brunt of being the embodied signifier of the past of the diaspora."[38] Gopinath's words ring particularly true here where we see Akunyili Crosby herself in these paintings, where she inserts herself as the boundary marker of ethnic/racial community and the embodied

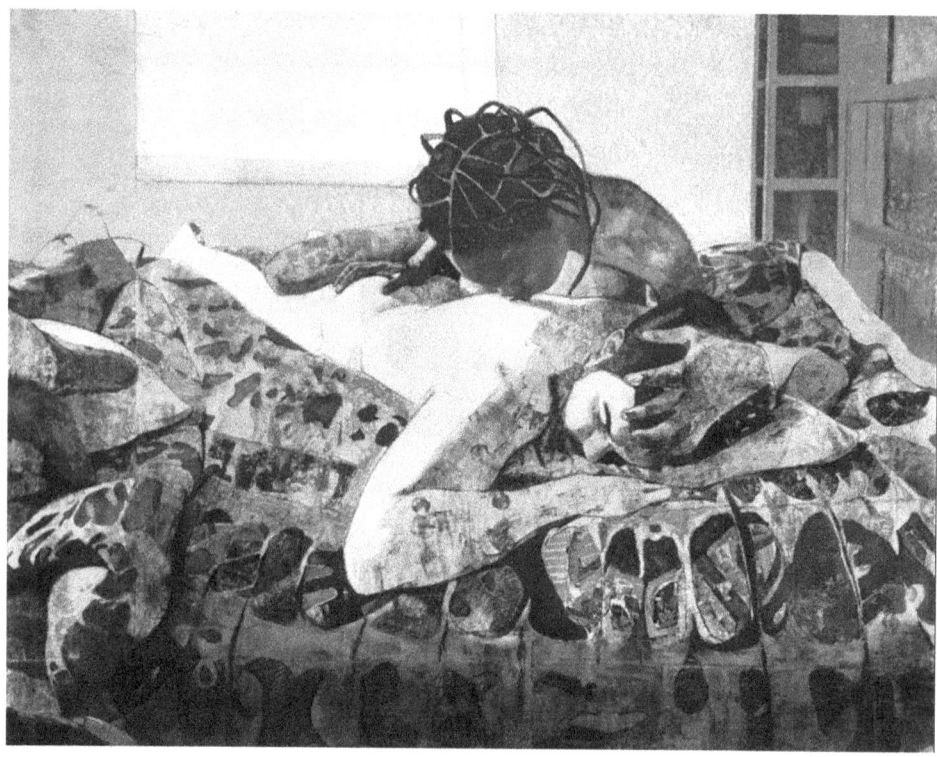

FIG. 2.4 Njideka Akunyili Crosby, *The Bridge* (2010). Charcoal, ink, acrylic, Xerox transfers, lace, and paper collage on paper, 5 ft. × 7 ft.

signifier of the "past," or the authentic culture of the diaspora. Her and her husband's bodies make an impression on a richly patterned blue and yellow material, reminiscent of traditional Nigerian ankara fabric, which creates a feeling of vastness and a rippling water effect. The back wall is a familiar pale green, a wall color common in Nigerian homes.

While the scene offers fewer details about the setting, the painting is reminiscent of her 2010 work *The Bridge* (figure 2.4) and her 2011 painting *Rebranding My Love* (figure 2.5). *The Bridge* captures the scene in *Thread* but from slightly farther away, allowing more details to fill the frame. The colors are pale and dark gray, white, and royal blue, with pops of orange and yellow in their forms. The collaging is far less prominent, making it easier to see small details in the face and skin. Moreover, there are visible charcoal lines around the back window and even in the forms. The window lets in bright white light that fills the room and bounces off their bodies. Akunyili Crosby has delicately painted her own face in gray, her eyes lowered with love and attention. The painting's

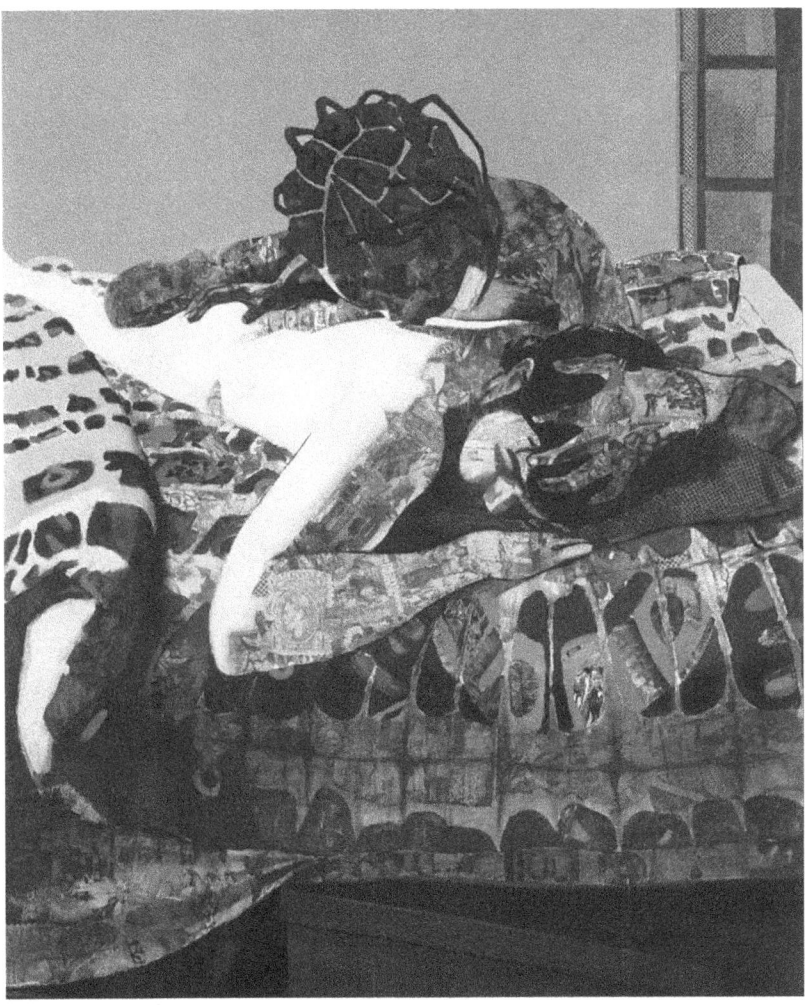

FIG. 2.5 Njideka Akunyili Crosby, *Re-branding My Love* (2011). Charcoal, acrylic, collage, and Xerox transfers on paper, 5.5 ft. × 4.5 ft.

color gives it a perhaps somber tone, and the style is less bold and more tentative than many of her other paintings.

In *Re-branding My Love*, the view is from a different angle as we see the tops of both Akunyili Crosby's and Justin's heads. Akunyili Crosby's hair is threaded in the same style, and a comforter with the same pattern covers the bed. Her figure straddles Justin, and her right knee, which pins down his right leg, almost seems to melt into him. She kisses his back, one hand in his hair and the other grabbing his buttocks. Justin's eyes appear closed, his arms peacefully tucked under his head. His skin is stark white except where his body is affectionately touched by Akunyili Crosby's figure, which casts orange-tinted collage shadows. The collaging in Akunyili Crosby's skin is tinted brown, allowing it to blend into her skin. The intensity of the tangerine-orange wall and the gold in the comforter is striking. Her style in *Re-branding My Love* is less crisp and more painterly, making it feel more emotional and sensual than *The Bridge*. Outside of the oranges and yellows, the collage hue is darker and utilizes more blues and purples. There is a dresser ledge that is painted hyperrealistically, further emphasizing the painterly style of the rest of the painting. Placed side by side, *The Bridge* and *Re-branding My Love* are almost compositionally identical, and yet the color and style of the two paintings communicate very different emotions, which we might understand as representative of her ambivalence about marrying a white man—the tension between her feelings of loss and sacrifice and her own full-body desire.

*Thread*, *Re-branding My Love*, and *The Bridge* all disrupt patriarchal gender norms that are invested in the construction of Nigerian women as pure, pious, and virginal. Akunyili Crosby pushes back on these cultural norms by shamelessly centering her own naked body and employing collage images of fashionable, confident women from Nigerian media, countering twenty-first-century conversations surrounding African women and their sexuality that discuss sexuality in terms of sin or exploitation and fail to engage pleasure and choice. In these three paintings, Akunyili Crosby is the key actor, in both cases on top of a submissive white body, which she kisses and grabs, unsettling the trope of the "efulefu," the lost conquered African woman who falls victim to the perverse pressures of the West and betrays her culture.

In *Thread*, *The Bridge*, and *Re-branding My Love*, the various elements of the environment, the patterns, and her use of collage compositionally bleed into Justin's body. I read this as a visualization of her anxieties about what it means to envelop and be enveloped by an outside culture. In these paintings, "culture," represented by the images of moments from Igbo history, pop idols, and family photos, does not move unilaterally but envelops them both. In *Thread*, we see an advertisement for the Nollywood film *Beyoncé & Rihanna 2*,[39] where actress Nadia Buari dons a straight blond wig; a photo of Kris Okoye, whom Akunyili Crosby has referred to as the "Nigerian Michael Jackson"; and a photo from her own wedding, which shows Justin with her and four other Nigerian women, all of them in traditional attire. Akunyili Crosby states in one interview, "I grew up on Madonna, Michael Jackson, MC Hammer, *The Cosby Show*, *Sesame Street*. As Nigeria got rich and oil money started coming in, the country was able to purchase programs from the United States, so that they became part of the fabric of Nigerian life."[40] Akunyili Crosby represents this transfer as a type of contamination that seeps into Justin's skin. Moreover, the images on her own skin are perhaps also a comment on the ways in which whiteness and Western culture have already transferred to her and shaped her desires by way of historical legacies of colonialism and imperialism; thus, the "battle" over losing her culture has, in many ways, already been lost.

I am fascinated by Akunyili Crosby's decision to render this scene, which is one of her most erotically charged images, over and over again. Her decision to revisit this imagery repeatedly confirms the power of the erotic to inform how we read the particularities of living in diaspora. In this scene, Akunyili Crosby asserts herself as a sexual agent, prioritizes her pleasure, owns her anxieties and her shame, and still proudly claims her Nigerian heritage and relationship to its geography as a home. Akunyili Crosby further emphasizes this when she contends:

> I'm Nigerian, I grew up under too many dictatorships, but I think that coup is a word I have in my head about my art. It's subtle and slips in there before you even know, so it turns out the image is changing your perception of a place before you even know what is happening. But political can refer to things beyond the government. I'm thinking of images I didn't see, but I wanted to see more—thinking of a woman of color and a white man in a very loving intimate relationship, being depicted in a very ordinary way; this is a power structure that is different from what I've seen before.[41]

Akunyili Crosby performs disbelonging as she positions herself both within and against her community by experimenting with visualizing how culture is expressed, transferred among individuals, and unconsciously rejected. This process appears again in her painting *Nwantinti* (2012) (figure 2.6), which is inspired by the French painter Edgar Degas. Rendered entirely in shades of reds, maroons, and pinks, the painting captures Akunyili Crosby sitting at the foot of a bed, locked in an intimate gaze with Justin, whose head she holds in her lap. There is an open pink closet door behind them and a door or window covered in dark purple metal bars. The walls, the bedspread, and their clothing feature photo transfers of Nigerian music icons from the past and present, photos from their wedding, family photos, and photos of political and religious figures. The painting is a celebration of love. The title of the painting, *Nwantinti,* comes from the popular 1976 love song "Love Nwantinti," which Crosby remembers from when she was growing up. In her words, "It became slang for cheesy, sappy love."[42] The painting is not only a formal exploration of color and

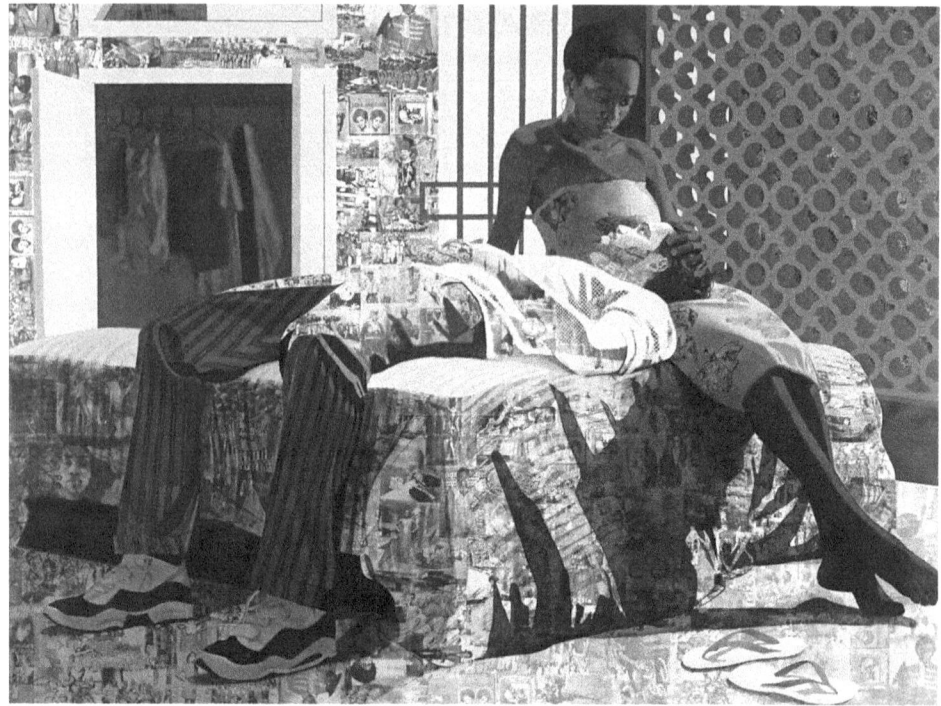

FIG. 2.6 Njideka Akunyili Crosby, *Nwantinti* (2012). Acrylic, charcoal, colored pencil, collage, and Xerox transfers on paper, 5.57 ft. × 8 ft.

composition but also a homage to Nigerian popular culture and Nigerian romance, which sit delicately juxtaposed against her own interracial relationship. On the material tied around her body, Akunyili Crosby has created a print that features wedding photos of a Nigerian man and woman who are most likely a couple, based on their matching traditional attire.

In "Orientations: Toward a Queer Phenomenology," Sarah Ahmed explains that the concept of orientations describes how life is directed vis-à-vis the requirements that we follow in the path of what has been set out for us. In pursuit of the "good life," we are told to imagine our futurity in terms of our ability to hit certain points along a life course.[43] Ahmed contends that this is how one "becomes straight." Writing of the role of the family photo displayed in the family home, she says:

> Everywhere I turn, even in the failure of memory, reminds me how the family home puts objects on display that measure sociality in terms of the heterosexual gift. That these objects are on display, that they make

visible a fantasy of a good life, depends on returning such a direction with a "yes," or even with gestures of love, or witnessing these objects as one's own field of preferred intimacy. Such objects do not simply record or transmit a life; they demand a return. Not only do they demand a return, but there is also a demand that we return to them, by embracing such objects as embodiments of our own histories, as the gift of our own lives.[44]

Here Ahmed explains that the role of the family photo is not simply to record, but to be a point of direction for us. The photos not only tell us what we did, but who we are and who we want to be. In this painting, Akunyili Crosby is quite literally wrapped in representations of a relationship ideal that does not resemble her own, while in a literal embrace with her white partner. Justin's Western attire, highlighted by his Air Jordans, further emphasizes his outsiderness in this scene.[45] Nonetheless, this scene, and arguably the presence of the family photo in all of her paintings, also positions their partnership as oriented toward both past and future understandings of the Nigerian family, regardless of the ways their interracial pairing disrupts normative narratives around transmission of culture to future generations, threatening the continuation of the type of Nigerian family represented on Akunyili Crosby's dress.

Akunyili Crosby's paintings vary in size, but she generally works large, creating paintings that are six and seven feet tall and wide. As a result, her works have a visceral effect on viewers, who are consumed by her worlds and the dense imagery. There is a sense that we are both in her worlds and just outside of them, looking in on intimate scenes that we wouldn't ordinarily have access to. And there is a sense that Akunyili Crosby wants us to notice our own response to the images of her and Justin together. Akunyili Crosby's visual rendering of fearless pleasure invites her viewers to linger with her in the space of her, to quote Audre Lorde, "deepest and non-rational knowledge" about the nature of her own longing, and also the pleasure she derives from being divided between multiple geographies and cultures. A kaleidoscope of color and texture, her paintings are archives full of figures and memories from her personal life and Nigerian popular culture, which she invites viewers to carefully excavate. By representing her erotic self while intentionally marking herself as someone intimately tied to Nigeria, Akunyili Crosby rerenders her diasporic reality as one where all parts of her, especially the aspects that are the source of her alienation, can coexist. Her erotic self does not defy but, in fact, defines her Nigerianness. Akunyili Crosby's diasporic homemaking here asks viewers to psychically travel with her across "multiple universes," rendering them as domestic sites of leisure, intimacy, and conflict. In doing this she creates a sense of movement and dislocation while simultaneously emphasizing the reality of settling and forming roots.

By exploring taboos and centering the erotic in her work about home, family, and belonging, Akunyili Crosby demonstrates what careful attention to affect and intimacy can reveal about the types of negotiations African diasporic women have to make in regard to how we see our bodies and our relationships, what parts of ourselves we reveal and to whom, and how obligated we are to the needs and expectations of our families and communities in the homeland. Akunyili Crosby visually maps these connections as we see her living in ways that are fully embodied, rather than censoring her desires, and envisioning landscapes of acceptance she creates for herself and her communities.

# 3

Erotic Agency and African Intimacy
in the Video Works of Zina Saro-Wiwa

*Environment for me is not just about oil pollution. It is vital to consider emotional, social and spiritual ecosystems in order to transcend the status quo.* —ZINA SARO-WIWA

Zina Saro-Wiwa's film *Sarogua Mourning* opens with the artist sitting in front of a three-paneled red backdrop. She looks vacantly at the camera, her head just barely tilted and her lips slightly parted. Her shaved head and bare shoulders are the only parts of her body in the frame, and she blinks slowly as if willing herself to cry—her breathing becoming slightly more audible (figure 3.1). At the 1:16 mark, her eyes well up with tears and she quickly averts her gaze downward, grabbing at the tip of her nose. She looks up again, immediately recomposed.

Suddenly words escape from her mouth: "I have to talk . . . it's about the idea of hanging onto pain and what this—" Saro-Wiwa pauses and appears

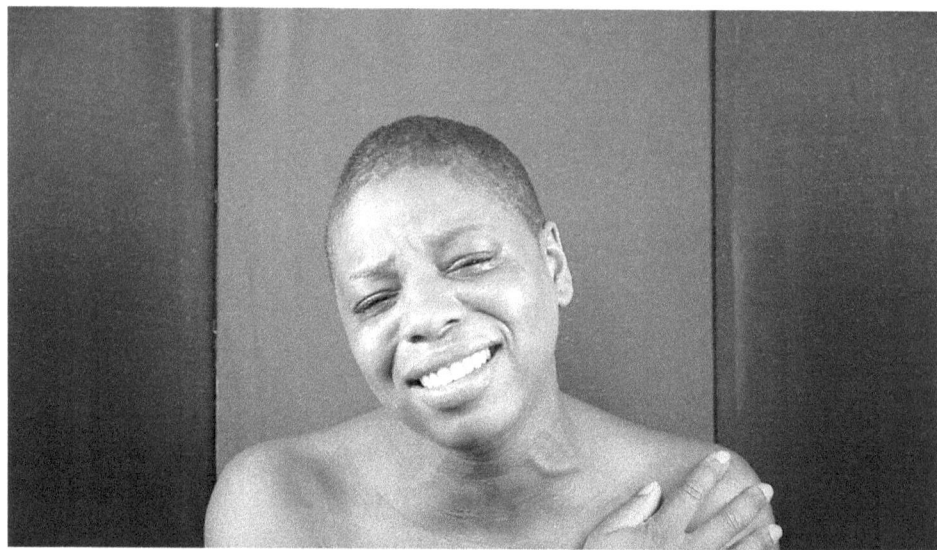

FIG. 3.1 Zina Saro-Wiwa, still from *Sarogua Mourning* (2011). Single-channel video, color, and sound, 11 minutes, 37 seconds.

to be holding back tears. She continues in a somewhat fractured stream of consciousness:

> Sometimes I think ... when I get upset about some guy or whatever ... because I am trying to hang on to a kind of ... pain. And that's what I've been looking for, I'm looking for pain, so I look for these guys who are in pain and who cause me pain. You need, like, emotional juices, something to masticate on, you know? And release itself on, because the other stuff is too hard. The other stuff is never-ending. So we're actually seeking catharsis ... small acts through these guys that you will get over. But your family member dying you might not get over, so you need something smaller to work through it and ... joy is hard. Letting go and releasing is really hard. And having nothing, especially if you're used to pain, is really hard. That's what this session is teaching me ... how to have joy.

Seconds after she utters the word *joy*, her eyes well up again and she begins to sob, attempting to maintain as much eye contact with the camera as possible. Her sobs are broken up by moments of deep breathing. She holds her head and grasps her chest. She looks from side to side and compulsively nods her head up and down.

At moments in the video, she appears to start to laugh, moving between laughter and sobs, at times stopping to breathe and lock eyes with the camera.

The video demands our attention and patience, as well as the ability to sit in our own discomfort. In the eleven-minute-and-thirty-seven-second video, Saro-Wiwa performs a delayed act of mourning—an offer of individual grief shared into an unseen but felt community beyond the camera's lens. The performance was initially shown at Stevenson Gallery in Cape Town, as part of the 2011 group exhibit *What We Talk About When We Talk About Love*, and was shown again in 2013 at the Pulitzer Foundation in Saint Louis as part of *The Progress of Love*. In June of 2015, the video was projected onto the Manhattan Bridge as part of "Light Year," a one-year program of projected video art. It was also shown during Art Basel Miami in 2021. The video then lived on Saro-Wiwa's website until the piece was purchased by the Museum of Fine Arts Houston and Smithsonian Museum of African Art.

In *Sarogua Mourning*, Saro-Wiwa attempts to use performance to construct her own cultural ritual. The title is inspired by precolonial Ogoni deities. Sarogua is both a rain god and a war deity. In fact, after naming the piece, Saro-Wiwa discovered that her father—environmental rights activist and writer Ken Saro-Wiwa—had evoked the deity in a poem he titled "For Sarogua, Rainmaker." In her description of the 2011 video installation, she reveals: "I did not cry for ten years after my father was killed. I found his very public death difficult to mourn partly because his legacy and story belonged to the wider world and not to me, but also due to a profound dissatisfaction with the Western mourning rites I found myself having to draw on at the time of his death and the death of my younger brother before him."[1]

Saro-Wiwa recorded the performance on her father's birthday, noting, "I didn't realise that at the time of shooting. The 10th of October 2011 would have been my father's 70th Birthday."[2] With a shaved head, she attempts to perform the act of mourning—the ritual she connects to rainmaking—for her camera. In the version that lived on her website before it was sold, the frame suddenly freezes at the 9:03 mark. Though perhaps not her original intention, it leaves an image of Saro-Wiwa mid-sob, with her left hand in the process of wiping her nose. The time on the video continues to run, and we are left with a feeling of incompleteness. Just on the verge of full catharsis. Longing for the good cry we could have had. For the release that never was.

In *Sarogua Mourning*, Saro-Wiwa responds to her inability to emote through a performance of emotional excess, which becomes an act of potential catharsis for viewers. Through her performance of unrestrained sadness, Saro-Wiwa invites the viewer into a moment of witnessing. Saro-Wiwa's speech in the performance describes the ways that she comes into contact with her pain through small acts, for example, in her romantic life. She implies that it is easier to experience and release her pain when it is triggered by something that she can get over. That major tragedies—for example, the death of a family member—are too overwhelming.

Through her piece, she maps the ways in which grand national narratives bleed together with stories of familial trauma and romantic heartbreak as she attempts to assemble individual triggers toward some sort of collective resolution—even, perhaps, collective healing. This excess is also performed in the way she vocalizes something between laughing and crying, which communicates both a feeling of release and the agonizing feeling of being unable to fully release grief. In this way, Saro-Wiwa's embodiment in the video illustrates critical theorist Amber Musser's theorizing of "brown jouissance," which Musser characterizes as "an embodied hunger that takes joy and pain in this gesture of radical openness toward otherness."[3]

The 2015 projection of *Sarogua Mourning* onto the Manhattan Bridge performs yet a different kind of excess. Nicole Fleetwood develops the term "excess flesh" to describe the ways "black female corporeality is rendered as an excessive overdetermination and as overdetermined excess."[4] She uses "excess flesh" to theorize the strategic ways black female artists deploy hypervisibility in the dominant culture. In her words, "excess flesh enactments work through the spectacular."[5] In the installation, Saro-Wiwa's larger-than-life black body weeping on the side of the bridge creates a performance of black excess as she refuses to let her emotionality be something that can be swept under the rug.

This prolonged and expansive emotionality also weaves through Saro-Wiwa's work beyond *Sarogua Mourning*, most notably her 2012–13 documentary project and video installation *Eaten by the Heart*, which I elaborate on later in this chapter. Saro-Wiwa's video artmaking is a home remaking practice that privileges African interiority by shifting our attention to affect, pleasure, and intimacy—a space theorized here as an example of what Audre Lorde calls the "erotic." In "Why We Get Off: Moving Towards a Black Feminist Politics of Pleasure," Joan Morgan addresses the tendency of black feminist theory, particularly in its engagement with the erotic, to essentialize the experiences of African American women while ignoring how this assumption might be different for black women throughout the diaspora. She writes, "All the women are white; all the men are black . . . but are all the blacks African American?"[6] While Morgan contends that diaspora studies has much to offer in terms of complicating what she sees as the African American essentialism present in black feminist scholarship, this chapter argues that black feminist investigations of the erotic and women's pleasure also have much to bring to diaspora studies. A deeper understanding of the erotic as it relates to diasporic identity and experience sheds light on the ways diasporic women practice disbelonging and reclaim their power by resisting oppressive social norms and conceptualizing their diasporic identities through the lenses of vulnerability, desire, and anti-respectability.

Saro-Wiwa's visual records of grief, intimacy, vulnerability, and love performances among Africans—both on the continent and throughout the diaspora—not only push the viewer past shame and repression to center feeling; they move beyond the realm of the aesthetic into the creation of fleeting affective diasporic communities. Her work demands a witnessing from others. It focuses on the interior emotional world of the subjects in her videos (at times Saro-Wiwa herself), offering viewers small paths to emotional release themselves. And by bringing these personal subjects and emotional releases into community through her video projects, she re-creates notions of community and collective affect. Political scientist Emma Hutchison defines an affective community as one where "the respective community is welded together, at least temporarily, by shared emotional understandings of tragedy."[7] I expand this notion by examining the ways Saro-Wiwa's affective communities are united not only by tragedy but also by expressions of the erotic.

Lorde defines the erotic as "the measure between the beginnings of our sense of self and the chaos of our strongest feelings."[8] For Lorde, the erotic is a resource, a kind of power rooted in what she calls "our unexpressed or unrecognized feeling."[9] Arguing that in order to perpetuate itself, every oppression must corrupt or distort the forms of power that create energy for change, she contends that, for women, this has meant a suppression of the erotic in particular. L. H. Stallings builds upon this idea in *Funk the Erotic: Transaesthetics and Black Sexual Cultures* with her concept of "funky erotixxx," which she describes as "an acknowledgment that what is profane or obscene has a lineage that exceeds its destructive imperialist mandates within Western Patriarchy and is sacred."[10] Present in Lorde's theory of the erotic is also a consideration of how ways of existing that trap women in roles of martyrdom—perpetually sacrificing for external systems and structures—limit our lives. She writes:

> When we live outside ourselves, and by that, I mean on external directives only rather than from our internal knowledge and needs, when we live away from those erotic guides from within ourselves, then our lives are limited by external and alien forms, and we conform to the needs of a structure that is not based on human need, let alone an individual's. But when we begin to live from within outward, in touch with the power of the

erotic within ourselves, and [allow] that power to inform and illuminate our actions upon the world around us, then we begin to be responsible to ourselves in the deepest sense.[11]

While Lorde speaks specifically of joy—where she writes, "The sharing of joy, whether physical, emotional, psychic, or intellectual, forms a bridge between the sharers. Which can be the basis for understanding much of what is not shared between them and lessens the threat of difference"[12]—I contend that the feeling and expression of joy and grief are so deeply intertwined that the two cannot be separated, something that Saro-Wiwa invites us to experience firsthand through her art. Also embedded in our embrace of the erotic is the power gained from what Lorde describes as "sharing deeply any pursuit with another person."[13]

Zina Saro-Wiwa was born in Port Harcourt, in the Niger Delta region of Nigeria. At the age of one she moved, with her mother and two siblings, to Sussex, England, only visiting Nigeria during school holidays. Over time, mounting political tensions involving her father, Ken Saro-Wiwa, made it increasingly dangerous for the family to visit. Ken Saro-Wiwa, then president and spokesperson for the Movement for the Survival of the Ogoni People, is most famous for leading a nonviolent campaign against the pollution of the land and water in Ogoniland by multinational oil companies, most notably Royal Dutch Shell. He also spoke out against the military dictatorship led by Sani Abacha, whom he criticized for failing to regulate foreign oil companies. In 1995, when Zina Saro-Wiwa was nineteen, he was executed by the government after being falsely accused of being involved in the murder of four Ogoni leaders. Zina Saro-Wiwa did not visit Nigeria again until she was twenty-four, when the government finally released his remains. She began connecting with her African heritage during a gap year in Brazil. Following her time in Brazil, she returned to the United Kingdom to complete a degree in economics and social history at Bristol University and worked for the BBC, where one of her projects included a two-part radio documentary about her time in the Brazilian state capital of Salvador da Bahia. Saro-Wiwa remained in broadcast journalism for ten years before deciding to move to New York in 2009, where she began her career as an artist.

While living in New York she directed and produced *This Is My Africa* (2008), a film about Africans living in London, which was picked up by HBO. She was also invited to curate a show at Location One Gallery in Manhattan, titled *Sharon Stone in Abuja*, after the 2003 Nollywood film. The show, which explored and reimagined the Nollywood film industry, featured commissioned works from Wangechi Mutu, Andrew Esiebo, and Pieter Hugo and a collaboration between Mickalene Thomas and Saro-Wiwa, who together created a Nollywood living room and two portraits. During this time, she traveled to Lagos to make her alt-Nollywood films *Phyllis* (2009) and *The Deliverance of Comfort* (2009). These films pulled heavily from Nigerian cultures of the everyday and Nollywood aesthetics and themes, while telling subversive stories and questioning social norms. In 2013, Saro-Wiwa moved back to Port Harcourt and opened an art gallery, Boys Quarters Project Space, in her father's old office. She divides her time between Nigeria and the United States.

Saro-Wiwa's work, which includes photography, documentary film, short film, and curatorial work, strives to reframe her migration story as well as the stories of Africans across the continent, considering how geography maps itself onto bodies through feeling and gesture. In her exhibition *Did They Know We Taught Them How to Dance?* Saro-Wiwa asserts: "Environment for me is not just about oil pollution. It is vital to consider emotional, social and spiritual ecosystems in order to transcend the status quo."[14] Here Saro-Wiwa is referring to how conversations about environmentalism in Nigeria almost exclusively focus on the pollution caused by oil extraction, when in actuality the Nigerian environment consists of so much more. In this chapter, I examine Saro-Wiwa's consideration of emotional ecosystems via her representations of love, intimacy, taboo, and pleasure, looking specifically to her 2012–13 documentary project and video installation *Eaten by the Heart*, which explores intimacy, heartbreak, and love performances among Africans, both on the continent and in the diaspora. I argue that Saro-Wiwa marks the black diasporic body as a site of erotic agency and, in doing so, simultaneously acknowledges and resists the burden of respectability and cultural norms and expectations that hide and dismiss the importance of emotional expression, intimacy, and vulnerability in the lives of African and African diasporic people.

Saro-Wiwa's work is political in its consideration of religion, cultural survival, and gender. Yet it is also concerned with what some may consider frivolous or indulgent, for example, affective expressions like the prolonged weeping in *Sarogua Mourning*. By offering viewers the opportunity to hear African and African diasporic subjects, particularly women, speak frankly about love, intimacy, and heartbreak, and witness the intimate act of kissing, her work serves as a visual record of African diasporic vulnerability. Her projects center private and taboo feelings, behaviors, and conversations, challenging the status quo of African film and media. In the process, she transforms them from being objects of shame to forming the basis for connection and community in an African diasporic context.

In *Postnationalist African Cinemas*, Alexie Tcheuyap historicizes the emergence of African cinema, which he contends was introduced as a colonizing mechanism by Europeans. Tcheuyap writes that these early films were designed to "manufacture otherness, disseminate colonial propaganda, market the 'civilizing mission,' and convey ideologies of superiority."[15] To counter this mission the Fédération Panafricanine des Cinéastes (FEPACI) emerged—an association of filmmakers from the African continent and the diaspora. Although the association began as a liberatory project, it quickly became prescriptive in its approach to film, defining African cinema as exclusively concerned with cultural struggles, education, information, and consciousness raising. According to Tcheuyap, until recently, these parameters excluded certain forms from the category of African cinema, particularly explorations of allegedly frivolous topics such as laughter, joy, pleasure, sexuality, and experimentation. Indeed, African curator Bisi Silva names the common misconception that matters of the heart are not as worthy as sociopolitical concerns when it comes to telling African stories, writing: "An exhibition taking love as the thematic underpinning may seem unusual in the context of presenting contemporary art from Africa. Most curatorial endeavors over the past few decades have focused extensively on more pressing 'grand' narratives such as history, colonialism, and the postcolonial as well as new social-political conditions, new identities, and new subjectivities that epitomize societies in transition. . . . Consequently we are led to think, 'What's love got to do with it?'"[16]

Saro-Wiwa's work shows us why love (as well as grief) has everything to do with it by pointing to the intricate ways history, colonialism, and sociopolitical conditions intersect and collide with African diasporic senses of self and community.

### Kissing and Heartbreak in *Eaten by the Heart, Part 1:* *How Do Africans Kiss?*

Taking a documentary approach, *Eaten by the Heart* captures individuals reflecting on intimacy, love, and relationships. The series was commissioned by the Menil Collection in Houston, Texas and supported by the Houston Museum of African American Culture for an exhibition titled *The Progress of Love.* It includes a three-part video series—*Eaten by the Heart: The Documentaries,* and *Eaten by the Heart: The Installation*—all shot interview style. While Saro-Wiwa uses the language of documentary to describe the videos, the participants are not named, making them anonymous to the viewer. Though Saro-Wiwa is not overt about who the participants are or where they come from, the varying amounts of familiarity between interviewers and respondents gives the sense that they are a mix of strangers, friends, and acquaintances. Through her work, she creates an affective community, as we see the same individuals appear in all three parts of the series. They look like African aunties, mothers, uncles, and cousins, but in a way that they are rarely seen. Instead, Saro-Wiwa films them in a way that gives room to move beyond our biases, habits, and "home training" to see African people differently than the way we've been told to see ourselves. This helps us imagine a different way of existing. This emphasis on affect and vulnerability extends into Saro-Wiwa's call for participation, put out by the African Studies Program at the University of Wisconsin–Madison, which read: "Video artist and documentary-maker Zina Saro-Wiwa is calling on Africans and African Diasporans aged eighteen to ninety to participate in a discussion and interview sessions discussing love, kissing, heartbreak and intimacy from the African perspective. Zina is also looking for Africans or African diasporans prepared to kiss for the camera."[17]

*Part I: Interview Excerpts or How Do Africans Kiss?* begins with a single question, "How do Africans kiss?" The eleven-minute film captures interviews with individuals from all over the African diaspora answering the deceptively simple question.[18] At the beginning of the film, we see a young black woman with her hair in Bantu knots, sitting in front of a white background, staring directly into the camera. We hear Saro-Wiwa, who is off camera, ask, "How do Africans kiss?" and the girl raises her eyebrows slightly as she repeats, "*How* do Africans kiss?" There is a quick cut to a young man in front of the white screen whose lips are in an exaggerated pucker. Then the screen cuts back to the same young woman, who hesitatingly answers with a smile, "I don't know. I don't really see Africans kiss." The answers offered at the beginning of the video repeat: "Africans do not kiss, Africans kiss badly, Africans kiss secretly. Kissing is not a part of African culture." An older woman in a deep-red headdress, with what sounds to my ears like a Nigerian accent, bluntly states, "I'm not comfortable seeing Africans kiss. I think that comes from the environment where I was raised." A younger woman interviewee expresses that while she does not find black people kissing strange, generally, she experiences physical discomfort when she sees Nigerians kissing in Nollywood films. Reflected in all of the responses is the feeling that for Africans, and especially Nigerians, the act of kissing is strange and troubling.

As the film progresses, the interviewees begin to consider why they might have these views on kissing. Two themes emerge: the difference between how kissing in Africa is perceived in rural areas versus in the city, and how where one is positioned in the diaspora determines their comfort with the act of kissing.

To the first point, a couple who appears to be middle-aged explains, "I think it all depends on the exposure . . . outside exposure . . . where you live, how you were brought up and everything. In the rural areas, I didn't see any kissing going on . . . in the city parties and stuff like that, we see kissing . . . but in general we hold our emotions in. We don't express it as much as it needs to be expressed." In this reflection, exposure to certain public displays of affection becomes a marker of geography, with the countryside being more conservative than the city. The interviewee also speaks to a type of repression, where she says, "we hold our emotions in. We don't express it as much as it *needs* to be expressed." By using the language of "need," she reveals that Africans are not naturally unexpressive and that this holding back is an act of restraint and one that is detrimental.

The theme of geography comes up again when another interviewee explains that where one is located in the diaspora is also a key factor in whether and how Africans kiss: "With the younger generations I think . . . um . . . there's definitely a little bit of spice when they kiss. Um . . . they're not shy about kissing anymore. They're a little bit expressive depending on what continent they're on. I think it's important to showcase that. I know I don't see that many couples in Nigeria of my generation kissing in public or whatever . . . it's just a kiss on the cheek but I do see couples here in the states who are a little bit more expressive."[19] Supporting this point, another interviewee shares that he did not become a good kisser until he came to the United States: "I became a good kisser when I arrived here in America. I became a good kisser. My first time . . . it's almost like I have a tongue in my mouth . . . it's like a meat in my mouth . . . and after like two three times trying to educate myself . . . you know about tongue in my mouth . . . you know it's almost like you want to throw up . . . but today it's a pleasure but it takes time with mind and with body to accept."[20] For both of these interviewees, sexual intimacy and expression is something that happens in a more liberated fashion outside of the continent. This also helps us better understand Saro-Wiwa as the interviewer, who speaks about how growing up in the West meant that she was used to seeing "certain types of white people kissing all of the time."[21] Both the location of the interviews (in the United States) and Saro-Wiwa's hyperexposure to white people kissing in Western culture understandably make her more aware of her lack of exposure to Africans kissing. Moreover, in the latter example, the interviewee expresses disgust as he describes feelings of wanting to throw up triggered by the experience of French kissing. Sianne Ngai writes in *Ugly Feelings*, "In its intense and unambivalent negativity, disgust thus seems to represent an outer limit or threshold of what I have called ugly feelings, preparing us for more instrumental or politically efficacious emotions."[22] Ngai argues that disgust, contrary to "weak" emotions such as envy, paranoia, and irritation, offers distinct possibilities. Building upon this, in her discussion of disgust and abjection in Julia Kristeva's *Powers of Horror*, Sara Ahmed writes, "Kristeva shows us that what threatens from the outside only threatens insofar as it is already within. . . . It is not that the abject has got inside us; the abject turns us inside out, as well as outside in."[23] In his story about his earliest experiences kissing with tongue, the interviewee describes a process that requires him to push through his own disgust in order to find—to learn—pleasure. It is only through facing another person's tongue, and the disgust it evokes, that he crosses a physical threshold.

Saro-Wiwa then asks interviewees, "How do you like to be kissed?" The first person to answer is a middle-aged man who hesitatingly says, "Hmmm ummm . . . probably on my lips . . . probably on my cheek." The uncertainty communicated by his use of "ummm" and "probably" gestures at his unpreparedness to answer that type of question and also seems reflective of how many African men, though often seen as the initiators of sex, are rarely put in a position where they are asked to articulate their desires, particularly around tender acts like kissing. After him, a young woman laughs and asks, "Are my parents going to see this video?" referencing the shadow of familial expectation and cultural burden African and African diasporic women in particular must consider. With this question, Saro-Wiwa pushes the interviewees to not only talk about "Africans kissing" as a reality, but also to name and articulate their own sensual desires, acknowledging the erotic within themselves.

In *Desire/Love*, Lauren Berlant argues, "Desire's formalism—its drive to be embodied and reiterated—opens it up to anxiety, fantasy, and discipline."[24] That is to say, the naming and adoption of desire beyond just a fleeting affect is an action that makes one vulnerable. This is precisely what Saro-Wiwa asks her interviewees to do. In the final parts of the film, Saro-Wiwa asks, "When was your heart last broken?" The mood within the film shifts from playful to somber as we see a young man pause for several seconds and smile uncomfortably, looking away from the camera, as if to shield his actual emotions, before saying, "I guess like . . . um . . . maybe nine months ago." He finishes the sentence and nods a few times as if relieved to have gotten the words out. We then hear Saro-Wiwa ask, "What happened?" from behind the camera. He pauses again and takes a breath. "Well . . . um." He shakes his head and smiles again. "I really don't want to talk about it." "When did you last feel loved?" Saro-Wiwa asks. Again he pauses, nervously licking his lips and averting his gaze. "The same time my heart was broken . . . nine months ago." "Can you tell me about that?" she asks again. "Um no . . . I really don't want to talk about it."

The camera lingers on this interviewee while he struggles to stay composed and speak without breaking down, though his voice trembles. By asking him to elaborate, Saro-Wiwa pushes the interview to a place where he is forced to articulate that not only does he not want to share, but he cannot share his last heartbreak. This is the only moment in the film when we hear Saro-Wiwa speaking to the interviewee multiple times. She sits behind the camera as a woman asking him, an African man, to be vulnerable in front of her, and she does not turn away in the face of his tears. In doing so, she creates space for his vulnerability by normalizing his experience through her performance of a feminist ethic of care, which centers the humanity and well-being of the interviewee, even as it interrupts our experience of the film.

Still, his refusal to elaborate speaks to the limits of the format. It is a safe space, but not entirely safe. Immediately following his interview, we see the older woman with the red headdress again. Although the viewer does not hear Saro-Wiwa ask a question, we can gather that it is the same: "When was your heart last broken?" The woman speaks deliberately. "I can smile now when I tell you that it was when my kids were buried. But the reason why I smile is because I feel strengthened by the love my husband has for me and by my faith in God. So that was when my heart was last broken, when I buried my children." She says it all very matter-of-factly, with a neutral look on her face. It is clear to the viewer that she is well practiced in sharing this difficult truth. After she speaks, we hear what sounds like a sob from behind the camera. By editing the film in such a way that we see this woman share something so devastating without so much as a tremble in her voice, but hear presumably Saro-Wiwa's disembodied gasp, as if by affective transmission, Saro-Wiwa illuminates the interconnectedness, and at times shared grief, between the interviewees and herself—this too is the erotic Audre Lorde speaks of.

In her filmed interviews, Saro-Wiwa also captures the often-unseen and unacknowledged burdens African women inherit and carry, and the struggles African women in the diaspora experience as we reconcile our desire to be seen as whole, complex individuals and our desire to perform the roles that are expected of us and that have been modeled by our mothers and grandmothers. Lorde writes, "The erotic is a measure between the beginnings of our sense of self and the chaos of our strongest feelings. It is an internal sense of satisfaction to which, once we have experienced it, we know we can aspire. For having experienced the fullness of this depth of feeling and recognizing its power, in honor and self-respect we can require no less of ourselves."[25] *Eaten by the Heart* is a container for participants to walk the line between discovering and asserting a sense of self and the chaos of grief, heartbreak, and desire. Participants are given the opportunity to experience this internal sense of satisfaction, which becomes a feeling that they can aspire to.

The people Saro-Wiwa chooses to interview have a range of skin tones, hairstyles, accents, and attire, and very rarely do they identify where in Africa they are from and whether they are "locals" or "diasporans." This heterogeneity reflects Tcheuyap's examination of how nation-building has become a less prominent motivation in African cinema, arguing that the early postcolonial goal to "write back" to colonial forces has given way to an interest in depicting what has historically been considered "non-representable" subject matter.[26] Although Saro-Wiwa is Nigerian, her project is primarily a diasporic one, concerned with shared experiences and understandings of intimacy among African subjects. In this sense, "African" as an identity is a unifying principle for everyone who has chosen to participate, and yet it does not erase their differences. Because the project is by Africans for Africans, it goes without saying that Africa is a diverse and multifaceted continent.

*How Do Africans Kiss?* is about more than kissing. The film also disrupts the veil of secrecy around touch and intimacy, secrecy that Saro-Wiwa works both with and against, not only by asking individuals to speak frankly about love and intimacy but also by allowing viewers to see it in real time. The video ends with the man who shares about learning how to kiss in the United States:

> Everything is love in Africa starting from birth . . . even when you pass away . . . it's love. If I [think of Ghana] I can take an example about funeral [*sic*]. It's amazing how many days it takes to get the body ready. That person is gone but you see the love and the connection there and all of the colors and seeing that body going underground six feet under and it's so much love so much passion and the elders are never forgotten, they're there, they're part of the young generation's life, they are everything and it's love.

The power in this video is its raw, unfiltered vulnerability. *How Do Africans Kiss?* is permission to be a deeply emotional, feeling African, and a reminder that the violence of colonialism does not strip the ability to love, to feel, to be soft. The film accomplishes this by inviting individuals from across the diaspora to collectively identify the erotic within themselves as they release gendered and cultural burdens and reject a culture of silence and secrecy. It is the communal experience of this sharing that makes it a sheltered space for this type of vulnerable storytelling and emoting even in a format intended for wide dissemination.

## Eaten by the Heart, Part II and III: Damien and Breathing Orchestra (2012–2013)

*Damien* opens as a black-and-white portrait of a young black man. Perfectly still, he stares directly at the camera, never breaking eye contact, his left eye squinting slightly (figure 3.2). Gradually color seeps into the image, the image growing warmer and more saturated in tone, until we can make out his brown complexion and bloodshot eyes (figure 3.3). Tears begin to pool at the base of his eyelids and eventually, after much blinking, one falls from his right eye. A few seconds later he vanishes into a white screen.

Though *Damien* is only three minutes long, time stretches while watching his face on the screen. Because video editing is often not intended to mimic real time, the experience of watching his face for the full three minutes is overwhelming. His eyes are locked on the camera and, in turn, our eyes are locked on his. Saro-Wiwa catches viewers in his gaze as we first wait to see if he will move, unsure if the video has started or if it is frozen, and then notice his slow blinks and the color that slowly fills the screen, turning him from a cool statue to a living being. At the end of the video, his eyes are so bloodshot that the whites of his eyes are entirely a deep pink. The acceleration of his blinking followed by the flash that is his tear falling is jarring against the stillness of the rest of the shot. This keeps us transfixed by his eyes, the locus of his vulnerability.

Many of Saro-Wiwa's videos focus on the different ways bodies communicate without words, asking the viewer to contend with the information they project onto what they are seeing. In the first half of *Damien*, he almost appears to be smirking, which is emphasized by the fact that the first half of the video is black and white, giving it a cold feeling. The look on his face could be interpreted as tough or intimidating. If we turn away too soon, which the video almost dares us to do in its slowness, that is our lasting impression. It is only once we are almost halfway through that it becomes evident that Damien is crying, and once a tear falls, the video ends abruptly. *Damien* captures the depths that exist when we take the time to see: in particular, the intense and tumultuous emotional landscapes that we all carry, as well as the "slow violence" of anti-blackness on the body. As film scholar Lakshmi Padmanabhan argues, long-take aesthetics in cinema help us better understand the affective experience of slow violence, not simply by watching it on a screen but through feeling it in our own bodies.[27]

Saro-Wiwa points to the ways black men may be perceived as smug, aggressive, or intimidating one moment, a façade that can crumble if you give it the

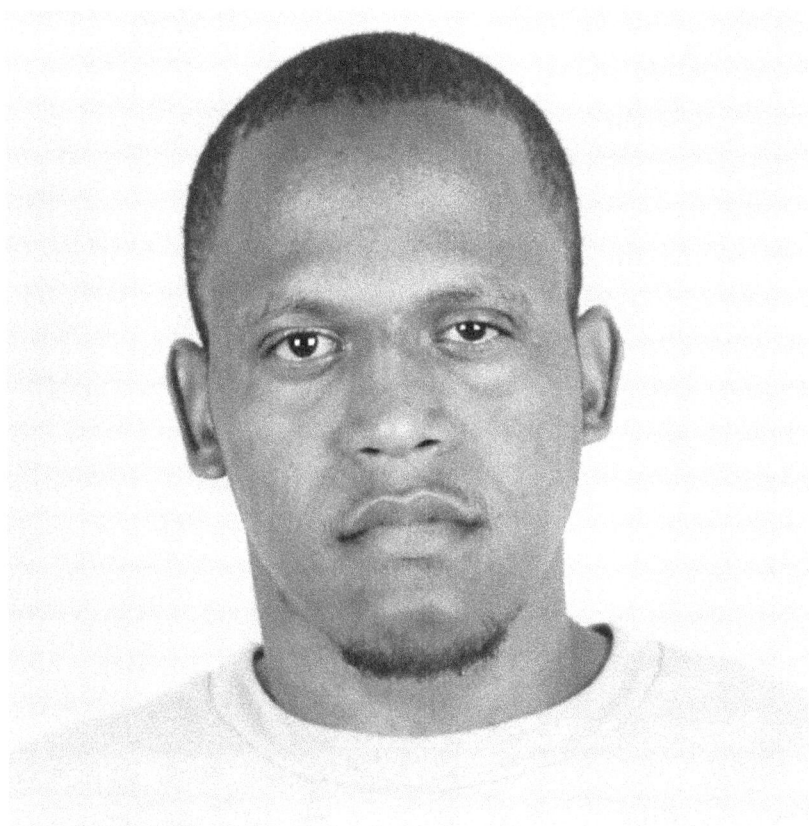

FIG. 3.2 Zina Saro-Wiwa, still from *Damien* (2012–13).

time. The video's placement in the series also has significance. While the first part of the *Eaten by the Heart* series gives us a traditional interview style, keeping our attention with bright colors, frequent cuts, and lots of dialogue, *Damien* demands more investment and patience. But once we see the payoff of this patience, we as viewers are more open to *Eaten by the Heart, Part III: Breathing Orchestra*, which requires an even greater amount of attention and patience (figure 3.4).

Building on the temporal stretching of *Damien*, *Breathing Orchestra* (2012–13) opens with the sounds of deep breathing. A close-up of a bald black man in a black-and-gray patterned sweater comes on the screen. His eyes are closed and his chest peacefully rises and falls.

"Many, many years ago when I was in the military, I um . . . fell in love, or what I thought was love and um . . ."

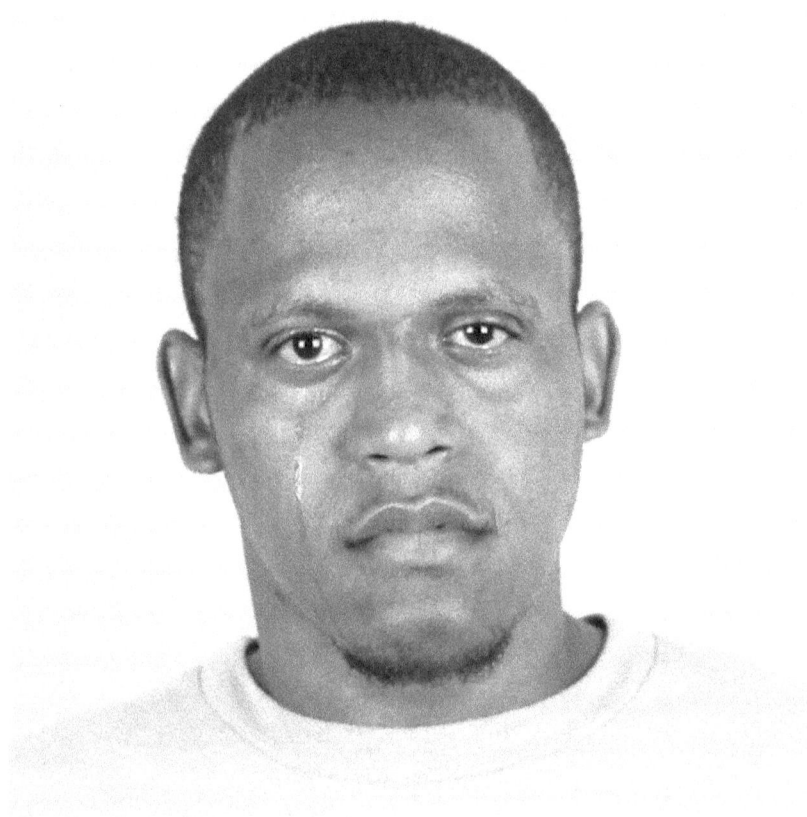

FIG. 3.3 Zina Saro-Wiwa, still from *Damien* (2012–13).

Another rectangle appears at the upper left corner of the first frame, this time with another bald black man, wearing a brick-colored shirt, whose eyes are also closed. Then a new voice:

"I didn't love myself."

Again and again, new rectangles pop up, containing snippets of new stories.

"I guess you might say, I have always been, what's commonly referred to as 'out' because I fell in love with a man in the military. Uh, I grew up having..."

"Well, I think it started with me being abused at eleven, first by a woman, then by a man, um so..." His story continues quietly but is hard to hear. A fair-skinned woman with big curly hair pops up on the screen.

"My parents loved each other very much. Um, I think their love was annihilating...."

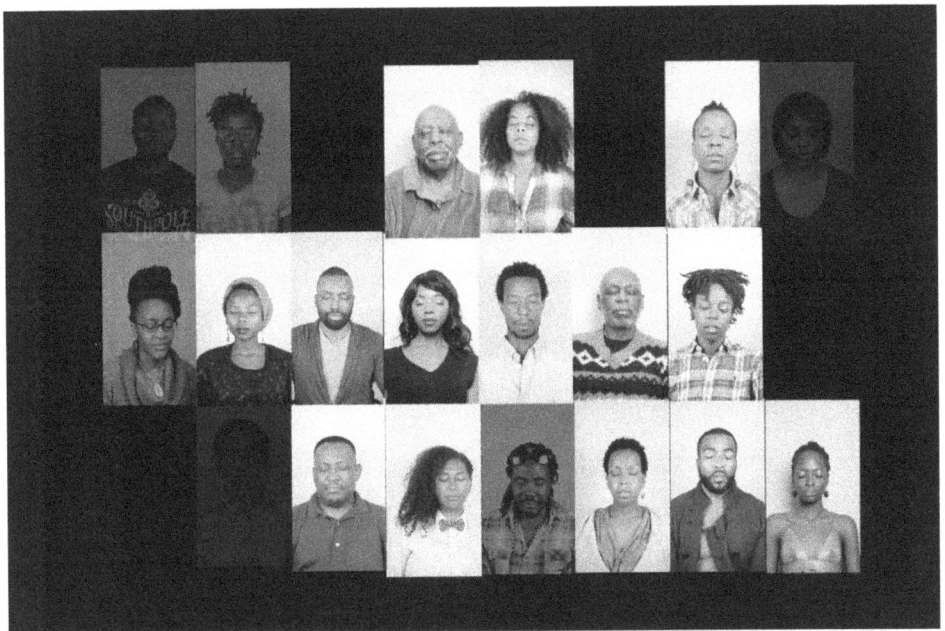

FIG. 3.4 Zina Saro-Wiwa, still from *Breathing Orchestra* (2012–13).

Another woman appears in the far-left corner. "When I think about black love, I don't, uh, get images of butterflies and hearts floating around. . . ."

"My mother came from traditional Indian, Islamic, family, Muslim. And she married this black African man. From Oboy, from the village."

The faces fill the screen one at a time, their words overlapping and blending.

"It feels like there are so many things going on with black people that they're not really . . ."

"I'm not alone. But I am lonely."

". . . images of butterflies and hearts."

"When I met my wife it was love at first sight. There was no doubt, you couldn't mistake it. I couldn't mistake it. The room disappeared, it was all very, very special. That was how I knew."

As the video continues it becomes harder and harder to make out the individual thoughts, and instead short phrases, some repeated from earlier in the video, rise to the surface.

". . . doesn't judge . . ."

"A lot of what it takes to be a dancer may also be what it takes to be a lover. . . ."

"Each of us are fractured but we bring something beautiful to the table if we look inside."

Although each rectangle pops onto the screen with its own story, Saro-Wiwa manages to capture the pregnant pauses in each segment, quieting the other voices when a new one enters. The voices overlap and blend, but they do not compete for the limelight, and Saro-Wiwa keeps them at a low murmur when there are many playing at once. The viewer is left waiting and wanting more, but having to patiently wait for the thoughts to reveal themselves and make sense.

When the last rectangle fills the screen, the viewer is left with twenty-four resting faces, just breathing for almost another two minutes. The image of them all on screen, chests rising and falling out of sync, creates the optical illusion that the surface of the screen itself is pulsating, and one by one the individual portraits vanish until there are none.

Here, we are offered stories of trauma, abuse, and fairy tale love from a variety of black diasporic cultural perspectives. Visually the video feels like a meditation inviting us to pause and breathe. Their peaceful faces and calm breathing ground the viewer even when the voices become more layered and the individual voices are harder to distinguish. Once the squares cover the screen, creating a living, pulsing group portrait, the viewer can't help but breathe with them. The video, which features individuals from the other two parts of the series, feels like an offering to the participants and the viewers.

Significantly, Saro-Wiwa's decision to begin this piece with a story about queer love in the military places the taboo topics of same-gender attraction and queerness front and center. This gives them a prominent space in the stories being told about African diasporic intimacy, even though most of the stories featured in the *Eaten by the Heart* series appear to be about hetero-sexual love. In this piece, the notion of "affective community" feels the most explicit, as our eyes linger on the faces of these individuals who have shared various parts of themselves throughout the series. In the three videos encompassing *Eaten by the Heart: The Documentaries*, we come to recognize and identify with certain interviewees with a tenderness that is connected to the vulnerability of what they have shared.

### Eaten by the Heart: The Installation (2012)

In 2012 Saro-Wiwa premiered a sixty-two-minute video installation at the Menil Collection of African and African diasporic couples and strangers making out.[28] The video opens with a rust-orange screen, indistinguishable sounds

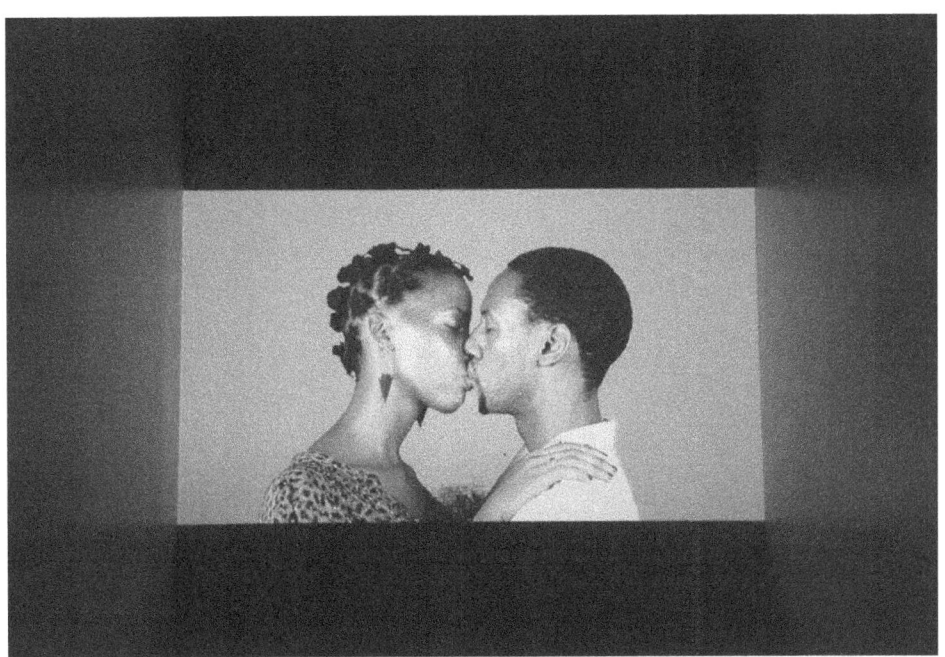

FIG. 3.5 Zina Saro-Wiwa, *Eaten by the Heart: The Installation* (2012).

of people speaking, the heavy bass of Afrobeat music playing in the distance, and cars honking. At the nine-second mark, a couple suddenly appears in the middle of the screen. The black static between their bodies and along the edges of their foreheads captures the mediated quality of the scene—it appears they are in front of a green screen. Their eyes are closed, and they kiss using ample tongue, as if unaware that they are in front of a camera (figure 3.5). After four minutes they pull away from one another and stare into each other's eyes before disappearing from the screen as quickly as they appeared. Saro-Wiwa writes of the performance, "So many of us cite with confidence that Love Is Universal. But the performance of love is, it seems, cultural. I wonder how the way we choreograph and culturally organize the performance of love impacts what we feel inside and who we become."[29]

The video features a diverse group of kissing couples of varying nationality, age, and sexual orientation. We recognize many of them from *How Do Africans Kiss?* Each couple was asked to stand in front of a green screen, allowing each pairing to have a different colored background. In the third video, a man and a woman stand against a blue background with the sounds of birds chirping. They are both wearing pink, and the man digs his hands into the woman's afro as they kiss. There is a push and pull between the two of them, with each expressing an equal amount of physical craving. When they are finished, they stare at each other and then at the camera, implicating the viewer. What is most captivating about the piece to me is all the ways we see African diasporic women exert sexual agency. They pull hair, they bite lips—they appear to be genuinely enjoying themselves. There are a couple of moments in the film where at the end of the kiss the men appear slightly embarrassed or ashamed, whereas the women always seem self-assured. The piece ends with two women kissing.

When the show premiered, museumgoers watched the film in an intimate dark room attached to the larger exhibit, where the kissing pairs were projected larger than life. I, on the other hand, first watched the film on my laptop at a neighborhood coffee shop. In an article in the *Houston Press*, Meredith Deliso writes, "It's a sweet concept, but I don't think most people can stand to watch an hour of other people making out. By the third couple, I had had enough."[30] Deliso's review exemplifies how the all-consuming nature of video installation forces viewers to encounter their own visceral responses. Isolde Brielmaier breaks down this relationship between the video installation and the visitor's body, writing: "The visitor's body is essential to the structure of video installation and the articulation of ideas. Within the context of the installation space, the visitor negotiates the specific site of the artwork as a way of experiencing and, in turn, creating meaning from the art. He or she quite literally and figuratively takes a position in the work. The very quality of video installation makes the visitor intensely aware of his or her body, and all of its sensory functions form a complex entity that is intertwined, engaged, and capable of perceiving."[31] What Brielmaier describes here is what Laura U. Marks refers to as *haptic* or *tactile visuality*, which describes images that "invite the viewer to respond to the image in an intimate, embodied way, and thus facilitate the experience of other sensory impressions as well."[32] The performance video is intense and uncomfortable. It feels almost intrusive. As a second-generation Nigerian American, this is the most I have seen Africans kiss in my entire life. The kissing is long and passionate. At times it includes lots of tongue. The couples vary in age, some appearing to be in their twenties and others seeming much older. Two of the couples appear to be same-sex pairings.

In my view, the performance's objective is simple. While there is so much writing that claims to be about African sexuality and intimacy only to pathologize it, Saro-Wiwa's performance video throws us directly in the midst of hot, passionate, sometimes sloppy making out. It presents African intimacy and love with no pretense. It does not allow us to overly intellectualize it. Instead, the colors and sounds consume and transform us. Perhaps this is the reason Deliso could only stand to watch three of the couples. Tcheuyap writes in his chapter on how postcolonial African films have addressed sex that "neither open intimacy or *sentimental confession* is popular in African cinema." He argues that in African films, the body and sexual organs in particular "seem to avoid and be avoided by the camera."[33] *Eaten by the Heart: The Installation* plays with this trope by taking an act as "PG" as kissing and allowing the viewer to experience it visually, emotionally, and intellectually. Saro-Wiwa pushes the act of kissing as far as possible and, in doing so, reveals much about sensuality, intimacy, and agency without the use of nudity.

On the theme of "sentimental confessions," the style and content of *Eaten by the Heart* is exceptionally confessional in nature. Confessional art has been defined as "a form of contemporary art that focuses on an intentional revelation of the private self. Confessional art encourages an intimate analysis of the artist's, artist's subjects' or spectators' confidential, and often controversial, experiences and emotions."[34] While Irene Gammel argues that calling this type of art "confessional" is inherently problematic, as it brings to mind the patriarchal history of the confessional and the priest, I argue that understanding *Eaten by the Heart* as a collective confessional speaks to the power of the piece, as well as the cathartic nature of the act of confessing.[35] In *Eaten by the Heart*, the subjects do not confess sins in a dark room to a hidden man but are given an opportunity to release a range of often repressed thoughts and feelings, which they may have been conditioned to carry as shame. They can share these confessions, publicly and in community, as part of a project dedicated to creating a safe space to practice vulnerability. Indeed, Saro-Wiwa's work illustrates Stuart Hall's assertion that representational art not only serves as a mirror but presents new possibilities that constitute new kinds of subjects. In his words: "I have been trying to speak of identity as constituted, not outside but within representation; hence of cinema, not as a second-order mirror held up to reflect what already exists, but as that form of representation which is able to constitute us as new kinds of subjects, and thereby enable us to discover who we are."[36]

*Eaten by the Heart* is a space of radical intimacy and vulnerability, and Saro-Wiwa's disregard for the ways shame and tradition become obstacles is precisely what allows her to approach people with the mission of filming them at their most vulnerable. Lorde writes, "Our erotic knowledge empowers us, becomes a lens through which we scrutinize all aspects of our existence, forcing us to evaluate those aspects honestly in terms of their relative meaning within our lives. And this is a grave responsibility, projected from within each of us, not to settle for the convenient, the shoddy, the conventionally expected, nor the merely safe."[37] That is to say, the erotic instructs us to want more of our lives and our communities and to seek it out or create it. Saro-Wiwa's films create new worlds and ephemeral communities where Africans across the diaspora can discuss sex and intimacy openly and connect across ethnicity, gender, sexuality, and age. In one interview Saro-Wiwa describes the impact watching white people kiss has had on her own expectations when it comes to intimacy: "I mean after decades of watching certain types of Caucasian people kissing all of the time and being very used to that kind of intimacy in the world, I always wonder, well how does that affect who you become? You know that kind of exposure and that kind of performance, who do you become after that. It's not just oh you ingest it, but also you metabolize it. And it turns you into someone, it turns you into someone who has expectations, it turns you into someone that recognizes love in a format or a different format."[38] Drawing on this experience of watching white people kiss, Saro-Wiwa uses *Eaten by the Heart* to create a new type of record that can shape the archive of what has been understood as acceptable African behavior. Saro-Wiwa does this by not merely tiptoeing around taboo or attempting to gently lure people into sharing, but by shattering the veil of secrecy, which allows for a brave and explicit naming of vulnerable emotions. In *Eaten by the Heart* Saro-Wiwa visually maps these connections, and we are given the opportunity to see African diasporic people existing, feeling, and loving in ways that are both emotional and fully embodied. In each of the works I discuss in this chapter, Saro-Wiwa utilizes the confessional style to disrupt the norm of shame and repression and invites participants and viewers to reflect on how experiences of love, lust, and grief, often-kept secret, have the power to unify and bring comfort when spoken aloud, and become the foundation for establishing alternative kinships in the form of fleeting affective communities.

# 4

---

## Queer Diasporic Girlhood in *The Adventures of Ada the Alien* and *Akata Witch*

*It's as much about beauty and make-believe, as it is a commentary on cultural hybridity. This isn't social science, it's magic-realism and the power of drawing to invent worlds for ourselves. I'm a storyteller, not an advocate.* —RUBY ONYINYECHI AMANZE

This chapter takes on the question of disbelonging and return through the lens of African diasporic girlhood. Looking to the work of visual artist ruby onyinyechi amanze and novelist Nnedi Okorafor, I examine two black girl figures: "ada the Alien"—a reoccurring character in amanze's drawings, inspired by her experiences navigating space as a returnee in Nigeria—and the protagonist in Okorafor's young adult novel *Akata Witch*: "Sunny," a Nigerian American girl who has moved to contemporary Nigeria with her family. This chapter considers what both characters tell us about African diasporic girlhood, the complicated act of return, and play and leisure as homemaking, worldmaking, and world-changing practices.

The characters of ada the Alien and Sunny are inspired by the stories of black girls who have "returned" to Nigeria, where they contend with their outsider status. Yet, through their storytelling, amanze and Okorafor disrupt easy understandings of time and space in order to complicate linear notions of return and overly simplistic ideas of belonging. In doing so, they highlight the full creative potential of diasporic subjectivities. These representations illustrate the tension inherent in the act of return and carve out space for the lead black girl characters to find ease as well as play within and through that tension.

Michelle Wright speaks to this tension in *Physics of Blackness*, where she calls for us to look to black speculative fiction for more complex theorizing of return in relation to the Middle Passage. She writes, "In creative discourse, it is Black speculative fiction that most often takes on these questions and problems of return brought about by a Middle Passage epistemology, sometimes to surprising effect."[1] Wright defines Middle Passage epistemology as a narrative of knowledge that centers the black experience primarily on slavery, either through a linear progress narrative or a reverse linear narrative arguing that no progress has been made.[2] She asserts that while return is accommodated easily by "nondiasporic epistemologies"—the epistemologies of Western civilization that uncritically chart a march forward—diasporic theorizing of return is far more self-reflexive in its approach, engaging the past ambivalently and ambiguously. Wright contends that within diasporic theorizations of return, "progress is often deconstructed; origins are often shifted and rendered fluid; and agency and Otherness often haunt textual expression, obliquely or directly."[3] In this chapter, I examine how amanze and Okorafor use speculative investigations to imagine alternative pathways and journeys for their African diasporic girl characters, who come to discover and embody their disbelonging through play and leisure.

Encompassing genres such as science fiction, horror, and magical realism, speculative fiction is concerned with the question "What if?"[4] While many scholars use the language of "speculation" to refer to utopian futures, my use of the term also allows space for fresh considerations of the present. I consider the speculative as an important part of how African diasporic girls perceive their reality, while also looking toward the future. As Keguro Macharia asks, "What speculative experiments are granted to African thinkers and theorists. What are we allowed to imagine and invent? What do we need to imagine and invent?" Sami Schalk argues in *Bodyminds Reimagined: (Dis)ability, Race and Gender in Black Women's Speculative Fiction*, that "by having racialized, disabled women protagonists who narrate their own texts and who live in future or alternative worlds in which the rules of reality are different, these books force readers to understand the experience of their intersectional identities from the main character's perspective, from within their bodyminds, their lives, and their societies.[5] By reading *Akata Witch* alongside amanze's drawings and pondering what Sunny and ada the Alien—as two diasporic black girls navigating connected diasporic realms—can teach us about worldmaking as diasporic homemaking, I attempt my own worldmaking. While Wright speaks explicitly about speculative fiction in writing, I ask what amanze's drawings and *Akata Witch* accomplish as liberatory worldmaking projects?

## Black Girlhood

In *Hear Our Truths: The Creative Potential of Black Girlhood*, Ruth Nicole Brown envisions black girlhood as freedom, writing, "Black girlhood makes possible the affirmation of Black girls' lives and if necessary, their liberation. Black girlhood as a spatial intervention is useful for making our daily lives better and therefore changing the world as we currently know it."[6] Brown's work emphasizes that we must celebrate black girlhood and affirm the experiences of black girls and their liberation if we are to support them in effecting positive change in their own lives and in their communities. In girlhood studies more generally, great strides have been taken to reinsert girls into the cultural narrative. As cultural anthropologist Aimee Meredith Cox writes of girlhood studies more generally: "The field of girlhood studies has questioned the changing nature of citizenship for young women who are defined primarily by their status as both female and adults in the making. Scholars across disciplinary orientations writing in this field have addressed the historical absenting of the experiences of girls in the context of youth cultural discourses, both in the academy and popular culture."[7] Yet because black girlhood studies is still an emerging area of study, the theorizing of the importance of play and leisure, particularly for black girls, is limited.[8] As a result of this gap in the literature, the internet has emerged as a key site for theorizing black girl subjectivity, beginning with #CarefreeBlackGirl and #BlackGirlMagic, which both emerged in 2013.

"Black Girl Magic" was created by educator and activist CaShawn Thompson, who intended it to be a celebration of the achievements of black women. The phrase steadily gained popularity, peaking in 2020 and exploding into a movement of sorts. In one interview, Thompson says, "I say 'magic' because it's something that people don't always understand. Sometimes our accomplishments might seem to come out of thin air, because a lot of times, the only people supporting us are other Black women."[9] Here, Thompson speaks to the ways the perceived "magic" of black girls is often a result of the ways they have been underestimated, ignored, and erased. In Linda Chavers's article "Why I Don't Love Black Girl Magic," she unpacks the troubling and dangerous assumptions that both contribute to and arise from this erasure:

> Black girl magic suggests we are, again, something other than human. That might sound nitpicky, but it's not nitpicky when we are still being treated as subhuman. And there's a very long history of black women being treated as subhuman by the medical establishment, in spite of the debt Western medicine owes to them. It doesn't begin or end with Henrietta Lacks and the cancer cells taken from her cervix without her or her family's knowledge or permission. It doesn't begin or end with black women receiving less anesthesia, if at all, in surgeries because of the widely held belief that black women felt no pain. It doesn't begin or end with black women receiving improper and dangerous prenatal care or compulsory sterilizations.[10]

Indeed, Chavers's comments point to the importance of knowing the difference between imagining oneself as beyond human and being denied humanity.

Centering the experiences and perspectives of black women and girls, I am interested in how imagining oneself as nonhuman and superhuman provides opportunities to resist and challenge societal barriers and expectations, particularly ones that are overly dependent on "reestablishing human recognition" as an "antidote to racialization."[11] In *Becoming Human: Matter and Meaning in an Antiblack World*, Zakiyyah Iman Jackson writes: "African diasporic cultural production does not coalesce into a unified tradition that merely seeks inclusion into liberal humanist conceptions of 'the human' but, rather, frequently alters the meaning and significance of being (human) and engages in imaginative practices of worlding from the perspective of a history of blackness's bestialization and thingification: the process of imagining black people as an empty vessel, a nonbeing, a nothing, an ontological zero, coupled with the violent imposition of colonial myths and racial hierarchy."[12] Identifying how African diasporic cultural production has long been concerned with reimagining the human, Jackson instead centers an "unruly sense of being/knowing/feeling existence."[13] Situating "Black Girl Magic" within this tradition offers new possibilities for an exploration of the intersection between black girlhood studies and black scholarship on the limitations of liberal humanism, which amanze's drawings and *Akata Witch* illuminate.

Their work also asks us to contend with the impulse driving the emergence of the "Carefree Black Girls" hashtag. While many have critiqued "Black Girl

Magic" for primarily being a celebration of the productive achievements of black girls, #CarefreeBlackGirls was created by film and culture critic Zeba Blay as "an assertion that Black women also get to be unabashedly themselves in the world that's constantly putting them into concrete boxes."[14] The concept speaks to the ways that black girls express individuality, freedom, and joy in the face of oppression and stereotypes. #CarefreeBlackGirls has also received criticism from black women who argue that the concept ignores the struggles that black girls and women face, flattening our livelihoods into shallow depictions of wealthy black women participating in leisure activities. In fact, YouTube video blogger Philogynoir argues that #CarefreeBlackGirls is exclusionary, classist, and ableist, stating, "every black isn't carefree, in fact especially black girls aren't carefree."[15] While my evocation of #CarefreeBlackGirls here does not attempt to dissociate from the struggles that black women face or separate black women into respectability categories, it understands that being carefree for black girls and women can serve as an active resistance to the social burdens that attempt to destroy and stifle joy. Carefree in this context means being free from the cares assigned to black girls and women by colonial mentalities and white supremacy. As actor and singer Cree Summers writes:

> I don't know a single black girl who's carefree because it ain't easy being a girl of color, period. God, I wish we were carefree. A lot of political things would have to dramatically change in this planet for a woman of color to be carefree. But I think what they mean by that is more of an aware black girl, a conscious black girl. The more conscious you are, maybe the less cares you have and maybe the more cares you have as well—it kind of goes hand in hand. Self-awareness and more self-love and also the ability to care for other black women. It has something to do with being politically aware of where you stand on this planet and I think it has to do with not accepting the definition that's been given to you by designing yourself.[16]

In this quote, Summers names being carefree as its own kind of work. It is black girls and women advocating for freedom of self-expression despite outside expectations. This understanding of "carefree" also informs my use of "play" in this chapter. Here I evoke Dotun Ayobade's utilization of "serious play," in his book *Queens of Afrobeat: Women, Play, and Fela Kuti's Music Rebellion*, which he develops to speak to how "the context of class, age, and gender inequities and the state of precarity of inhabiting all of these subject positions [can mean] the ludic posture assumes repercussive dimensions."[17] In this chapter, I understand play as regularly occurring in relationship to and/or alongside danger and violence, and as I illustrate in my discussions of Sunny's encounter with her father at the end of *Akata Witch*, negotiating risk is a fundamental part of imagining and leisure for African girls. In this chapter, I recuperate "Black Girl Magic" as an acknowledgment of the often-invisible worldmaking potential of black girls and engage "Carefree Black Girls" as black girls practicing a type of easeful disbelonging that centers play. Exploring both concepts through the experiences of Sunny and ada the Alien, who utilize carefree play and leisure as well as magic to reorder and reimagine their realities, we see these characters create worlds where their differences and peculiarities are not only accepted but essential. Lastly, my discussion of the political power of play and leisure is ultimately a discussion of pleasure. As Schalk reminds us, "Pleasure does not exist outside of oppression because none of us exist outside of these systems of power, but pleasure can nonetheless arise in the midst of oppression, in the face of it, in spite of it, or sometimes even because of it."[18]

## Notes on *Alien* and *Akata*

Through their work, amanze and Okorafor reclaim the terms *alien* and *akata*, which have been used to separate and divide individuals into categories that maintain colonial logics and white supremacist heteropatriarchy. In amanze's and Okorafor's hands, the terms illuminate the complexities of black subjectivity and the tensions between what it means to be nonhuman and superhuman. Their storytelling reanimates subjects that are often flattened into identity discourse and exhibits a disregard for borders and identity labels. To fully appreciate their interventions, a note on the history and theorizing of the terms is necessary.

In "Alien Feminisms and Cinema's Posthuman Women," Dijana Jelača considers how posthumanism emerges in what she calls "the wake of humanism's failed promises."[19] Noting how the doctrine of humanism is one that "combines the biological, discursive and moral expansion of human capabilities into an idea of technologically ordained, rational progress," Jelača contends that humanism has historically favored Western/European whiteness and the normative subject. Jelača uses *alien* to refer to more than extraterrestrial entities, extending the term to apply to that which is simultaneously "familiar and strange, humanoid and posthuman" and refusing to adhere to hegemonic ideas around subjectivity, gender, and identity. In her words, "Alien—broadly construed as both of and not of this world and a liminal figure who is elusive and concrete at the same time—resides at and haunts the human-posthuman spectrum, refusing to conform to a strict binary between the two."[20]

We see these traits in ada the Alien, who possesses the body of a black girl, but with glowing yellow skin. She is both familiar and strange, not only in how she looks but in how she traverses space. I see akata doing similar work. Like alien, akata, which is distinct from *oyinbo*, suggests a familiarity—one that acknowledges a shared origin while also signaling outsiderness. On the one hand, it signals a black Americanness that is distinct from Africanness and, depending on the context, might indicate "lesser than." This is the better-known meaning. Discourses around the word *akata* often focus on the rift between Africans and African Americans, and feelings of judgment and misunderstanding on both sides.

*Akata* is commonly used by Nigerians to refer to black Americans and has also been said to refer to undomesticated or "wild cats" in the Yoruba language. In *Akata Witch* Sunny's character reframes the slur, as she balances the realities of being Nigerian American, being a girl, being magical, and having albinism. Readers of *Akata Witch* are asked to look to the figure of the akata girl as the moral compass of the community, and centering her well-being offers a truer picture of the moral and ethical future of a community. The words *alien* and *akata*, which amanze and Okorafor reclaim as terms of empowerment, illustrate how blackness, diasporic-ness, and girlhood are nuanced, diverse, and simultaneously entangled in difficulties and joy.

Amanze's drawings and *Akata Witch* are also notable in the way they feature and center queer kinship ties beyond the nuclear family. I borrow Alexis Pauline Gumbs's use of *queer* as an intervention into how we think about "the social reproduction of the meaning of life."[21] The queer families where both Sunny and ada the Alien experience belonging are chosen and include individuals who are part human and superhuman. They serve as gateways to self-discovery for both black girl characters. Hershini Bhana Young considers the role of what she calls differential embodiment and movement in expanding and reimagining our understandings of black community in the face of imperial violence. She writes: "The tremendous violence that characterizes contemporary African diasporic life, profoundly altering the very makeup of black bodies, leads me to ask, How can we enact a different kind of black sociality based on differential embodiment and the movements that result? How can this sociality enable us to reimagine the human in ways that move away from individual, discrete, 'normal' bodies that seem capable of independent functioning toward alternate corporealities that are hybrid, multiple, reliant on one another, and often seen as 'monstrous failures'?"[22] Amanze's worlds reimagine the African subject in her depictions of hybrid figures that span space and time, all coexisting, and in *Akata Witch*, Sunny finds imperfect belonging among a motley crew of friends primarily bonded by their magical powers. Cultural theorists Lauren Berlant and Michael Warner discuss the importance of alternative understandings of family in order to create queer worlds, writing, "Making a queer world has required the kind of intimacy that bears no necessary relation to domestic space, to kinship, to the couple form, to property, to the nation."[23] By interrogating representations of queer intimacy in amanze's drawings and *Akata Witch*, we see them blur the familial, platonic, romantic, and generational hierarchies in worlds that exist somewhere between utopias and what Foucault refers to as "heterotopias"—spaces of otherness that exist in non-hegemonic conditions, unlike utopias, which are most often imagined perfect worlds.[24]

### *The Adventures of ada the Alien*

Amanze created ada the Alien when she arrived in Nsukka, Nigeria (the same year she met Wura-Natasha Ogunji, whose work I discuss in the first chapter). Although ada the Alien's features are almost identical to amanze's, she describes ada the Alien as borrowing her likeness but not *being* her. In a process of magical transference, she created a figure who likewise is forced to navigate a complicated return. She explains, "I wanted to tell stories about my time in Nigeria and my experiences and how I was moving through this space as an alien even though it is also my home. This is why I developed this character: to use her and her voice to tell this story."[25]

Amanze was born in Port Harcourt in the Niger Delta region of Nigeria. Following her birth, her family relocated from Nigeria to the United Kingdom, where she resided until the age of thirteen. Amanze earned a bachelor of fine arts from the Tyler School of Art at Temple University and went on to earn her master of fine arts from Cranbrook Academy of Art in Michigan. In 2012, she became the recipient of a Fulbright Scholars Award in Drawing to the University of Nigeria, Nsukka. During her time in Nigeria, amanze found that her outsider identity extended beyond her fair skin, freckles, dreadlocks, and British accent to her chosen medium of drawing: "I quickly discovered that drawing's role in contemporary Nigerian art is a second-tier one. There is a very clear-cut hierarchy of mediums, and drawing just doesn't carry the same weight as something like painting. It exists, and is very much a part of the history of art in Nigeria, but if you're talking about what is being exhibited, bought, and generally respected in Nigerian art, it isn't drawing. That's an almost laughable idea."[26]

For amanze, however, drawing as a medium has opened up possibilities. Its position as a less-respected medium in Nigeria gave her space to push the boundaries of the form. Drawing is also an ideal place to explore girlhood since drawing, for many, is the first way they learn to make art as children. Amanze embraces mistakes and stains on the paper's surface, seeing them as evidence of her human-ness: "I'm not a machine. I'm not trying to be a machine. That human-ness, including mistakes and failures, is something that I am open to and it is part of the conversation between me, and the materials, and the process."[27] Amanze's incorporation of mistakes and failures into her work speaks to a carefreeness that extends to her characters, whom she also allows to be messy, flawed, and easeful.

*Ada* in Igbo is both a title and a name that refers to the eldest daughter in a family. Traditionally, the role of the Ada is to take on a leadership role in the family. Ada the Alien takes the Ada out of the heteronormative family and traditional home, instead expanding the spaces and beings that she has access to and the ways she can take leadership. By doing this, she asks us to consider what it means to be the eldest daughter outside of the traditional Igbo family structure and reimagine the potential of her roles and responsibilities by offering another way for the eldest daughter. The playful ada the Alien thus obfuscates this hefty, burdensome role.[28] Ada is fluorescent yellow, her color inspired by Western images of glowing green and yellow aliens, which amanze applied to her own experience in Nigeria for a number of reasons. Most noteworthy is her physical appearance and accent, which she experienced as immediate markers of her outsiderness. Over time, amanze created additional characters to fill in the magical universe ada the Alien navigated, and this became her series *Aliens, Hybrids, and Ghosts*. In her artist statement she writes, "In a non-linear and fluid narrative, her large scaled drawings explore space, play, magic and hybridity. . . . Navigating fictional and conflating worlds, a cohort of aliens, hybrids and ghosts play effortlessly and access magic as their mundane, yet expansive norm."[29]

In addition to ada the Alien, recurring characters in the series include audre the Leopard, Pidgin, Twin, Tritón, Ofunne and the army of Ghosts, Unidentified Colored Blobs, and Zebra. As the title of the series suggests, the characters fall into three categories: aliens, hybrids, or ghosts. Amanze takes familiar forms such as animals, the alien, and the astronaut in scenarios like travel, leisure, and daydreaming, remixing them in unfamiliar ways. She uses Xerox transfers to create new hybrid forms, names and categorizes her characters by their habits and history, and links forms and figures according to diasporic logics. These tactics make her worlds legible as full-fledged realities with their own set of rules and a particular order, which privileges queerness and hybridity. Philosopher Nelson Goodman writes of worldmaking: "Much but by no means all worldmaking consist of taking apart and putting together, often conjointly; on the one hand, of dividing wholes into parts and partitioning kinds into subspecies, analyzing complexes into component features, drawing distinctions; on the other hand, of composing wholes and kinds out of parts and members and subclasses, combining features into complexes, and making connections. Such composition or decomposition is normally effected or assisted or consolidated by the application of labels; names, predicates, gestures, pictures, etc."[30]

Not only does amanze enact such nuance in her creations, she also utilizes worldmaking in her drawings in order to reject a narrative of displacement as trauma, which she has said viewers of her works often place upon the images. Insisting on the playfulness and ease of her characters, who exist comfortably and, most importantly, playfully, amanze contends:

> I do think we (humans) figure things out by playing. But I also think, play in a certain context is a privilege reserved for a few, and I don't just mean children. . . . My African-packaged body embraces the freedom of play in this America that says otherwise—that says I should be traumatized or anguished or cautious or angry. But joy is a birthright . . . an entitlement that cannot be stolen. I play in life and I play in art, and I've stopped apologizing for not being sad. To invent feels like the ultimate freedom. To claim space to pleasure feels like revolution.[31]

For amanze, play is a political act, an act of defiance, particularly in the United States, where her black African body is expected to be primarily a site of trauma and anger. Her drawings utilize a vast amount of white space and compositions that disrupt firm ideas of time or place and often show her characters flying or falling. They are infinite landscapes of play, leisure, and queer community.[32]

### Ogbonno Soup Is Sweeter Since We Met

The political and revolutionary potential of pleasure and play for queer subjects is evident in amaze's tender work *Ogbonno Soup Is Sweeter Since We Met* (figure 4.1). The thirty-eight-by-fifty-inch drawing shows ada the Alien lying with audre the Leopard, who embraces her from behind. In the mixed-media drawing, audre the Leopard is rendered as a black-and-white photo transfer head of a leopard with the arms of a human. Amanze has described audre the Leopard as ageless (but appearing older and androgynous). Audre the Leopard is queered not just by the leopard head and human body, but also through their

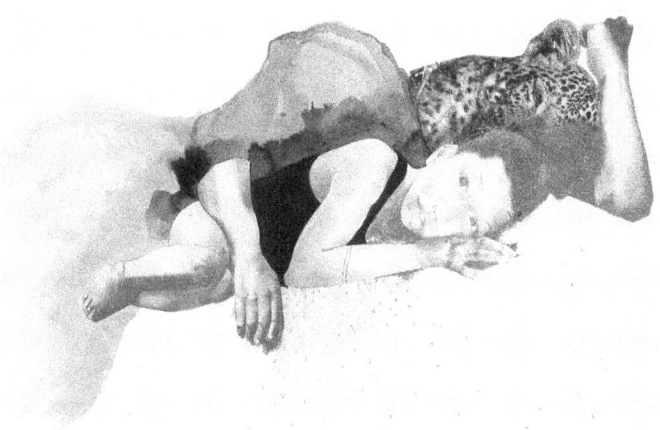

FIG. 4.1 ruby onyinyechi amanze, *Ogbonno Soup Is Sweeter Since We Met* (2014). Pencil and ink, photo transfer, 38 in. × 50 in.

use of the nonbinary pronouns they/them. Amanze has also said in numerous interviews that audre the Leopard's character is Ogunji, an unsurprising detail considering the close friendship the two developed during this time. In both Igbo and Yoruba culture, the figure of the leopard symbolizes strength, tenacity, agility, and vitality, and leopard skins are used and worn in a variety of rituals. Moreover, the leopard's nocturnal nature and lack of predators also make it a powerful symbol.[33]

Audre's body appears to be under a plush comforter done in black ink wash, making only their arms visible. Their right arm, which is drawn in pencil, is filled in with yellow, giving them an alien glow. It drapes over ada the Alien's torso, while their left arm supports their own head. Ada the Alien lies in front of audre the Leopard in a black tank top. Her legs and feet, drawn in graphite, are exposed and appear to belong to a small child or a baby. Her arms are tucked underneath her head as she stares straight at the viewer. On ada the Alien's arm, we see one of amanze's tattoos: two parallel lines that circle her forearm. The two figures float on top of an intricate network of lines connected by drawings of black-eyed peas; the black-eyed peas, found in dishes across West Africa and southern parts of the United States, call to mind diasporic connections.

The piece conjures feelings of rest, safety, and security. Ada the Alien's figure is both woman and child, symbolizing the connection between black women and black girls. Amanze writes in one interview, "My niece called me a Woman-Child. Something in her recognizes me as her kindred, only taller and able to do more things. When we enter other worlds, she knows I am believing in full."[34] In *Black Girlhood Celebration*, Ruth Nicole Brown argues that black girlhood is "the presentations, memories, and lived experiences of being and becoming in a body marked as youthful, Black, and female," and that "Black girlhood is not dependent, then, on age, physical maturity, or any essential category of identity."[35] Indeed, amanze acknowledges the black girl within her despite being technically in the body of a black woman. Her decision to render herself as a girlchild talks back to the ways black girls are denied childhood and asserts the innocence and vulnerability of black girls as deserving of comfort and love. Furthermore, the fact that audre the Leopard, who represents Ogunji, is the one holding ada the Alien points to the ability of black women and girls to show up and care for one another. The scene evokes for us the ways carefreeness is both magical *and* work.

The title of the piece, *Ogbonno Soup Is Sweeter Since We Met*, also speaks to the ways experiences of home are altered by and through those we encounter and connect with. Amanze has said that although she isn't a writer, she enjoys language and often uses her titles to "give fragmented snippets of the reality."[36] Even the altered spelling of "ogbono" in the piece's title, to include two n's, captures the ways language changes and shifts, and new spellings emerge during processes of migration. When they encounter one another, ogbono soup tastes different to ada the Alien and audre the Leopard. Psyche Williams-Forson argues that "Food is a critical expression of cultural identity and an important marker of cultural borders."[37] Although there is no ogbono soup in the image, its distinct ingredients of assorted meat and/or fish, seeds from the bush mango plant, palm oil, and ground crayfish perform a deconstructed cultural reference, giving it a distinct smell, which also informs the scene for those familiar with the dish.

The title of amanze's drawing implies that our social bonds can also affect how we experience the pleasure of food, either because we have the privilege of sharing it with someone whom we feel connected to or due to the shared memory of a particular dish. In *Feeding the Family: The Social Organization of Caring as Gendered Work*, Marjorie DeVault writes, "part of the intention behind producing a meal is to produce 'home' and 'family.'"³⁸ Brinda Mehta elaborates on the relationship between imaginings of home and food, writing:

> The migrants' attitude to food unearths deep association with what I call a "homeland imaginary." . . . [The] sensory construction of the distant island home is a way of localizing space in the metropolis. Recreating the fragrances of "home" through the culinary occupation of space . . . symbolizes the act of creolizing dominant space whereby the familiar of the birthland is both conjured and physically actualized through fragrant whiffs of memory. . . . [T]he recipes for these culinary performances [are where] home is imagined through associative ingredients, flavours, smells, tastes, and colours. In other words, food . . . delineate[s] recognizable mappings of home.³⁹

While *Ogbonno Soup Is Sweeter Since We Met* gestures toward familiar mappings of home, the image also queers those cartographies. Amanze's are the maps of disbelonging, those that offer us incomplete dishes while magically invoking our olfactory senses. And we are invited to navigate these spaces and ingredients, not with those the state or tradition deem family, but with the chosen family members who reorganize the boundaries of culture as they rework our taste buds. The scene draws new maps on and with our tongues as it offers us new names for our food, for ourselves. Amanze has spoken extensively about and expressed gratitude for the other in-between individuals who have helped her understand her particular experience and story. While ada the Alien and audre the Leopard are the characters in this particular drawing, it is a declaration intended for the many individuals who have helped bring deeper meaning to the seemingly commonplace experience of eating ogbono soup.

### Kinfolk [Diptych]

Utilizing graphite, ink, photo transfers, colored pencils, and metallic enamel, *Kinfolk [Diptych]* (2015) (figure 4.2) is split between two fifty-by-thirty-eight-inch sheets. The work features several familiar figures from amanze's drawings, who lounge and play across an immense white plane. On the far-left side of the drawing is the top half of a reclining nude female astronaut whose legs we can imagine continue beyond the borders of the paper.⁴⁰ Her arms are folded behind her head, which rests on a light graphite sketch of a woman's head, rendered as if carved from stone. Supporting the figure's back and neck is a constellation of drawn black-eyed peas. Sharing the panel with the reclining figures are photo transfers of pigeons—calling to mind the special ability of homing pigeons to find their way back home over long distances—as well as tiny Xerox photo transfers of pathos and fiddle-leaf houseplants, which are both floating and anchored to drawn geometric lines, a lamp, and a light switch. Amanze uses minimalist lines and shading to differentiate spaces within the vast white plane, simultaneously creating a sense of insular domestic space, outer space, and nature. In the same panel, directly opposite the reclining ada, is a reclining blue figure. The figure appears to be human but has no face or recognizable features. Its body is filled with blues and dark grays, and it appears pensive, with its right arm folded under where the mouth would be and the left arm propping up its body. This figure may be Tritón, who amanze describes as "a bit of a bore, but for all those who come from the water."[41] In the second panel, two headless figures with ankara arms are potato sack racing with "Ghana Must Go" bags. This is Twin. Amanze describes Twin's character as "a double-bodied, headless entity, full of mischief, childlike. [They are] acrobats by profession. This cheeky doer requires supervision. In the narrative, they are usually childlike and adventurous. They climb trees. They do handstands. They're a little bit naughty. This is part of why they don't have heads, it's more to do with their physicality."[42]

The Ghana Must Go bags are named after the inexpensive large waterproof bags that many carried during the mass expulsion of Ghanaians from Nigeria in 1983. A number of African and African diasporic artists, including South African artist Dan Halter and Ghanaian artist Senam Okudzeto, have used them as a material to explore globalization, migration, and exile. Amanze uses the Ghana Must Go bags to signify movement and travel. Between Twin's legs, clad in Ghana Must Go sacks, an *okada*—the popular name for motorcycles in Nigeria (not drawn to scale)—floats between their feet. Above Twin on the page is Pidgin, a pigeon with a blue face and green glittered body suit. His arms are spread as if floating in water, and he wears floaties made from Ghana Must Go bags on both arms. Amanze describes Pidgin as part pigeon and part-human:

> Pidgin is an in-between character and can be playful and silly like Twin but can also be more serious and take on different responsibilities. The inspiration for the name Pidgin comes from Pidgin English, the Creole language in Nigeria. I am interested in this idea that you can have a language that is essentially a broken, mixed-up, inauthentic language and how you can travel throughout Nigeria (North, South, East, West) and use this to communicate. There are so many official languages and you can't assume that you can speak the same language to someone two hours away from you.[43]

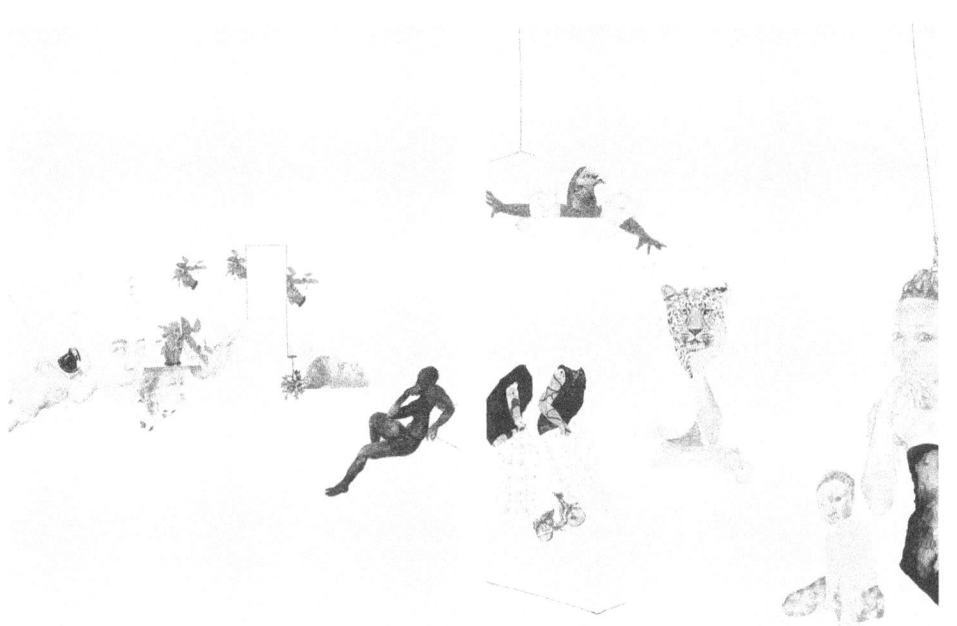

FIG. 4.2 ruby onyinyechi amanze, *Kinfolk [Diptych]* (2015). Graphite, ink, photo transfers, colored pencils, metallic enamel, each 50 in. × 38 in.

Shooting out from one of Pidgin's hands is a constellation of pencil-drawn black-eyed peas, which form a halo around audre the Leopard's head. Positioned in the middle of the frame, audre the Leopard stares straight at the viewer, head resting in their left hand and right hand resting on an invisible surface in front of them. Wrapped around audre the Leopard's resting fingers is a thin string that connects their form to ada the Alien, who is just at the right edge of the panel. To the left of her is an opaque peach-colored figure whose head, drawn in graphite and colored pencil, is modeled after a bronze head from Ife. Though their body is at an angle, their head turns so they can gaze directly at us. The figure's legs, which are also rendered in gray tones, look almost reptilian. His hands appear to mold something we cannot see out of clay. This is merman, inspired by people in the Niger Delta River region of Nigeria, "who often refer to themselves and their cultures as 'Riverine' (or coming from the water)."[44]

The abundance of white space in *Kinfolk [Diptych]* makes the piece appear minimalist, but it is dense with meaning and symbolism. Amanze uses simple accessories such as the astronaut helmet, floaties, houseplants, and Ghana Must Go bags to capture diverse landscapes and represent temporal shifts. Amanze writes: "The magical potential of space (in all of its dimensions) is its malleability: its ability to shift, overlap, take form or infinitely expand. There is a point where land and sea invert, time travel happens daily and flying and walking are interchangeable. The drawings embrace these spatial freedoms, and playfully flirt with design, architecture and utopic mythology."[45]

Amanze conveys female agency with the reclining astronaut, who lies naked and unconcerned with who may or may not be gazing upon her body. Her nude body combined with the astronaut helmet allows us to imagine the figure in two places at once, both lounging and exploring outer space. With the astronaut's arms folded behind her head, amanze uses the helmet to create a sense of leisure, exploration, curiosity, and freedom. Though this figure's skin is a shade of yellow deeper and warmer than the neon tone amanze uses for ada and audre, the fact that she is still a shade of yellow perhaps identifies her as a past or future version of ada in the series. Moreover, in amanze's 2014 work *ada rests in places unknown*, we see ada depicted as a reclining nude donning a similar astronaut's helmet.

Amanze has described the disembodied drawings of heads, which appear throughout her drawings, as the ghosts she has drawn from people who share her experience of being in between: "Sometimes that is important to me, pulling in people who I share this story with, and I share it with many people. Sometimes the ghosts are unknown to me. For the ghosts, it goes back and forth, and it is important for me that these characters are reflecting real people that I know and real people that I haven't met yet. These are people, characters in the story that I don't have a personal relationship with. They could be made up, in some way they are made up but they also exist wherever they are."[46] The ghosts connect amanze's works to a larger community of diasporic women who share her experience of outsiderness. By inserting these women as ghosts, amanze addresses the way these women remain with her and within her, an invisible network of kindred spirits, as she navigates her own disbelonging. While ghosts often represent trauma or types of hauntings, these ghosts represent for amanze a connectedness with those she may not know but shares a story with. Amanze creates a new narrative around these types of characters:

> It isn't trauma in this story at this point. If I tell my story that I am from Nigeria, and the UK and the US very quickly it can go to displacement and loss, and not belonging in a negative way. It is important for me in this story that this is not the energy that is conveyed, that these characters are not lost. They are quite at home. They have created a world for themselves where they exist. They exist comfortably. They exist playfully. They

have fights. They have interactions as normal people would but that idea of it being a traumatic experience to be from many places is not the story that I am interested in telling.[47]

Sociologist Avery Gordon asserts that the ghost "is not the invisible or some ineffable excess. The whole essence, if you can use that word, of a ghost is that it has a real presence and demands its due, your attention."[48] Amanze's treatments of the ghosts in her works make it impossible not to see them, as they are at times larger than the other forms and sketched realistically in pencil, making them appear as full-fledged characters in her drawings.

In *Kinfolk [Diptych]*, hybridity and queerness are not only celebrated but also necessary. Modifications to the human form speak to the tension black women face in nonhumanity and the superhuman but gives us a way out through new possibilities. As Malik Gaines reminds us, the expressive power of imagination "exceeds the rational containment of the body into legible, manageable, individual subject-status."[49] Pidgin can fly but not swim, so he needs floaties. Twin represents multiplicity on multiple levels—they are two bodies but only one character and travel on foot, hopping in a Ghana Must Go bag while also riding an okada.[50] Ada the Alien is at once exploring outer space, daydreaming, staring directly at the viewer, and perhaps even floating in water. Furthermore, gender and species are of no consequence, and amanze's manipulations of space are also manipulations of time. Her use of the astronaut helmets, in particular, brings to mind Wright's discussion of the relativity of time depending on space. It is this that allows ada the Alien to be in two places at once in *Kinfolk [Diptych]*.

José Esteban Muñoz identifies queer worldmaking as a tool of survival used by marginalized subjects to create worlds of "transformative politics and possibilities."[51] Through her visual queer worldmaking, amanze creates her own community of the disbelonged, where aliens, ghosts, and black girls thrive in conditions of their own creation, and experimentation, play, and leisure are central.

### Pools as Sites of Leisure: *The Divers* and *10 Litres of Air [The Diver II]*

In *The Divers* (2016) (figure 4.3) two forms, which appear to be "Twin," with hot pink, green, and electric blue ankara-printed arms and legs and wearing tan swimsuits, dive into a body of water in synchronized fashion on the left edge of the paper. In the center, ada the Alien wears a gray, aquamarine, yellow, and white striped blouse and is represented as just a head, torso, and arms.

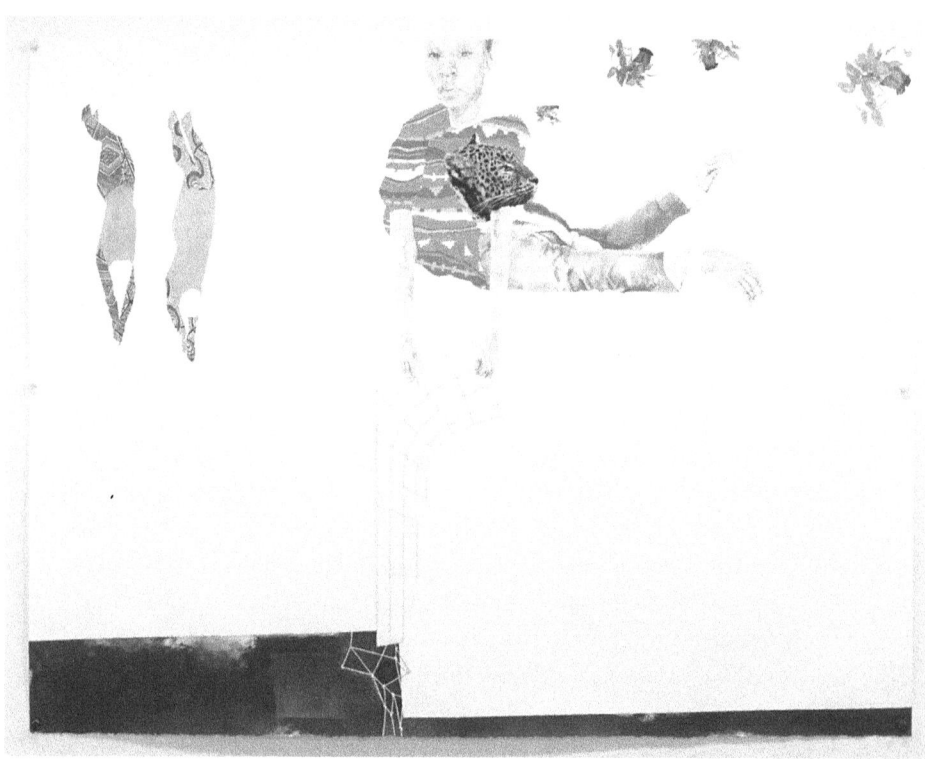

FIG. 4.3 ruby onyinyechi amanze, *The Divers* (2016). Graphite, ink, photo transfer, acrylic, colored pencils, 38 in. × 50 in.

She holds audre the Leopard (also represented as a head, torso, and arms but wearing an aquamarine suit jacket and white button-up) under her arms. In ada the Alien's hands, which hang below, is what looks like a yellow perspective grid used for animation, as if she is using her hands to create or manipulate the world below. Photo transfer houseplants float in the space above their heads.

In *10 Litres of Air [The Divers II]* (2016) (figure 4.4), a similar scene is depicted, but this time audre the Leopard appears to be cradling ada the Alien. It is less clear whether ada the Alien, who is wearing an astronaut helmet and dressed in a swimsuit made of the same material as her billowy blouse in *The Divers*, is floating or falling. Ada's left hand is spread, with pigeons and a ghost face just outside of her grasp. Below them is a rectangular blue mass where Twin, now further into the dive, is mere inches from entering. Low on the left side is a yellow greenhouse. The rectangular blue mass is reminiscent of a swimming pool surrounded by cement and also a portal to outer space or another dimension.

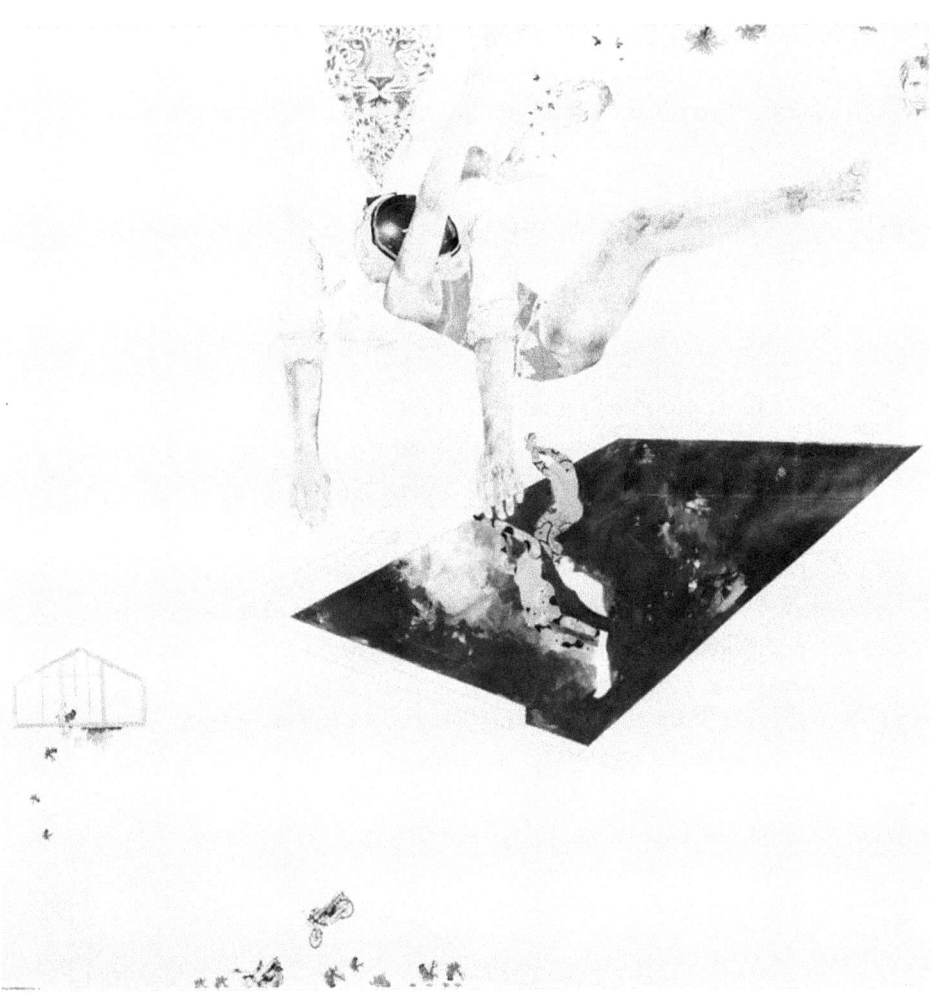

FIG. 4.4 ruby onyinyechi amanze, *10 Litres of Air [The Divers II]* (2016). Graphite, ink, photo transfers, fluorescent acrylic, colored pencil, 72 in. × 72 in.

The painterly quality of the blues and blacks with clouds of white give the appearance of infinite depth. Pools appear often in amanze's drawings as sites of leisure that many of her characters enjoy. The blue void is legible as both water and space, both indicators of diaspora, as water calls to mind water spirits like Yemanya and Oshun, as well as the transatlantic slave trade, and outer space evokes an Afrofuturistic imagination. Amanze combines them to create a site of imagining, remembering, and leisure. Moreover, the water is also connected to the birthplace of amanze's mother, who is from River State, which is part of the Delta region:

If I am in Nigeria, identity-wise, I am just considered to be from where my father is from. Where my mother is from, and that lineage, is not recognized as part of my identity. But thinking about where she is from, you may hear phrases to do with riverine people, or people from a riverine area, or riverine languages. This fascinated me, the idea that someone can identify with or connect their identity to water, or connect their identity with land in a different way. I remember stories of my mother being in water, swimming, or catching fish, and how present water was in forming her identity. I started thinking about the merman as a riverine creature and then thinking about mythologies and spirits or creatures that come out of the water. There are many of them and they take many different forms, the mermaid and the merman being one.[52]

Because in Nigeria the birthplace of the father is considered the birthplace of all the children, amanze reclaims her matrilineage by thinking about her own connection to water. Additionally, in *10 Litres of Air*, amanze utilizes simple pencil lines in the style of an architectural drawing, further adding to the worldmaking aesthetic. Viewers are easily able to insert themselves and their ideas onto the paper, which is still a work in process. Her use of blank space and surreal details invites viewers to fill in the gaps and imagine ourselves reclining in outer space or flying with birds.

What does it mean for ada the Alien to be a character who is in amanze's likeness but who is also not her? How does this speak to the double consciousness of the Carefree Black Girl who creates various versions of herself in order to capture all of her complexities, and also to survive?

Ada the Alien, audre the Leopard, and Twin may all be her creations, but the goal is to have them be able to live as their fullest selves. The relationships that amanze depicts seamlessly and queerly move among the familial, platonic, and romantic, embracing the full range of dictionary meanings of kin. Amanze writes that her works are not utopian fantastical futures but represent the present. Indeed, her works suggest, as I have argued, that the speculative is not simply a tool used to fantasize the future but rather a lens through which we might see the present.

What does it mean to speculate about the present/current condition? How might we not only imagine what we have not become, but also find language to articulate that which already exists but goes unseen? In *Cruising Utopia*, Muñoz writes, "Queerness is that thing that lets us feel that this world is not enough, that indeed something is missing."[53] Amanze's queer and hybrid characters do not exist in opposition to Nigeria or Nigerian culture, but expand how we understand and conceive of culture and identity. Her works capture the act of being both here in the present and also in a queer future where we can imagine beyond what already is. In her drawings, she uses compositional gaps, mixed-media hybrid creatures, and scenes of leisure and play to create fantastical worlds of disbelonging. In doing so, amanze not only rejects trauma narratives but offers an alternative story complete with new characters. She highlights the complex personhood and potential of black girls in diaspora, who are able to blossom, experiment, and create through their own process of self-discovery and self-definition.

### Akata Witch

In *Akata Witch*, the main character, Sunny, goes on a similar journey of self-discovery, which is a necessary first step if she is to save the world from total destruction. *Akata Witch* begins one evening after the power has gone out in an unnamed Nigerian city. Twelve-year-old Sunny Nwazue lights a candle and lies on the floor to stare at it, as she often does: "I lay on my belly and just stared and stared into it. So orange, like the abdomen of a firefly. It was nice and soothing until . . . it started flickering. Then, I thought I saw something. Something serious and big and scary."[54] In the flame, Sunny sees "raging fires, boiling oceans, toppled skyscrapers, ruptured land, and dead and dying people." She states, "It was horrible. And it was coming."[55] The rest of the novel follows her as she discovers her own magic, which includes the ability to see into the future, and chronicles her journey to stop her visions from becoming a reality.

Okorafor refers to herself as an Africanfuturist and Africanjujuist, defining Africanfuturism as distinct from Afrofuturism, which she says she tried to embrace before realizing "it wasn't working."[56] While Afrofuturism more broadly describes the creative reimaginings of science and technology toward black liberation, according to Okorafor, Africanfuturism is directly and firmly rooted in "African culture, history, mythology and point-of-view as it then branches into the Black Diaspora, and it does not privilege or center the West."[57] Africanfuturist texts also heavily engage the themes of technology and space travel. While many of Okorafor's works are Africanfuturist texts, *Akata Witch* is distinctly Africanjujuist. In Africanjujuist works, African spiritual practices and cosmologies merge and blend with fantasy. Similar to amanze's drawings, *Akata Witch* asks us to reconsider a reality that takes into consideration the endless possibilities for black girls in diaspora. In this contemporary Nigerian reality that Okorafor creates, beings move among multiple realms and travel through time, and disbelonging helps save the world.

Born in Cincinnati, Ohio, to two Igbo parents, Okorafor was raised in the suburbs of Chicago until the age of six. As a child, she aspired to be an entomologist—a researcher of insects and their relationship to humans and the environment. The suburbs gave her ample space and plenty of "empty weed filled lots to explore."[58] In the suburbs she describes experiencing racism, as the first black family to move into their neighborhood: "In the 80s of South Holland, Illinois it was like the 60s. My family was one of the first black families to move into that neighborhood. Thank goodness I was a fast runner. I learned early what it was to save my own ass from the bad guys."[59]

Okorafor was inspired by trips she took with her family to Nigeria in the late 1990s. In a 2017 TED Talk, she speaks of how her outsiderness as an American led her to notice things that most Nigerians took for granted, like the growing role of technology in Nigerian life, including cable television in the village, cell phones, and constantly buzzing generators. In her words, "My intrigue finally gave way to stories. I started opening doors."[60]

At the age of twelve, Okorafor was diagnosed with scoliosis. Her condition worsened for several years until, at the age of nineteen, she was told she would need a spinal surgery with a 1 percent chance of causing paralysis, or risk being "severely crippled" by the age of twenty-five. When Okorafor woke up from surgery, she was paralyzed from the waist down and spent the following summer learning to walk again. She asserts that her paralysis led her to begin writing. In her words: "My experience with paralysis *is* why I started writing . . . being paralyzed forced me to disregard the physical for a while and travel inward. That's where I found much of the weird stuff you find in my work. That's where I discovered the storyteller within. Friends of mine say that the whole paralysis thing was fate. Maybe, but it still sucked."[61] Faced with an abrupt change in how she interacted with the physical world, the once hyperathletic Okorafor was forced to retreat into her own world and imagine life beyond the limitations of her physical form.

Okorafor has been candid about the tension she experienced between the norms in her Nigerian family and her creative aspirations. When asked about the biggest hurdle she had to overcome to become a writer, Okorafor answers: "My family and, I guess, culture. In my family, and amongst Igbos as a whole, the most respected careers are in medicine and engineering. Writing is a hobby. I remember my father scoffing at the idea (he was a cardiovascular surgeon and a Chief of Surgery in Chicago). I definitely had to prove myself. So when I decided I was serious, I knew I had to do more than just get published. I had to get a PhD in writing (Nigerians love degrees) and get published by a top publisher."[62]

Similar to what amanze shares about how drawing is perceived in Nigeria, writing being seen as a hobby is what allowed Okorafor to not only navigate her paralysis but ultimately create worlds where others could find liberation.[63] *Akata Witch* was published in 2011 as a young adult fantasy novel, and was followed by two more books: *Akata Warrior*, published in 2017, and *Akata Woman*, published in 2022. The novels have been celebrated for featuring a strong black girl character and taking place on the African continent.

In *Akata Witch*, we come to know Sunny through her complex outsider identities. She declares, "My name is Sunny Nwazue and I confuse people." With this statement, Sunny names the ways she understands her outsiderness vis-à-vis how her community receives and responds to her.[64] Sunny's character is described as "Nigerian by blood, American by birth, and Nigerian again," noting that the process of being Nigerian and returning to Nigeria are actually two separate experiences and nodding to the ways disbelonging as an orientation requires us to move back and forth. Sunny is the only girl in her family, with two brothers, and also the youngest. The most glaring feature marking her outsiderness is her physical appearance. Though she has what she calls "West African features," like her mother, she also has albinism, making her much fairer than the rest of her family. In her words, "I've got light yellow hair, skin the color of 'sour milk' . . . and hazel eyes that look like God ran out of the right color. I'm albino."[65] Like ada the Alien's neon yellow skin, Sunny's albinism marks her as an outsider in most spaces, a visual reminder that she does not quite belong. In his review of *Akata Witch*, Haroon Ghori writes: "As a person of color growing up with albinism, Sunny's character particularly resonated with me. Her interactions with her classmates and countrymen strongly resembled my own. The odd looks and comments that Sunny deals with from her Nigerian counterparts are familiar to any 'albino of color' as we see the confusion in the faces around us—as if we're pieces in a puzzle that don't fit correctly. Between the devices we use to protect ourselves from the sun, the blond or white hair, and the pale skin, we're seen as misfits even among our own societies."[66] Sunny's albinism makes her sensitive to the intense Nigerian sun, and although she is an extremely talented soccer player, she must play at night. Despite the teasing at school, Sunny soon becomes close friends with Orlu, Chichi, and Sasha. Orlu is described as a nice, quiet boy who likes to build things, and he and Sunny become friends when he defends her against bullying classmates. Orlu is also the child of two Leopard People, individuals with magical powers, and neighbors with Chichi. We eventually learn that he is dyslexic, which also gives him the power to undo juju.[67] Chichi is described as "fine boned and elfin," and always wearing dirty clothing.[68] She lives in a small hut with her mother, who is also a Leopard Person, and does not go to school. Chichi possesses many talents, including time travel. Though Chichi is small, the group of friends suspects that she is actually much older than they are. Last, there is Sasha, a black American boy who was sent to Nigeria after getting in trouble in the States. Throughout the book he speaks frankly about being black in America and dealing with the Chicago police.

Sunny soon learns that she has the ability to shape-shift, which allows her to move between the spirit realm and the human realm. Eventually, she unites with Orlu, Chichi, and Sasha, and the four of them form the Oha Coven. Over the course of the book, the Oha Coven and the older mentors who watch over them become Sunny's chosen family. Among them, she finds belonging as they learn about the many parts of her.

Early in *Akata Witch*, Sunny is called several names by her peers at school including "stupid, pale faced akata witch," "stupid oyinbo akata witch," and *onyocha*. As I discuss earlier in this chapter, akata is a sometimes-derogatory name used to refer to African Americans, while *oyinbo* and *onyocha* are typically used to refer to white foreigners. What makes these names particularly wounding coming from Sunny's classmates is the fact that Sunny is the child of two Nigerian parents and living in Nigeria, so she "should be" considered Nigerian. Calling her akata is intended to hurt her, and it does. Sunny's Nigerian identity is used as a bartering chip when her schoolmates and even her brothers are upset with her—if she behaves, she is allowed to remain Nigerian, but if she acts out of line it can be taken away.

Although Sunny is only twelve years old, she is distinctly aware of the ways that her diasporic identity, her disability, her inability to adhere to normative beauty standards, and her gender prevent her from experiencing full belonging. In her essay "Nnedi Okorafor: Exploring the Empire of Girls' Moral Development," Sandra Lindow explains this stage of Sunny's development, writing: "Okorafor depicts her YA protagonists at a place where they are transitioning to a Post Conventional level of moral development. They have gut-level recognition that the social norms of their communities are narrow-minded and prejudicial, but initially they don't know other possibilities."[69] According to psychologist Lawrence Kohlberg, conventional morality describes the taken-for-granted values and ethics of a community, or in other words, the internalization of what is required to be considered "good." Postconventional morality is the development of an individual sense of ethics and morals.[70] In *Akata Witch*, forming her own moral compass necessitates that Sunny practice disbelonging by making the decision to disregard many of the cultural codes and values she has been taught to accept and embracing her outsiderness. These new morals are also developed through Sunny's difficult relationship with her father, who she feels sees her as inadequate, for both not being a son and not being an ideal daughter. She shares, "Sometimes I hated my father. Sometimes I felt he hated me too. I couldn't help that I was not the son he wanted or the pretty daughter he'd have accepted instead."[71] In order to find herself, Sunny must learn to disregard her father's ideas of what makes her valuable.

While Sunny's albinism is cause for teasing and ridicule, Okorafor also makes it a marker of her mutability and connection to the spiritual realm. In Sunny's early interactions with Chichi, her outsiderness is named, but we soon learn that, unlike Sunny's classmates, Chichi sees something more in her: "People say stuff about people like you. That you're all ghost, or a half and half, one foot in this world and one in another. Sunny rolled her eyes. Not this again, she thought. So cliché. Everyone thinks the old lady, the hunchback, the crazy man, and the albino have magical evil powers."[72]

In *Akata Witch*, Okorafor engages stereotypes about people with disabilities, going so far as to have Sunny name it in her interaction with Chichi. She is aware that the idea of the "magical albino" is a trope and her truth. Beyond this moment, Sunny talks about her disability at times in regard to how others treat her—but it is not the primary obstacle she must overcome, and as she realizes she is a Leopard Person, both not-human and superhuman, her relationship to her albinism shifts.

Scholarly articles on the prevalence and experiences of children with albinism in Nigeria are sparse, and oftentimes problematic, using overly general and othering language. In 2018, a demographic and socioeconomic study of persons with albinism (PWAs) conducted in Nigeria's Oyo and Plateau States revealed that PWAs suffer most discrimination in public places.[73] In Nigeria, children with albinism often first face discrimination from their own families. Jake Epelle, founder of the Albino Association in Nigeria, shares that upon his birth he was rejected by his birth mother, who refused to recognize him as her child:[74] "My early infancy days were characterised with teasing and taunting by family members, childhood friends and school mates. While on the other hand, I found solace in my father and step mum who took great care of me and showed me incredible love and affection. I attended public schools and indeed had a hard time with seeing the blackboard: I had to go close to the blackboard amidst teasing and derogatory name calling and even sometimes insults and assaults by both the teachers and student alike."[75]

Here, Epelle describes how his albinism limited his social relationships and experiences of care and safety, both at home and at school. Anthony Olagunji's thesis on the experiences of PWAS in Nigeria echoes Epelle's personal experiences, asserting that children with albinism are more likely to experience social bullying, parental neglect, and abuse, which often leads to poor academic performance, truancy, and loss of interest in education. These disadvantages are even greater for women with albinism, who experience sexism as well.[76] Okorafor's decision to show Sunny moving freely through space in a Nigerian context, without her albinism perpetually putting her at risk and determining every interaction, is significant. Okorafor asks us to reconsider how we view and understand normativity, creating an entire world where nonnormative bodies hold power, authority, and unique perspectives.

Another area where Sunny experiences outsiderness is as a Free Agent, meaning that neither of her parents are Leopard People, though she suspects that her maternal grandmother, whom her family no longer talks about, was also a Leopard Person. Her identity as a Free Agent is occasionally the cause of angst—because the rest of her coven were raised as Leopard People, they know much more than she does and are more comfortable with the Leopard world. Sunny's feelings about not being raised by Leopard People strongly parallel discourses about Nigerian Americans raised in the United States or by parents who are not Nigerian by birth, as she similarly navigates feelings of inadequacy and not knowing. The Leopard Society in *Akata Witch* is inspired by the Ékpè Society, an ancient institution inhabiting the forest regions of West and Central Africa.[77] Over the course of the book, Sunny's various outsider traits and newfound comfort with being a Leopard Person become an indicator of her connection to her Nigerian heritage and ancestors, which give her the powers needed to fight the villain, Black Hat Otokoto. Sunny's identity as a Free Agent is also significant because the connections that she makes in Nigeria and the family she creates as a Free Agent are outside of her connections to her family and require her to embrace a world that her family fears.

In *Akata Witch*, Sunny must embrace disbelonging because she never experiences full belonging in the human world or in Leopard Knocks—a marketplace in a realm accessible only to Leopard People. She does this by embracing her own mutability, play and leisure, and her alternate kin networks. In the human world her powers, albinism, place of birth, and gender make her life difficult. And in Leopard Knocks, although her powers and albinism do not stand out, the fact that she is both Nigerian and American perplexes people, and her gender still prevents her from fully participating. Throughout the book, Sunny does not discover a seamless belonging in any one place, but rather by moving between multiple places and spaces.

Like ada the Alien, the setting for *Akata Witch* disrupts easy understandings of place and time, and because the characters can travel between Leopard Knocks, where almost anything is possible, and the human realm, they can experience the world similarly to ada the Alien and her kin, existing in multiple places at once—moving from water, to earth, to air, and back to earth in an instant—and manifesting reality through thought alone. The experience of girlhood for ada the Alien and Sunny is summed up in the last line of *Akata Witch* when Sunny says to Orlu, "Feels weird doesn't it?" as she reflects on all they have been through. Orlu replies, "You'll get used to it. . . . Having two lives is better than none."[78] With this line, Orlu's character asserts that to survive and thrive in multiplicity—to embody the tension between being human and superhuman—is better than the alternative, which is often the case for black girls, whose lives are so often devalued.

Sunny's centering of rest and play paves the way for greater realizations and shifts in herself and her immediate environment. Her leisure aids in her survival. Notably, when Sunny has the powerful vision of the world ending, an event that ultimately the Oha Coven comes together to stop, she is staring into a candle flame, which she describes as soothing, even recalling the nostalgia of fireflies. "I have always been fascinated by candles. Looking into the flame calms me down."[79] For Sunny, the act of looking at the candle flame is meditative, and ultimately it creates the conditions for her to access pertinent information. Later, after Sunny is initiated into the coven, she accompanies Sasha, Orlu, and Chichi to Leopard Knocks. Sunny, exhausted and confused from the experiences of the day, exclaims, "I thought today was supposed to be fun." Orlu answers, "Would you rather have fun or learn the meaning of your life?"[80]

In actuality, Sunny's adventures in *Akata Witch* are both. For example, in order to enter Leopard Knocks, the four children are forced to cross a bridge, and Chichi explains to Sunny that to cross the narrow bridge, she must transform into her spirit self, described as one's true essence. This is so vulnerable that seeing someone's spirit self is described in the book as similar to viewing them in their underwear. Sunny's spirit face looks like the sun, and her spirit name is Anyanwu, which means "eye of the sun" in Igbo. This is somewhat incongruous because her albinism prevents her from spending time in the sun, but it is also a reflection of how her spiritual and indigenous knowledge allow her to extend beyond her human form. Soon she hears music and feels a levity that allows her to dance across the bridge, feeling fearless:[81] "She felt so good and confident that she laughed, thinking, Man, this is going to be easy. With her peripheral vision she could see golden points radiating from her face. Her spirit face had sunrays too! She laughed again, feeling a wave of pleasure as the classical music hit a crescendo. . . . She felt not an ounce of fear."[82] It is only after she is almost across the bridge that she realizes there was a river monster waiting for her to fall, and it is through pleasure and play that she can cross the bridge without falling into the river monster's grip.

Later in the book, during the annual Zuma Festival in Leopard Knocks, she is allowed to play soccer even though she is a girl. She blows everyone away. Despite the ridicule and attention, her primary motivation is her pleasure. "By the second half Sunny could barely think straight, she was in such ecstasy."[83] Moreover, at the end of the day, her skin is unharmed even after spending the entire day in the sun. While Ghori problematizes this moment, arguing that "the novel does a disservice as she frees Sunny from a burden that every other albino must consciously shoulder or risk the consequences,"[84] I suggest that we can also read this scene as a metaphor for how the "ecstasy" Sunny experiences when dancing on the bridge or playing soccer as a girl stems from the ways she balances the limitations of a human body with her ability to exceed and experience beyond her form. Sunny's albinism doesn't permanently go away; rather, she experiences instances of superhuman possibility and sensation.

Finally, Sunny's kin networks in the book are necessarily queer, as among the Leopard People normative categorizations across age and human/animal affinities seem not to apply, though gender remains somewhat static. Gumbs defines *queer intergenerationality* as "the practice of being present to what can be generated and shared between moments in time and encounters, that is not necessarily linked to generations in the patriarchal family sense."[85] Chichi may very well be an old woman, but her friends cannot know for sure. As a result, she straddles the line between feisty elder and peer, disrupting linear notions of kinship hierarchies and order according to age. Similarly, boundaries between human, plant, and animal are often blurred and, as a result, systems of relationality do not follow the rules of the human world. For example, when they first enter Leopard Knocks, Sunny notices a man made of leaves: "Iroko leaves were falling around her, and as she watched, one of the leaf piles took a humanoid shape. It sloppily cartwheeled over to a man and fell apart, burying the man in its green leaves. As the leaves covered him, the man looked more annoyed than afraid."[86] Emphasizing that the man was more annoyed than afraid, Okorafor normalizes this type of human/plant hybrid in the world of Leopard Knocks. This queering of relationality is facilitated by how Sunny moves between the categories of human, superhuman, and nonhuman. As literary scholar Deborah Williams writes in her essay "Witches, Monsters, and Questions of Nation: Humans and Non-Humans in *Akata Witch* and *Trail of Lightning*": "In both novels, we see that the heroines become non-human; it is a process and a practice that involves learning how to see self, other, and world differently. These monstrous female bodies demonstrate Braidotti's point that post-human feminism serves to 'criticize narrow-minded self-interests, intolerance, and xenophobic rejection of otherness.' . . . a critique that is further enabled by the form of the speculative novel. Fantasy and speculative fiction, says Okorafor, can be 'the most accurate way of describing reality.'"[87] Other significant kin relationships that Sunny forms are with the outsider women who mentor her and play a key role in her discovery of self. They are, in many ways, crucial to her survival, as we are reminded of the ways her parents are unable to fully see and support her in her difference, though we see her mother make attempts. This is most explicit at the end of the book after the Oha Coven defeats Black Hat Otokoto, leading to Sunny having to defeat the demon Ekwensu, and she has a final confrontation with her father. Upon arriving home, her brother asks where she has been and she replies, "Trying to save the world." When her dad angrily asks where she has been all day, she answers with a shaky voice, "I was up to nothing unholy or shameful or dirty. I was with my friends and—."[88] The way Sunny starts her explanation shows that she is well aware of the regulations and expectations that govern her body and actions. Before she can finish, Sunny's father lashes out at her and begins to yell, declaring that Sunny will "come to no good" like her grandmother. Speaking to Sunny's mother, he recalls, "Your mother started disappearing at night around this age, no? Didn't you tell me that? Then one day she came home carrying you in her belly! She's lucky the guy married her." He then turns back to Sunny, disgusted, and says, "A beating won't save you. Look at you, you're lost. I can't stand it!"[89] Although Sunny's grandmother's "strangeness" was because she was a Leopard Person, his inability to understand women outside of their roles as mothers and wives limits his imagination to worries about pregnancy. His investment is in maintaining her purity, even though she is only twelve, and he feels the need to police her behavior with violence. Following the confrontation, Sunny's mother brings her pepper soup, and they have a heart-to-heart. Sunny's mother knows that there are things that she cannot know about Sunny but says to her, "I trust you." In a scene built around soup, Okorafor makes space for recognition without understanding, as they both see that they cannot and will not fully understand one another, and that is okay.

A key mentor for Sunny is her Auntie Chinwe, who exemplifies disbelonging in several ways, as the "free spirit" of their family. Auntie Chinwe, who lives in the United States, married an African American man and was considered a disappointment by Sunny's grandfather.[90] Chinwe is also a disappointment because she chose to study dance rather than medicine.[91] While Sunny's mother still speaks to her, we get the sense that Auntie Chinwe has been excommunicated from the family, and it is her Auntie Chinwe who directs her to a box of her grandmother's secrets, which confirms that she was a Leopard Person. Sunny's aunt's decision to marry a non-Nigerian, nontraditional career path, and lack of shame about these decisions all encompass her disbelonging. Though she has made decisions that relegate her to the margins of her family of origin, she still plays an active role in emotionally supporting Sunny and Sunny's mother in Nigeria. Moreover, by directing Sunny to the box of secrets, she takes the initiative to help pass on the history of the family's matriarchal connection to Leopard People. Another key mentor is a woman by the name of Sugar Cream. Sunny first learns of Sugar Cream at a bookstore in Leopard Knocks. She is the author of a book titled *Nsibidi: The Magical Language of the Spirits*, which Sunny is surprisingly able to read.[92] When Sunny unethically uses her powers in a fight at school, she finally meets Sugar Cream, who she has been hoping will mentor her, even though Sugar Cream has never taken a mentee before. Despite Sunny's mistake, it is clear early on that Sugar Cream likes her, and she shares her story with Sunny. Sugar Cream has severe scoliosis and tells the story of being found in the forest and raised by monkeys: "When I was very small, I walked out of the forest. A young man found me. I was like a little monkey, wild and feral. Some people think that actual monkeys might have even looked after me for a while. Somehow I'd survived in the bush. I couldn't have been over three years old."[93]

She receives the name Sugar Cream because the young man offers her tea with "lots of sugar and lots of cream" when he discovers her. The young man raises Sugar Cream as his daughter, and she eventually goes on to be the head of the Leopard Knocks Library Council. Though Sugar Cream does not know who her family is, she is a woman of great self-knowledge and presence, and undeniably Nigerian, having mastered the ancient language of Nsibidi. Her connection is primarily to the land and animals. Chinwe and Sugar Cream represent a number of taboos and nonnormative performances of Nigerian womanhood, and they are content in doing so. Through them, Sunny can come to a place of accepting herself. Here mentorship offers a model for loving and supporting black girls and also reveals how critical distance from home allows women to create spaces of wholeness for others.

In *Akata Witch*, Okorafor creates a world where a black girl hero reaches her fullest potential by embracing her disbelonging. Through the support and guidance of her chosen family, she can find comfort within her own body and grow her magical capabilities, and this occurs through her strategic embrace of play and leisure. The consideration of diasporic disbelonging, play, leisure, kinship, and worldmaking through the lens of black girlhood is important because it creates an opening for an alternative record of what it has meant to be a Nigerian diasporic girl and what it can mean to be a Nigerian diasporic woman. Sunny and ada are examples of Cox's assertation that, "young Black women propose the possibility that the body may be a space to which we may finally come home, or where we make a new one. Staying in the body, therefore, may very well mean moving in and, most importantly, beyond it to locate new ways of imagining oneself and of remaking one's surroundings."[94] Amanze's drawings and *Akata Witch* consider the value in imagining beyond our human forms, current realities, and present communities by showing us two characters simply existing as black girls. This dynamic reflects disbelonging as an intergenerational practice—a practice that is not simply a tool for resistance but also a way of coming of age, of coming into self, and shaping the world.

# Conclusion

## REDEFINING BELONGING
## VIS-À-VIS TETHERING

When Chimamanda Adiche's *Americanah* came out in 2013, I read it three times that year. It was one of the first popular representations of complicated, nuanced African womanhood that I had encountered, and at the time there was really nothing like it. Despite its compulsory heterosexuality, "daughter of diaspora" tropes, and too tidy ending, it spoke to something deep inside me. Today there are more complex representations of African womanhood than there were just a decade ago.[1] Popular African creators like Akwaeke Emezi, Eloghosa Osunde, and Taiye Selasi, to name just a few, have done a great deal to expand understandings of how marginalized genders in the African diaspora think of ourselves and our relationship to homeland.

While I do not claim that the works I analyze in this book alone caused the shift in contemporary depictions of Nigerian womanhood, the works of these diasporic artists have undeniably contributed to the shifting consciousness, both on the continent and throughout the diaspora, by adding to the archive of happenings, videos, and visual art embracing taboo and remixing tradition. The artists showcased in *Transatlantic Disbelonging* have created new language and images to describe the experience of being a woman in diaspora, and these have shifted both representations and discourse in meaningful ways. As Zina Saro-Wiwa reflects when speaking about *Eaten by the Heart*:

> I wanted people to see [depictions of African intimacy] and maybe be uncomfortable or maybe get used to it. Also start a conversation, which I think it did, and then suddenly you see more kissing happening in Nollywood. Information now goes out much more quickly and so you say, "Well we don't really see much of this" and then suddenly you have video and it proliferates very quickly. But really at the time, there was so little of that. But quite soon afterwards, I would say there was a bigger conversation around that kind of intimacy, and you see more of it.[2]

In this quote, Saro-Wiwa names the way a single viral video or work of art has the power to change what is understood as acceptable or familiar, seemingly overnight. In a 2020 conversation with Emezi, amanze describes noticing a similar shift: "I think now, in recent years, there has been a shift in now feeling like there's language, and I think [Emezi's] work is an important part of that, in a way that's different from the visual arts. That there's actual language now that is speaking for these other realities and other ways of being that I can identify with and feel that you're kin and that it's not so lonely anymore."[3]

Notably, amanze locates how literature, in particular, has the power to offer language that African and African diasporic people can use to describe our experiences, something that she says is distinct from what visual art does. This language not only aids in self-understanding but also creates a feeling of kinship. In both of these quotes, Saro-Wiwa and amanze offer observations about how they have witnessed culture change as a result of their art, as well as that of their peers. Worldmaking isn't something that only happens in our imaginations, they suggest, but an action that begins in imaginations and has real-life ramifications.

It has become increasingly clear that it is within the realm of aesthetics that some of the most critical conversations about the nuances of African diasporic subjectivity are occurring. This book and the work of the artists highlighted in it bring to light the critical role art plays in subject formation for diasporic women, as a site that reflects our lived experiences and allows us to imagine and create something new.

This cultural shift over the last decade has cultivated a new generation of Nigerian women and nonbinary artists working in experimental forms like installation and performance art, and these forms have led to the creation of new spaces where artists can show and witness this type of work. One example is The Treehouse, which Ogunji founded, following in the legacy of the Center for Contemporary Art, in 2018. An alternative art space in the Ikoyi neighborhood of Lagos, its name reflects its location on the top flat of a seven-story building. When asked about the importance of alternative art spaces in Lagos, Ogunji explains: "A diverse art ecology is one thing we have been missing in this city. There is the idea that art is about making something you have to sell to a collector; however, that is only one part of it. As an artist, this is important but it should not be the focus. The focus should be on supporting artists and pushing them to create visual language that expands their imagination and expands us as the audience."[4]

Since its opening, The Treehouse has emerged as a remarkable site of witnessing and collaboration in the Lagos art scene and has hosted over forty artists—both local and from across the black diaspora—who are exploring a range of themes including African womanhood, food, queerness, and the natural environment. At The Treehouse, artists are able to show work and discuss themes that may not be so readily received in more traditional art spaces.

One artist who has shared work at The Treehouse is Taiwo Aiyedogbon, whom I met in August of 2014 while completing the Omo Yemisi Adedoyin Shyllon Art Foundation Fellowship in Lagos. During our Zoom conversation in 2022, Aiyedogbon shared that her first experience with performance art was in 2012, as part of a performance workshop she was invited to by Nigerian transdisciplinary artist and professor Odun Orimolde. This was also where she met Ogunji, and she would go on to perform in *Will I still carry water when I am a dead woman?* For Aiyedogbon, who studied sculpture at Yaba College of Technology, the shift in the art world has been noticeable. During our conversation, she shared that the number of performance artists in Lagos has grown exponentially since those early days, and the vast majority of them are women. "I remember always knowing that Wura was doing performance," she said, "and there was hardly, aside from ruby and then the rest, there were hardly people I knew who were doing performance aside from Dr. Odun Orimolade."[5] In recent years, she has noticed a direct link between the performance workshops and the number of new performance artists working in Lagos. Still, she has a hard time believing it when younger performance artists reach out to her wanting to collaborate and learn from her, the same way she used to reach out to Ogunji and Jelili Atiku when she was discovering the form. During our conversation, she shared, "At times I feel like I'm still learning, I'm still in a learning process, and when people tell me, 'Oh, we're looking up to you' I look at myself like I've not even gotten anywhere."[6]

For Aiyedogbon, being a performance artist has opened doors for an incredible number of collaborations, including with those in the diaspora. Speaking about the urgency she feels to stay focused on her artistic career when she sees many of her peers settling down and getting partnered, she says, "I've got to make generational wealth, not just for my family, but for other people's families. For younger females behind me. . . . It's crazy when you see how women are being treated in spaces." In the interview Aiyedogbon speaks on often being the only woman in performance art spaces and being dismissed and/or disrespected while also being told that she holds "special privilege" as a woman—a fact that is continuously disproven not only by how she is treated in art spaces but also by the disproportionate responsibilities she holds living at home with her parents and siblings.[7] For artists like Aiyedogbon, their creative practice is also a rejection of the status quo. Due to performance art's recent legibility as a commodity in the West, she can imagine a financially independent future and a future that is her own to shape. Aiyedogbon's experiences as a woman artist in Nigeria illustrate the homemaking and life-changing capabilities of artmaking for African women.

By switching to an examination of how disbelonging is lived and practiced, *Transatlantic Disbelonging* attends to the everydayness of diaspora and considers what possibilities lie alongside and beyond trauma narratives of loss and displacement for diasporic women. Studying diasporic homemaking captures the ways diasporic subjects navigate, think about, and construct their identities. In much of diaspora studies, the main focus is on national boundaries and national borders, which are absolutely important to center, as they have real and often-violent implications for individuals. What I argue is that by considering the everyday, affect, the erotic, and psychic constructions of home, we can attend to the ways that people make up for the shortcomings of home and belonging.

The idea of home for many of us in diaspora is so often a site of disappointment, trapped between nostalgia and the harsh realities of globalization and modernity. So why do we cling so furiously? Many of us cling to the idea of home and homeland as our entry points to belonging because we have been told that these are places, when we find them, that will always desire us—where our belonging is guaranteed. The works I highlight in this book offer the option to let go of the fantasy of this type of belonging and find comfort in the fullness of in-between-ness. It gives us permission to release the singular belief that the experience of existing in the in-between is inherently traumatic and acknowledge that this is the very nature of diaspora. It allows us to consider the ways in which diasporic connections are broken and created anew.

While this book focuses on instances of disbelonging in fine art and literature, disbelonging as a strategy is not limited to these genres. In recent years, social media has evolved as a key site where disbelonging is practiced and refined as both a survival strategy and a tool of critique. As I write now, TikTok and Instagram have been the sites where I have most consistently witnessed acts of disbelonging in the last five years. In my article "#AfricanAunties: Performing Diasporic Digital Disbelongings on TikTok," I do close readings of "auntie" performances by African woman creators, arguing that these performances come to shape how these creators imagine and form kinship ties within the African diasporic communities they understand themselves to be a part of. I contend that in this digital context, "disbelonging allows the creators of African auntie TikToks to embrace the personal and cultural importance of their African aunties, while explicitly rejecting the forms of surveillance, discipline and shame that govern their communities in their day to day lives."[8] Along with these displays, Nigerian culture has seen the rise of the "Alté girl," emerging out of the "Alté movement," a music genre that pulls from a diverse range of genres and often features glitchy experimental sounds and saturated visual storytelling. According to a 2021 *Teen Vogue* article, the central premise of the Alté movement is "to stay true to yourself in spite of existing traditions or cultural restrictions."[9] The article describes the movement as beginning in 2007, as more young Nigerians gained access to the internet—two years before Saro-Wiwa coined "alt-Nollywood" as a genre. Music writer Tanya Akinola writes, Alté is "an amalgamation of global influences obtained through slow speed early-00s internet connections, the rise of MTV, and their own transcontinental experiences."[10] She adds that backlash on Twitter from locals has dismissed the movement as "being different for different's sake."[11] This idea of being different for different's sake is central to the idea of disbelonging, which offers difference as important fertile ground for self-making in the afterlife of colonialism.

While most conversations about Alté culture focus on music, I see the movement as having deep ties to the rise of experimental contemporary art in Nigeria and diasporic collaborations both in person and online. Conversations about the rise of Alté culture and the experiences of those within the subculture fail to closely examine the particular experiences of Alté women in a cultural context where women have been policed more aggressively than men. Moreover, conversations about Alté culture are hyperfocused on music and fashion. In Lagos musician Jake Doe's love song to alternative girls, "Alté Girl," he describes a woman with colored hair and piercings who doesn't mind standing out. He sings, "This one's for my Alté girl / Living in the Alté world / That creates her universe / Every star belongs to her." The Alté girl he describes is perpetually creating the worlds that will see, hold, and affirm her. The Alté girl is a woman who is using disbelonging as a mode of self-fashioning and worldbuilding.

It is fair to say that, in online spaces, disbelonging as I outline it in this book has become somewhat normalized, particularly among middle-class Africans and African diasporic young people. It's hard to believe that just a decade ago—when I started this project—dyed hair, revealing outfits, or public displays of affection were rare and taboo, even in a city like Lagos. Today, we see African women content creators using their platforms to be open about their sexuality, share instances of abuse they experienced in their households growing up, and revel in the many ways they disappoint their families through memes. Before these platforms were used in the way they are today, these conversations happened primarily in the realm of visual art and new media, and that is where I locate the significance of the artists I discuss in this book.

I wonder what art might teach us about embodying the hesitation,

the slipping,
the feeling not enough,
the forgetting,
the not having the right words,
the tension,
the melancholy,

and even still, the overwhelming joy of being in dispersal—from the homeland, from family, and within oneself—with ease? Disbelonging allows us to think about how people are creating the conditions for freedom and survival, and art becomes a key way to study modes of homemaking, as the visual and literary lend themselves to imagining, creating, and rendering new worlds. By looking to visual art, performance art, and video, I draw attention to the often-hidden negotiations made and survival tools used by black diasporic women.

\*\*\*

There is much about the experience of diaspora that is difficult to articulate, particularly the day-to-day affective experience of longing and belonging, and the quiet, seemingly mundane compromises made by women every day as we navigate bringing together our personal needs, desires, and obligations to our beloved communities. The art of Ogunji, Akunyili Crosby, Saro-Wiwa, amanze, and Okorafor each offers unique insights into the diasporic negotiations that are so often invisible in diasporic stories, by tending to the messy contradictions and fantasies embedded in the act of return, the power of the erotic, the liberatory potential of leisure and play, and their implications for black girls.

My focus on the Nigerian diaspora specifically brings to light the limitations of African American and African binaries when discussing diasporic return and belonging. This project bridges the fields of African American studies and African studies by underlining the overarching contentiousness and instability of belonging, geography, and even blood lineage for black subjects both living on the continent and scattered across the Americas. Additionally, by using gender as a critical lens through which to study diaspora, I have foregrounded issues that have long been considered frivolous or irrelevant but have held revolutionary potential for black women across the globe. These issues include sexual agency, pleasure, play, queer social bonds, and worldmaking, all of which, I argue, are and have been at the center of liberation for women, and are critical tools used by women to heal and build home and community. Along the way, this book has asked what we might discover when we do not assume that displacement is always internalized as traumatic for diasporic subjects. These women artists demonstrate how art creates the conditions to imagine an affective experience of diaspora beyond trauma, and the possibility of creating belonging anew.

In his meditation on generational healing, the late Vietnamese Buddhist monk and Zen master Thich Nhất Hạnh writes, "We don't need to go back to our native land, to Ireland, to China, to find our roots. We just need to be in touch with every cell in our body. Our father, our mother, and all of our ancestors are present in a very real way in each cell of our body, even in the bacteria."[12] In this quote, Nhất Hạnh decenters land as a necessary component for discovering our roots, or creating belonging, and redirects us to the body for answers. Selasi's TED Talk echoes this sentiment that a country is an insufficient basis for understanding an individual, stating: "To say that I came from a country suggested that the country was an absolute, some fixed point in place in time, a constant thing, but was it? In my lifetime, countries had disappeared—Czechoslovakia; appeared—Timor-Leste; failed—Somalia. My parents came from countries that didn't exist when they were born. To me, a country—this thing that could be born, die, expand, contract—hardly seemed the basis for understanding a human being."[13]

The myth of national identity and the vocabulary of "coming from" confuses us into placing ourselves into mutually exclusive categories. In fact, all of us are multi: multilocal, multilayered. To begin our conversations with an acknowledgment of this complexity brings us closer together, not further apart. What might it look like to center a study of diaspora that seeks to analyze how we might, as individuals, connect with every cell in our bodies rather than physically rooting in a place? How might this create space for people who have never found home in one place and perhaps never will? And if we can accept that ultimately belonging is not always found in one place, where might that lead our study?

After addressing these questions through the case studies in this book, I am left wondering: How might we consider a theorizing of home that accounts for the ways we as black women find and make home in our own bodies? One possible answer to this question is by looking for the homes black diasporic subjects create within and through our creative production. The visual gives us new language to more accurately represent diasporic processes beyond surveying place of birth and nationality. In *Scenes of Subjection*, Saidiya Hartman writes: "The significance of becoming or belonging together in terms other than those defined by one's status as property, will-less object, and the not-quite human should not be underestimated. This belonging together endeavors to redress and nurture the broken body; it is a becoming together dedicated to establishing other terms of sociality, however transient, that offer a small measure of relief from the debasements constitutive of one's condition."

I consider Hartman's words alongside amanze's insistence that her work not be read through the lens of trauma. Each of the artists that I analyze actively moves beyond the trauma narratives associated with their specific diasporic journeys. Instead, they are interested in the possibilities these circumstances create. Disbelonging, as an analytic, allows us to see and trace how loss, displacement, isolation, and not knowing shape the ways diasporic subjects practice belonging. Disbelonging creates an option that is not insider or outsider, but both, in a way that is expansive and liberating.

The decentering of the romanticized home within diaspora studies also allows for the study of rhizomatic connections as sites of meaning. I have examined what studying those who do not fit can tell us about the freedom of existing elsewhere, in between, and nowhere at all. *Transatlantic Disbelonging* highlights the ways that we cannot take home for granted but must instead make a commitment to being present for all of the ways home comes into being.

In 2013, Ogunji and amanze performed their piece *Twin: Art + Performance* at the Museum of Contemporary African Diasporan Art in Brooklyn, as part of an exhibit called "Six Draughtsman," which amanze curated as part of her Fulbright. The performance, which ran for close to three hours, was restaged in 2020 at Frieze, New York. In *Twin: Art + Performance* their hands are attached with string, and they draw with their free hands on a transparent piece of glass, allowing their sense of one another to inform their drawing. Their position on the opposite side of the plexiglass separates them from the audience both spatially and temporally, as the durational performance and the repeated motions lull them into an altered state. Although the performance is happening in New York, they are also elsewhere, looking out at us through the world they have created. They are attached to each other, allowing them to reach the farthest points of the glass surfaces as well as access inspiration from the movements of the opposite body. Obscured by both the plexiglass and the mark-making, they are seeing us and we are seeing them through the small gaps in the waxy black lines, and the black in their dresses blurs with the images. In reality, we can see them only through their creation. They are performing as the drawing and through the drawing, thus creating new ways of existing and new ways of presenting themselves. The same way amanze's drawings allow her to travel through space and time, she and Ogunji's friendship exists in a variety of realms. The drawing also represents particular ways of holding one another that exceed their physical forms and ways of relating.

Ogunji and amanze met in Nigeria, where they had both traveled for their art. In fact, they were both showing work in an exhibit titled "No One Belongs Here More Than You" at the Center for Contemporary Art in Lagos. The starting point for their relationship was thinking about what it means to belong, what it means to claim belonging, and what it means to refuse to be denied belonging, and their friendship grew within this space. In this way, their creative practice has facilitated their engagement with Nigeria as they understand their connection to Nigeria as being connected to the process of creation and making. Their friendship grows and deepens through their creative collaborations, and these collaborations inform the parts of each other they're able to know and understand.

Ogunji and amanze, as artists and as the characters of audre the Leopard and ada the Alien, are often tethered. In *Kinfolk [Diptych]* a thread connects them; in *Queens*, it is a strip of Aso Oke fabric; in *beauty*, a synthetic hair extension. As I consider the recurring theme of them being tethered to one another, I am left with these questions: What does it mean for them to be tethered to one another rather than to a place? And what does this type of relationality say about new ways we might imagine diasporic belonging? My use of *tether* here is intentional. It does not gesture toward belonging to another in a way that is purely centered on the freedom of the individual. Instead it considers what it might mean to participate in a type of consensual restriction informed by our desire to be connected to others. On the notion of black women's conjoinment, Hershini Bhana Young looks to Solange Knowles's music video for "Cranes in the Sky," writing: "I am arguing that Solange's performances of conjoinment point us toward what Spillers calls the 'living laboratory' of black flesh that refuses blackness as a site of pessimistic negation, instead imagining new ways of breathing, moving, and being that are not merely compensatory. These alternate black (female) morphologies (fourteen-legged, periwinkle, vaginal area connected to ass, and multiple headed) rewrite the boundaries of an atomized body to dismantle both possessive individualism and the group identities used to disenfranchise black people."[14] Here, Young invites us to imagine how conjoinment—and, I would add, tethering—offers new possibilities for what black bodies can do, and how and where they can belong.

A series of messages exchanged between amanze and Ogunji and published in *BOMB* magazine speak to the delicate balance between the individual and the collective that disbelonging attempts to reconcile. In the messages, the two artists discuss making "ugly" work, artistic integrity, whether one can be an artist for an entire lifetime, and where they are both finding inspiration. Sent between Brooklyn and Lagos, the letters are nonlinear and poetic and communicate an immense amount of mutual love and respect. In a 2015 message to amanze, Ogunji writes:

> Now that the drawings are out in the world and maybe also because I have passed over this water of the atlantic, I can think about them differently, reflect. this moment is causing me to reflect . . . on the arc of my life as an artist. the work I was making 15 or 20 years ago was very much about the black female body and myself. It was about my experience in America in many ways. And the experience of race/blackness and being a woman and history.
>
> I find myself wanting to create from another kind of space entirely, as if you could have a space devoid of identity, a space not hampered by the structures that other people or society or community (hate that word) or even history puts on us. Can I create from the current moment something that is purely mine and not reactive?[15]

Sharing her frustration with what she sees as a reactivity to racialized and gendered subjugation and American history in her earlier work, Ogunji describes desiring to mentally access a space where she can create outside of these frameworks—to access in the moment of creation something that is purely hers. At the same time, the letters, along with their collaborative performance, communicate a deep desire to be connected and to work through the act of creation with others, particularly in light of the inescapable history written onto her black female body. Gesturing at the power and importance of love and friendship, despite her frustration around legibility and the pressures of art world deadlines, amanze signs off in one letter, "i almost hate having shows. they're disruptive sometimes. but you, i love."[16] In this exchange we are reminded of the ways that artmaking is not only worldmaking and homemaking for these diasporic women artists, as I have argued in this book, but also a critical site of witnessing messiness and contradiction. Perhaps most importantly, here artmaking is a self-making practice where new ways of relating to ourselves and our environments are invented and reinvented, and we are able to experiment with expanding and exceeding our physical forms and preexisting structures beyond anything we have been taught or shown.

# Notes

## INTRODUCTION. DISBELONGING: A STRATEGY FOR OUR COLLECTIVE SURVIVAL

1. Also written *dis-belonging* and *(dis)belonging*.

2. Brown, "Listening to the Land/Playing Off the Crowd."

3. Bedoya, "Placemaking and the Politics of Belonging and Dis-Belonging."

4. An exciting departure from the tendency to understand disbelonging and unbelonging as an imposed position is the work of Iván A. Ramos, who, in *Unbelonging: Inauthentic Sounds in Mexican and Latinx Aesthetics*, employs *unbelonging* to discuss how Latinx artists use discordant sounds of punk metal and rock to embrace alienation and create new spaces where they can embrace their existence outside of the mainstream (5). Ramos describes unbelonging as "a strategy of rejection used by those who have already been rejected, a tactic expressed by rejects" (21).

5. Ellis, *Territories of the Soul*, 6.

6. Nyong'o, *Afro-Fabulations*, 202.

7. Muñoz, *Disidentifications*, 4.

8. Gopinath, *Impossible Desires*, 16.

9. Gopinath writes, "I use the notion of 'impossibility' as a way of signaling the unthinkability of a queer female subject position within various mappings of nation and diaspora." Gopinath, *Impossible Desires*, 15.

10. Campt, *Image Matters*, 52.

11. Macharia, "Africa: Queer: Anthropology."

12. Gopinath, *Impossible Desires*, 5.

13. Gopinath, *Unruly Visions*, 128.

14. Joseph, *Against the Romance of Community*, vii.

15. Bauman, *Community*, 4.

16. Stack, *Call to Home*, 18.

17. Rowley, "'It Could Have Been Me' Really," 527.

18. Examples of these narratives include Hartman, *Lose Your Mother*, and Brand, *A Map to the Door of No Return*.

19. I use quotes here to point to the many nontransatlantic journeys African subjects living on the continent make—migrations that are often left out of conversations about diaspora, migration, and exile.

20. Chambers-Letson, *After the Party*, 6–7.

21. Similarly, in *Coloring Whiteness: Acts of Critique in Black Performance*, Faedra Carpenter calls for a shift toward considering artist intention, writing, "The inclusion of artists' voices is a valuable element in this study and, moreover, their perspectives help keep us mindful of the importance in acknowledging artistic intention when analyzing audience reception or formulating scholarly opinions. Well known is the fact that creators cannot ensure how audience members will receive any, single message. This is in part the wonder and frustration of art; the impact and meaning of its reception is shaped by its audience as well as its devisers. Quite often, however, our focus is placed on a spectator's judgment with relatively little attention paid to the art maker's vision." Carpenter, *Coloring Whiteness*, 14.

22. Smith, *Enacting Others*, 23.

23. Ater, *Remaking Race and History*, 6.

24. Machida, *Unsettled Visions*, 9.

25. Ater, *Remaking Race and History*, 6.

26. Conquergood, "Performance Studies," 149.

27. Madison, "Co-Performative Witnessing," 828.

28. A "bid for connection," coined by John Gottman and Julie Gottman, describes attempts to gain attention, affection, or acceptance.

29. Weheliye, "My Volk to Come," 62.

30. Edwards, "The Uses of Diaspora."

31. Shepperson, "The African Abroad or the African Diaspora," 46.

32. Edwards, "The Uses of Diaspora," 54.

33. Gilroy, *The Black Atlantic*, 51.

34. Hall, "Cultural Identity and Diaspora," 235.

35. Okpewho and Nzegwu, *The New African Diaspora*, 5.

36. Okpewho and Nzegwu, *The New African Diaspora*, 6.

37. Gopinath, "Archive, Affect, and the Everyday," 166.

38. Bhabha. "The World and the Home."

39. Wilderson, "Grammar and Ghosts," 122.

40. Imoagene, *Beyond Expectations*, 29.

41. Kebede, "The African Second Generation in the United States," 128.

42. Kebede, "The African Second Generation in the United States," 130.

43. Kebede, "The African Second Generation in the United States," 120.

44. Chacko, "Fitting In and Standing Out," 229.

45. Chacko, "Fitting In and Standing Out," 233.

46. Falola and Heaton, *A History of Nigeria*, 17.

47. Falola and Heaton, *A History of Nigeria*, 9.

48. Arthur, *Invisible Sojourners*, vii.

49. Coritz "Over Half of Those Who Reported Their Race as Black or African American Identified as African American, Jamaican or Haitian."

50. "Sub-Saharan African Immigrants in the United States."

51. Castellote and Okwuosa, "Lagos Art World," 183.

52. In Nigerian contexts these individuals may also colloquially be referred to as "IJGBs," which stands for "I Just Got Back."

53. Adjepong, *Afropolitan Projects*, 3–4.

54. Adjepong, *Afropolitan Projects*, 4.

55. Adjepong, *Afropolitan Projects*, 4.

56. Adjepong, *Afropolitan Projects*, 5.

57. Wemega-Kwawu, "The Politics of Exclusion."

58. Tsing, *Friction*, 4.

59. Tsing, *Friction*, 6.

60. Macharia, *Frottage*, 5.

61. Castellote and Okwuosa, "Lagos Art World," 187.

62. Castellote and Okwuosa, "Lagos Art World," 187.

63. hooks, *Art on My Mind*, xiii.

64. Clifford, "Diasporas," 313.

65. Nketiah's essay builds on the work of Evelyn Brooks Higginbotham, who coined the phrase "politics of respectability." Though Higginbotham discusses respectability politics specifically as it related to the work of the Women's Convention of the Black Baptist Church during the Progressive Era, the emphasis on "sexual conduct, cleanliness, temperance, hard work, and politeness" mirrors the white supremacist colonial logics of respectability that are still emphasized on the African continent today. Still, I intentionally pull away from using "respectability politics," which has a history specifically rooted in the United States.

66. Nketiah, "Why Respectability Politics Is Failing African Women and Girls."

67. Nketiah, "Why Respectability Politics Is Failing African Women and Girls."

68. Van Dyke, *Everyday Narcissism*. Moreover, while not specifically about the African diaspora, Marianne Hirsch's work on postmemory—the deep connection of second generations to traumatic experiences that preceded their birth—Cathy Schlund-Vial's engagement with traumatic memory among 1.5-generation Cambodian artists, and Machida's work on second- and third-generation Japanese American artists writing about internment have greatly influenced my work and research questions. Hirsch, *The Generation of Postmemory*, 33.

69. Herman, "Complex PTSD," 377.

70. Herman, "Complex PTSD," 378.

71. Gqola, *Female Fear Factory*, 18.

72. Ezepue and Nwafor, "October 1," 1.

73. Ezepue and Nwafor, "October 1," 3.

74. Ezepue and Nwafor, "October 1," 2.

75. Njenga, "Trauma in African Women and Children," 28.

76. Biggs, *Healing Stage*, 22.

77. Laenui, "Processes of Decolonization."

78. Laenui, "Processes of Decolonization," 4.

An early version of chapter 1 appeared in *Text and Performance Quarterly*.
Epigraph: Wura-Natasha Ogunji and ruby onyinyechi amanze, "Paper as Body:
A Conversation."

1. *Trouble* in Nigerian pidgin.

2. Ogunji, "Will I still carry water when I am a dead woman?"

3. Madison, Acts of Activism, 112.

4. Madison, Acts of Activism, 113.

5. Kazeem, "Performances That Seek to Interrupt."

6. *Oyinbo* is Yoruba for white person or foreigner.

7. See Saidiya Hartman's *Wayward Lives, Beautiful Experiments*.

8. Radical rudeness has been recently repopularized by Ugandan women's rights
activist, scholar, and mother Stella Nyanzi. See Nothias and Kagumire, "Digital Radical
Rudeness."

9. Abstract for Summers, "Radical Rudeness."

10. Gaines, *Black Performance on the Outskirts of the Left*, 56.

11. Wright, *Physics of Blackness*, 74.

12. Wright, *Physics of Blackness*, 83.

13. Layiwola, "Transcultural Conversations," 146.

14. In *Appropriating Blackness*, E. Patrick Johnson asks us to interrogate our attach-
ments to the idea of authenticity writing, "I do not wish to place a value judgement on
the value of authenticity, for there are ways in which authenticating discourse enables
marginalized people to counter oppressive representations of themselves. The key here is
to be cognizant of the arbitrariness of authenticity, the ways in which it carries with it the
dangers of foreclosing the possibilities of cultural exchange and understanding. As Henry
Louis Gates Reminds us: 'No human culture is inaccessible to someone who makes the
effort to understand, to learn, to inhabit another world,'" 3.

15. Jones, "Yoruba Diasporic Performance," 323.

16. DeFrantz and Gonzalez, *Black Performance Theory*, 37.

17. Defrantz and Gonzalez, *Black Performance Theory*, 37.

18. La Pastina, "A Food Connection."

19. Boym, *The Future of Nostalgia*, xiv.

20. Lara, "Wura-Natasha Ogunji, Interviewed on February 25, 2006."

21. Lara, "Wura-Natasha Ogunji, Interviewed on February 25, 2006."

22. *Sankofa* in the Twi language of Ghana translates to "Go back and get it." The idea
of return is embedded in its meaning, and it is evoked throughout the African diaspora
to encourage people to learn about their African origins.

23. Ogunji, "How Does That Sound Look?"

24. Murphy and Sanford, *Osun Across the Waters*, 5.

25. Schneider, "Of the Pomegranate."

26. Wura-Natasha Ogunji, email interview with author, October 25, 2014.

27. De León, "Catching Up with Wura-Natasha Ogunji."

28. Meigh-Andrews, *A History of Video Art*, 8.

29. For more about the feminist art movement, see Broude, Garrard, and Brodsky, *The Power of Feminist Art*.

30. Oliver, "Between Artifice and Authentic," 38.

31. Oliver, "Between Artifice and Authentic," 39.

32. Ogunji, "Videos."

33. De León, "Catching Up with Wura-Natasha Ogunji."

34. De León, "Catching Up with Wura-Natasha Ogunji."

35. "Can Trauma Be Passed Down to the Next Generation Through DNA?"

36. Ogunji, "Videos."

37. Ogunji, "Videos."

38. Hartman, *Scenes of Subjection*, 61.

39. McMillan, *Embodied Avatars*, 7.

40. Russell, "Digital Dualism and the Glitch Feminism Manifesto."

41. Russell, "Digital Dualism and the Glitch Feminism Manifesto."

42. Ogunji, "Videos."

43. Ogunji, "First Rain in Abuja."

44. Ogunji, "Sweep."

45. Young, *Falling, Floating, Flickering*, 61.

46. Young, *Falling, Floating, Flickering*, 61.

47. Layiwola, "Transcultural Conversations," 148.

48. Muñoz, *Disidentifications*, 196.

49. Udobang, "Will I Still Carry Water When I Am a Dead Woman?"

50. Houlberg, "Notes on Egungun Masquerades Among the Oyo Yoruba."

51. Ogunji, "Will I still carry water when I am a dead woman?"

52. Willis, "Negotiating Gender, Power, and Spaces," 323.

53. Willis, "Negotiating Gender, Power, and Spaces," 328.

54. Willis, "Negotiating Gender, Power, and Spaces," 324.

55. Quashie, *The Sovereignty of Quiet*, 45.

56. Daniel, "The Little Can That Could."

57. Daniel, "The Little Can That Could."

58. "Crude Politics."

59. Udobang, "Will I Still Carry Water When I Am a Dead Woman?"

60. Ogunji, "Will I still carry water when I am a dead woman?"

61. "Witnessing the Present, the Artist as Citizen."

62. Lærkesen, "Wura-Natasha Ogunji."

63. Ogunji, "Will I still carry water when I am a dead woman?"

64. Layiwola, "Transcultural Conversations," 150.

65. Ogunji, "beauty."

66. Ogunji, "beauty."

67. Lærkesen, "Wura-Natasha Ogunji."

68. Ogunji, "beauty."

69. Ogunji, "beauty."

70. Ogunji, "Queens."

71. Akinwotu, "Waves of Change."

72. "Eko Atlantic City Project to Create 150,000 Jobs, Lagos Commissioner Says."

73. Ajibade, "Can a Future City Enhance Urban Resilience and Sustainability?," 87.

74. Ajibade, "Can a Future City Enhance Urban Resilience and Sustainability?," 89.

75. Ogunji, "Queens."

76. Hayden, "Contested Terrain," 9.

77. Ogunji, "Queens."

78. Campt, "Performing Stillness," 158.

79. Campt, "Performing Stillness," 168.

80. Young, *Embodying Black Experience*, 42.

81. Brah, *Cartographies of Diaspora*, 181.

82. Livermon, *Kwaito Bodies*, 30.

83. Livermon, *Kwaito Bodies*, 30.

84. Quashie, *The Sovereignty of Quiet*, 45.

85. Ogunji, email interview by author.

CHAPTER 2. AMBIVALENT INTERRACIAL LONGING IN
*I ALWAYS FACE YOU, EVEN WHEN IT SEEMS OTHERWISE,
THREAD, THE BRIDGE,* AND *RE-BRANDING MY LOVE*

Epigraph. Chika Odua, "Njideka Akunyili Crosby: A Nigerian Visual Artist."

1. Njideka Akunyili Crosby, in discussion with the author, November 2016.

2. I am grateful to Dr. Moyo Okediji for this observation. Also see Atoke, "Atoke's Monday Morning Banter."

3. "Leading Contemporaries, Njideka Akunyili Crosby."

4. "Leading Contemporaries, Njideka Akunyili Crosby."

5. "Leading Contemporaries, Njideka Akunyili Crosby."

6. Dedieu, "Njideka Akunyili Crosby's Intimate Universes."

7. Odufunade, "Primary Colors."

8. Valentine, "Njideka Akunyili Crosby Painting Sells for Record 3.1 Million."

9. Although Akunyili Crosby had visited Nigeria since her departure, she didn't show work in the country until 2017, despite her extremely successful career in the United States.

10. Davies, "Artist Joins Nigeria's 'Cultural Explosion.'"

11. Bhabha, *The Location of Culture*, 1.

12. Odua, "Njideka Akunyili Crosby."

13. Epprecht, "The Making of African Sexuality," 770.

14. Epprecht, "The Making of African Sexuality," 770.

15. Epprecht, "The Making of African Sexuality," 773.

16. Frottage, 96.

17. Epprecht, "The Making of African Sexuality," 773.

18. Diabate, "Genital Power," 8.

19. Dosekun, *Fashioning Postfeminism*, 33.

20. Bakare-Yusuf, "Nudity and Morality," 122.

21. Dosekun, *Fashioning Postfeminism*.

22. Dosekun, *Fashioning Postfeminism*.

23. Clark, "Feminisms in African Hip Hop," 394.

24. Gopinath, *Impossible Desires*, 18.

25. A traditional Nigerian top typically worn by men.

26. During her 2017 Art X Lagos talk, which was Akunyili Crosby's first public talk in Nigeria, artist and curator Temitayo Ogunbiyi asks her specifically about the Nigerian artists who inspired her creative path. Akunyili Crosby names Yinka Shonibare, J. D. Okhai Ojeikere, and writers such as Chinua Achebe, Chimamanda Ngozi Adiche, and Wole Soyinka. While her answer speaks to the strong literary influence in her work, the lack of Nigerian women visual artists also illustrates the dominance Nigerian men artists have had in popular conversations about hybridity and diaspora.

27. Akunyili Crosby, *I Refuse to Be Invisible*, 28.

28. Wooford, "Africa as Muse," 9.

29. Crawford, "African-Caribbean Women, Diaspora, and Transnationality."

30. Nalley, "Public Display of Affection?"

31. Esekheigbe, "6 Nigerian Women Talk About Overcoming Purity Culture."

32. In her article "Nudity and Pleasure," Diabate argues that in recent years there has been what she calls a "pleasure turn" on the African continent, defined as the increasing visibility and availability in major African cities, and in their online spaces, of objects related to erotic pleasure; these include erotica, pornography, sex toys, fattening pills and butt-enhancing underwear, chat rooms, aphrodisiacs, erotic dances, strip clubs, naked bodies, advertisements for surgical enhancements of male sexual parts, and sexy clothing. Even as public opinion about heterosexual expressions of affection has perhaps begun to shift, Nigeria's 2014 anti-gay law threatens individuals with up to ten years in prison for public displays of affection with members of the same sex.

33. Njideka Akunyili Crosby, in discussion with the author, November 2016.

34. See *Osuofia in London 1* and *2*, which are among the highest grossing Nollywood films of all time.

35. Nigerian Constitution, Constitute Project, https://www.constituteproject.org/constitution/Nigeria_2011.

36. Appadurai, "Disjuncture and Difference in the Global Cultural Economy," 18.

37. Stallings, *Funk the Erotic*, 150.

38. Gopinath, *Impossible Desires*, 14.

39. In *Fashioning Postfeminisms*, Dosekun writes, "According to the women in *Fashioning Postfeminisms*, nowadays it is highly mediated and circulated figures like Beyoncé and Rihanna contributing to the transnational dissemination of the spectacularly feminine, including a specifically *black* look." Here Dosekun points to the ways figures like Beyoncé and Rihanna have shaped a distinctly feminine Nigerian aesthetic, despite the fact that these imported stylings have often been considered un-African, 31.

40. Akunyili Crosby, *I Refuse to Be Invisible*, 22.

41. Akunyili Crosby, *I Refuse to Be Invisible*, 29.

42. Sjostrom, "Nigerian-Born Artist Explores Expatriate Identity at Norton Museum."

43. Ahmed, "Orientations," 559.

44. Ahmed, "Orientations," 559.

45. Also, the fact that Justin is wearing his sneakers inside a bedroom, which is not the norm in most Nigerian homes, marks him as an outsider.

## CHAPTER 3. EROTIC AGENCY AND AFRICAN INTIMACY IN THE WORK OF ZINA SARO-WIWA

An early version of chapter 3 appeared in *Women Studies Quarterly*.

Epigraph: Zino Saro-Wiwa. "Did You Know We Taught Them How to Dance?"

1. Saro-Wiwa, "Sarogua Mourning (2011)."

2. Saro-Wiwa, "Sarogua Mourning (2011)."

3. Musser, *Sensual Excess*, 5.

4. Fleetwood, *Troubling Vision*, 9.

5. Fleetwood, *Troubling Vision*, 9.

6. Morgan, "Why We Get Off," 40.

7. Hutchison, *Affective Communities in World Politics*, 4.

8. Lorde, "Uses of the Erotic: The Erotic as Power," in *Sister Outsider*, 54.

9. Lorde, "Uses of the Erotic," 54.

10. Stallings, *Funk the Erotic*, xv.

11. Lorde, "Uses of the Erotic," 342.

12. Lorde, "Uses of the Erotic," 341

13. Lorde, "Uses of the Erotic," 341.

14. Saro-Wiwa, "Did You Know We Taught Them How to Dance?"

15. Tcheuyap, *Postnationalist African Cinemas*, 3.

16. Silva, "Performing Love, Enacting Life," 113.

17. "*Eaten by the Heart*: An Exploration of Love, Intimacy and Heartbreak in Africa and the African Diaspora."

18. Saro-Wiwa, dir., *Eaten by the Heart*.

19. Saro-Wiwa, *Eaten by the Heart*.

20. Saro-Wiwa, *Eaten by the Heart*.

21. Saro-Wiwa, "The Archive on African Time."

22. Ngai, *Ugly Feelings*, 354.

23. Ahmed, *The Cultural Politics of Emotion*, 86.

24. Berlant, *Desire/Love*, 20.

25. Lourde, "Uses of the Erotic," 340.

26. Tcheuyap, *Postnationalist African Cinemas*, 33.

27. Padmanabhan, "The Weather in Tsai."

28. Saro-Wiwa, *Eaten by the Heart*.

29. Saro-Wiwa, *Eaten by the Heart*.

30. Deliso, "The Menil Hosts a Big Show on Love."

31. Brielmaier, "Transformers."

32. Marks, *The Skin of the Film*, 2.

33. Tcheuyap, *Postnationalist African Cinemas*, 194.

34. Jackson and Hogg, "Confessional Art," 123.

35. Gammel, *Confessional Politics*, 3.

36. Hall, "Cultural Identity and Cinematic Representation," 80.

37. Lorde, "Uses of the Erotic," 342.

38. Saro-Wiwa, "The Archive on African Time."

## CHAPTER 4. QUEER DIASPORIC GIRLHOOD IN *THE ADVENTURES OF ADA THE ALIEN* AND *AKATA WITCH*

Epigraph. amanze, "Biography."

1. Wright, *Physics of Blackness*, 73.

2. Wright, *Physics of Blackness*, 8.

3. Wright, *Physics of Blackness*, 73.

4. Jackson and Moody-Freeman, "Introduction," 2.

5. Macharia, "Africa: Queer: Anthropology."

6. Brown, *Hear Our Truths*, 1.

7. Cox, *Shapeshifters*, 12.

8. See Cox, *Shapeshifters*.

9. CaShawn Thompson, quoted in Thomas, "Why Everyone's Saying 'Black Girls Are Magic.'"

10. Chavers, "Here's My Problem with #BlackGirlMagic."

11. Jackson, *Becoming Human*, 1.

12. Jackson, *Becoming Human*, 1.

13. Jackson, *Becoming Human*, 2.

14. Bustos, "With the Help of Online Social Networks."

15. Philogynoir, "Why I'm Not a Carefree Black Girl."

16. Uwumarogie, "Cree Summer."

17. Ayobade, *Queens of Afrobeat*, 18.

18. Scalk, *Bodyminds Reimagined*, 143.

19. Jelača, "Alien Feminisms and Cinema's Posthuman Women."

20. Jelača, "Alien Feminisms and Cinema's Posthuman Women," 380.

21. Gumbs, "Speculative Poetics," 130.

22. Young, *Falling, Floating, Flickering*, 1.

23. Berlant and Warner, "Sex in Public," 558.

24. In *Strange Affinities: The Gender and Sexual Politics of Comparative Racialization*, Roderick Ferguson and Grace Hong write of heterotopias, "Heterotopias are disturbing, probably because they secretly undermine language, because they make it impossible to name this and that, because they shatter or tangle common names, because they destroy syntax in advance and not only the syntax with which we construct sentences but also that less apparent syntax which causes words and things (next to and also opposite one another) to 'hold together.'" Most importantly, heterotopias are localizable, examples being cemeteries, ships, and gardens. Amanze in particular is explicit about her works not being utopias, but actual representations of the here and now.

25. Greslé, "ruby onyinyechi amanze."

26. Corbett, "Curator and Artist ruby onyinyechi amanze."

27. Greslé, "ruby onyinyechi amanze."

28. Arie, "'I Was Born a Leader'—Ada."

29. amanze, "About."

30. Goodman, *Ways of Worldmaking*, 7.

31. amanze, "Aliens, Hybrids, and Ghosts."

32. In her 2020 exhibition at Goodman Gallery titled, *The Ones That Stayed*, amanze said goodbye to a number of these characters and introduced a new cohort including: ada, audre (formerly ada the Alien and audre the Leopard), Bird and the inanimate characters Swimming Pool, Moped, Window and Other Architectural References. Amanze's willingness to stay goodbye to elements of an old world and introduce new characters deftly speaks to her commitment to home and belonging as an iterative process.

33. Miller and Ojong, "Ékpè 'Leopard' Society in Africa and the Americas," 267.

34. amanze, "Aliens, Hybrids, and Ghosts."

35. Brown, *Black Girlhood Celebration*, 1.

36. "Multiple Black Realities."

37. Williams-Forson, "Other Women Cooked for My Husband," 437.

38. DeVault, *Feeding the Family*, 79.

39. Mehta, "Culinary Diasporas," 35.

40. This figure seems to reference amanze's 2014 drawing *ada rests in places unknown*, which shows a nude neon-yellow ada lounging beneath a hanging houseplant with her arms behind her head.

41. amanze, "Aliens, Hybrids, and Ghosts."

42. Greslé, "ruby onyinyechi amanze."

43. Greslé, "ruby onyinyechi amanze."

44. "'Myth-Making, Space-Shifting.'"

45. amanze, "Statements."

46. Greslé, "ruby onyinyechi amanze."

47. Greslé, "ruby onyinyechi amanze."

48. Gordon, *Ghostly Matters*, xvi.

49. Gaines, *Black Performance on the Outskirts of the Left*, 19.

50. In *Animate Planet: Making Visceral Sense of Living in a High-Tech Ecologically Damaged World*, Kath Weston asks, "what happens to people's visceral understanding of what it means to be human when damage to ecosystems has muddied any interior/exterior divide," arguing that "the goal is to learn from the new animacies and to identify the intimacies embedded in them, but at the same time to read them as symptom." Weston, *Animate Planet*, 19.

51. Muñoz, *Disidentifications*, 195.

52. Greslé, "ruby onyinyechi amanze."

53. Muñoz, *Cruising Utopia*, 1.

54. Okorafor, *Akata Witch*, 1.

55. Okorafor, *Akata Witch*, 2.

56. Wabuke, "Afrofuturism, Africanfuturism, and the Language of Black Speculative Literature."

57. Wabuke, "Afrofuturism, Africanfuturism, and the Language of Black Speculative Literature."

58. Jones, "If It Scares You, Write It."

59. Jones, "If It Scares You, Write It."

60. Okorafor, "Sci-Fi Stories That Imagine a Future Africa."

61. Tan, "Nnedi Okorafor Interview on the Nebula Awards Website."

62. Tan, "Nnedi Okorafor Interview on the Nebula Awards Website."

63. Okorafor is the author of eighteen young adult and adult novels. In July of 2017 she announced via Twitter that her novel *Who Fears Death* had been picked up by HBO to become a TV series, with novelist and *Game of Thrones* producer George R. R. Martin joining the project as executive producer. In October of 2017, Okorafor also announced via Twitter that she would pick up where author Ta-Nehisi Coates left off and write the next three issues of Marvel's *Black Panther* comic book. Alter, "Nnedi Okorafor and the Fantasy Genre She Is Helping Redefine."

64. Alter, "Nnedi Okorafor and the Fantasy Genre She Is Helping Redefine."

65. Okorafor, *Akata Witch*, 3.

66. Ghori, "Review: *Akata Witch* by Nnedi Okorafor."

67. Another word for magic.

68. Okorafor, *Akata Witch*, 15.

69. Lindow, "Nnedi Okorafor," 50.

70. Lindow, "Nnedi Okorafor," 49.

71. Okorafor, *Akata Witch*, 5.

72. Okorafor, *Akata Witch*, 23.

73. "Persons with Albinism Suffer Most Discrimination in Public Spaces."

74. Aghaji, "Out of the Sun."

75. "Jake Epelle, Founder of the Albino Foundation."

76. "The Stigma of Albinism in Nigeria Explored in Research."

77. According to Ivor Miller and Mathew Ojong, the Ékpè, which translates to leopard, have four major roles in precolonial life, "First, the conferment of full citizenship holding a title in Ékpè accorded one the status of full citizen with rights to make decisions having implications for the entire community, much like the respect accorded to the toga virilis in ancient Rome. Ékpè was also the no-nonsense community police, with the power to discipline and, as a measure of punishment, to confiscate the property of a community member who disobeyed the law. And Ékpè provided entertainment, with dances, music and body-mask performance, for members. Finally, Ékpè was a school for esoteric teachings regarding the human life as a cyclic process of regeneration, with the eventual reincarnation of that being." Miller and Ojong, "Ékpè 'Leopard' Society in Africa and the Americas," 267.

78. Okorafor, *Akata Witch*, 349.

79. Okorafor, *Akata Witch*, 1.

80. Okorafor, *Akata Witch*, 63.

81. Okorafor, *Akata Witch*, 68.

82. Okorafor, *Akata Witch*, 69.

83. Okorafor, *Akata Witch*, 259.

84. Ghori, "Review: *Akata Witch*."

85. Gumbs, "Speculative Poetics," 130.

86. Okorafor, *Akata Witch*, 73.

87. Williams, "Witches, Monsters, and Questions of Nation," 16.

88. Okorafor, *Akata Witch*, 338.

89. Okorafor, *Akata Witch*, 330.

90. Okorafor writes that Sunny's grandfather derogatorily called him an akata.

91. Okorafor, *Akata Witch*, 288.

92. The language of Nsibidi is the oldest written language in Africa, and only a select few understand it. On the first page of the book, below the title, is the Nsibidi symbol for "This is all mine."

93. Okorafor, *Akata Witch*, 187.

94. Cox, *Shapeshifters*, 29.

## CONCLUSION. REDEFINING BELONGING VIS-À-VIS TETHERING

1. See Emezi, *Freshwater*; Mohammed, Nagarajan, and Aliyu, *She Called Me Woman*; Osunde, *Vagabonds*; George, *Maame*.

2. Saro-Wiwa, "The Archive on African Time."

3. "Multiple Black Realities."

4. Oluwajoba, "The Rise of Alternative Art Spaces in Lagos."

5. Taiwo Aiyedogbon, in conversation with the author, April 4, 2022.

6. Taiwo Aiyedogbon, in conversation with the author, April 4, 2022.

7. Taiwo Aiyedogbon, in conversation with the author, April 4, 2022.

8. Akinbola, "#AfricanAunties."

9. Nelson, "Origins of the Alté Movement."

10. Akinola, "An Introduction to Nigeria's Innovative 'Alté' Scene."

11. Akinola, "An Introduction to Nigeria's Innovative 'Alté' Scene."

12. Nhất Hạnh, *Reconciliation*.

13. Selasi, "Don't Ask Where I'm From."

14. Young, *Falling, Floating, Flickering*, 68.

15. amanze and Ogunji, "just a note; artist to artist."

16. amanze and Ogunji, "just a note; artist to artist."

# Bibliography

Achebe, Chinua. *No Longer at Ease*. London: Heinemann, 1960.

Achebe, Chinua. *Things Fall Apart*. London: Heinemann, 1958.

Adichie, Chimamanda Ngozi. *Americanah*. New York: Alfred A. Knopf, 2013.

Adjepong, Anima. *Afropolitan Projects: Redefining Blackness, Sexualities, and Culture from Houston to Accra*. Chapel Hill: University of North Carolina Press, 2021.

Aghaji, Nonye. "Out of the Sun." DW, September 25, 2013. https://www.dw.com/en/activist-reaches-out-to-nigerias-albinos/a-17036768.

Ahmed, Sara. *The Cultural Politics of Emotion*. New York: Routledge, 2015.

Ahmed, Sara. "Orientations: Toward a Queer Phenomenology." *GLQ: A Journal of Lesbian and Gay Studies* 12, no. 4 (2006): 543–74. muse.jhu.edu/article/202832.

Ajibade, Idowu. "Can a Future City Enhance Urban Resilience and Sustainability? A Political Ecology Analysis of Eko Atlantic City, Nigeria." *International Journal of Disaster Risk Reduction* 26 (December 2017): 85–92.

Akinbola, Bimbola. "#AfricanAunties: Performing Diasporic Digital Disbelongings on TikTok." *Text and Performance Quarterly* 42, no. 3 (2022): 284–97. https://doi.org/10.1080/10462937.2022.2044071.

Akinbola, Bimbola. "African Intimacy and Love with No Pretense: The Erotics of Diaspora in Zina Saro-Wiwa's *Eaten by the Heart*." *Women's Studies Quarterly* 50, nos. 1–2 (2022): 68–85. https://www.jstor.org/stable/27187209.

Akinola, Tanya. "An Introduction to Nigeria's Innovative 'Alté' Scene." *Dazed*, July 5, 2019. https://www.dazeddigital.com/music/article/45115/1/introduction-to-nigeria-alte-music-scene.

Akinwotu, Emmanuel. "Waves of Change: Nigeria's Lagos Battles Atlantic Erosion." *Phys.org*, July 10, 2019. https://phys.org/news/2019-07-nigeria-lagos-atlantic-erosion.html.

Akunyili Crosby, Njideka. *I Refuse to Be Invisible*. West Palm Beach, FL: Norton Museum of Art, 2016.

Alter, Alexandra. "Nnedi Okorafor and the Fantasy Genre She Is Helping Redefine." *New York Times*, October 6, 2017. https://www.nytimes.com/2017/10/06/books/ya-fantasy-diverse-akata-warrior.html.

amanze, ruby onyinyechi. "About." *ruby onyinyechi amanze*. http://rubyamanze.com/about.

amanze, ruby onyinyechi. "Aliens, Hybrids, and Ghosts." *Anatomía de una Escena*, February 27, 2017. http://backroomcaracas.com/escritura-expandida/aliens-hybrids-and -ghosts-en/.

amanze, ruby onyinyechi. "Biography." Morgan Lehman Gallery. Accessed June 18, 2015. https://www.morganlehmangallery.com/exhibitions/ruby-onyinyechi-amanze/press -release.

amanze, ruby onyinyechi. "Statements." *ruby onyinyechi amanze*. http://rubyamanze.com /statements.

amanze, ruby onyinyechi, and Wura-Natasha Ogunji. "Just a Note; Artist to Artist." *BOMB*, August 23, 2019. https://bombmagazine.org/articles/just-a-note-artist-to-artist/.

Appadurai, Arjun. "Disjuncture and Difference in the Global Cultural Economy." *Theory, Culture and Society* 7, nos. 2–3 (June 1990): 295–310. https://doi.org/10.1177 /026327690007002017.

Arie, Ivery. "'I Was Born a Leader'—Ada." *Ivery Arie: The Contemporary African Woman*, May 23, 2018. https://iveryarie.wordpress.com/2018/05/23/the-ada-2/.

Arthur, John. *Invisible Sojourners: African Immigrant Diaspora in the United States*. Westport, CT: Praeger, 2000.

Ater, Renee. *Remaking Race and History: The Sculpture of Meta Warrick Fuller*. Berkeley: University of California Press, 2011.

Atoke. "Atoke's Monday Morning Banter: Bow, Kneel and Greet." *Bella Naija*, August 11, 2014. https://www.bellanaija.com/2014/08/atokes-monday-morning-banter-bow -kneel-greet/.

Ayobade, Dotun. *Queens of Afrobeat : Women, Play, and Fela Kuti's Music Rebellion*. Bloomington: Indiana University Press, 2024.

Bakare-Yusuf, Bibi. "Nudity and Morality: Legislating Women's Bodies and Dress in Nigeria." In *African Sexualities: A Reader*, edited by Sylvia Tamale, 116–29. Cape Town: Pambazuka Press, 2011.

Bauman, Zygmunt. *Community: Seeking Safety in an Insecure World*. Cambridge, UK: Polity, 2001.

Bedoya, Roberto. "Placemaking and the Politics of Belonging and Dis-Belonging." *GIA Reader* 24, no. 1 (Winter 2013). https://www.giarts.org/article/placemaking-and -politics-belonging-and-dis-belonging.

Berlant, Lauren. *Desire/Love*. Brooklyn: Punctum Books, 2012.

Berlant, Lauren, and Michael Warner. "Sex in Public." *Critical Inquiry* 24, no. 2 (Winter 1998): 547–66. https://doi.org/10.1086/448884.

Bhabha, Homi. *The Location of Culture*. London: Routledge, 1994.

Bhabha, Homi. "The World and the Home." *Social Text* nos. 31–32 (1992) 141–53.

Biggs, Lisa. *The Healing Stage: Black Women, Incarceration, and the Art of Transformation*. Columbus: Ohio State University Press, 2022.

Boym, Svetlana. *The Future of Nostalgia*. New York: Basic Books, 2001.

Brah, Avtar. *Cartographies of Diaspora: Contesting Identities*. Oxford: Routledge, 1996.

Brand, Dionne. *A Map to the Door of No Return: Notes to Belonging*. Toronto: Vintage Canada, 2001.

Brielmaier, Isolde. "Transformers: Video Installation, Space, and the Art of Immersion." In *Cinema Remixed and Reloaded: Black Women Artists and the Moving Image Since 1970*, edited by Andrea Barnwell Brownlee and Valerie Cassel Oliver, 55–61. Atlanta: Spelman College Museum of Fine Art/Contemporary Arts Museum of Houston, 2008.

Broude, Norma, Mary D. Garrard, and Judith K. Brodsky, eds. *The Power of Feminist Art: The American Movement of the 1970s, History and Impact.* New York: Harry N. Abrams, 1996.

Brown, Julia Arielle. "Listening to the Land/Playing Off the Crowd: Black Public Performance Interventions in Artmaking and Placemaking." *Public Art Dialogue* 7, no. 2 (2017): 230–41.

Brown, Ruth Nicole. *Black Girlhood Celebration.* New York: Lang, 2009.

Brown, Ruth Nicole. *Hear Our Truths: The Creative Potential of Black Girlhood.* Springfield: University of Illinois Press, 2013.

Bustos, Kristina. "With the Help of Online Social Networks, Women Like Issa Rae Are Promoting Better Representations of Black Women." *The Riveter*, March 10, 2015. http://www.therivetermagazine.com/beyond-the-black-girl-nerds-hashtag/.

Campt, Tina. *Image Matters: Archive, Photography, and the African Diaspora in Europe.* Durham, NC: Duke University Press, 2012.

Campt, Tina. "Performing Stillness: Diaspora and Stasis in Black German Vernacular Photography." *Qui Parle: Critical Humanities and Social Sciences* 26, no. 1 (June 2017): 155–70.

"Can Trauma Be Passed Down to the Next Generation Through DNA?" *PBS*, August 31, 2015. http://www.pbs.org/newshour/extra/daily-videos/can-trauma-be-passed-to-next-generation-through-dna/.

Carpenter, Faedra Chatard. *Coloring Whiteness: Acts of Critique in Black Performance.* Ann Arbor: University of Michigan Press, 2014.

Castellote, Jess, and Tobenna Okwuosa. "Lagos Art World: The Emergence of an Artistic Hub on the Global Art Periphery." *African Studies Review* 63, no. 1 (March 2020): 170–96. DOI:10.1017/asr.2019.24.

Chacko, Elizabeth. "Fitting In and Standing Out: Identity and Transnationalism Among Second-Generation African Immigrants in the United States." *African and Black Diaspora: An International Journal* 12, no. 2 (2018): 228–42. https://doi.org/10.1080/17528631.2018.1559789.

Chambers-Letson, Josh. *After the Party: A Manifesto for Queer of Color Life.* New York: NYU Press, 2018.

Chavers, Linda. "Why I Don't Love BlackGirlMagic." *Elle*, January 31, 2016. https://www.elle.com/life-love/a33180/why-i-dont-love-blackgirlmagic/.

Clark, Msia Kibona. "Feminisms in African Hip Hop." *Meridians* 17, no. 2 (2018): 383–400. https://doi.org/10.1215/15366936-7176538.

Clifford, James. "Diasporas." *Cultural Anthropology* 9, no. 3 (1994): 302–38.

Commander, Michelle D. *Afro-Atlantic Flight: Speculative Returns and the Black Fantastic.* Durham, NC: Duke University Press, 2017.

Conquergood, Lorne Dwight. "Performance Studies: Interventions and Radical Research." *TDR* 46, no. 2 (Summer 2002): 145–56.

Corbett, Rachel. "Curator and Artist ruby onyinyechi amanze on the Ancient, Universal Language of Drawing." *Artspace*, November 26, 2013. http://www.artspace.com /magazine/interviews_features/expert_eye/ruby_onyinyechi_amanze-51862.

Coritz, Alli. "Over Half of Those Who Reported Their Race as Black or African American Identified as African American, Jamaican or Haitian." *Census.Gov*, October 17, 2023, www.census.gov/library/stories/2023/10/2020-census-dhc-a-black-population .html.

Cox, Aimee Meredith. *Shapeshifters: Black Girls and the Choreography of Citizenship*. Durham, NC: Duke University Press, 2015.

Crawford, Charmaine. "African-Caribbean Women, Diaspora, and Transnationality." *Canadian Woman Studies* 23 (Winter 2004): 97–103.

"Crude Politics." *The Economist*, March 28, 2015. https://www.economist.com/news /middle-east-and-africa/21647361-broken-oil-industry-source-many-woes-crude -politics.

Daniel, Richard M. "The Little Can That Could." *Invention and Technology* 3, no. 2 (Fall 1987). https://www.inventionandtech.com/content/little-can-could-1.

Davies, Catriona. "Artist Joins Nigeria's 'Cultural Explosion.'" *CNN*. October 23, 2012. http://www.cnn.com/2012/10/22/world/africa/nigerian-artist-njideka-akunyili/.

Dedieu, Jean-Phillippe. "Njideka Akunyili Crosby's Intimate Universes." *New Yorker*, November 5, 2015. http://www.newyorker.com/culture/photo-booth/njideka-akunyili -crosbys-intimate-universes.

DeFrantz, Thomas F., and Anita Gonzales, editors. *Black Performance Theory*. Durham, NC: Duke University Press, 2014.

de León, Alec. "Catching Up with Wura-Natasha Ogunji." *National Performance Network*, July 20, 2012. http://npnweb.org/2012/07/20/catching-up-with-wura-natasha -ogunji/.

Deliso, Meredith. "The Menil Hosts a Big Show on Love." *Houston Press*, January 16, 2013. https://www.houstonpress.com/arts/the-menil-hosts-a-big-show-on-love -6365778.

DeVault, Marjorie. *Feeding the Family: The Social Organization of Caring as Gendered Work*. Chicago: University of Chicago Press, 1994.

Diabate, Naminata. "Genital Power: Female Sexuality in West African Literature and Film." PhD diss., University of Texas at Austin, 2011.

Diabate, Naminata. "Nudity and Pleasure." *Nka: Journal of Contemporary African Art* 1, no. 46 (2020): 152–66. https://doi.org/10.1215/10757163–8308270.

Dosekun, Simidele. *Fashioning Postfeminism: Spectacular Femininity and Transnational Culture*. Springfield: University of Illinois Press, 2020.

"*Eaten by the Heart*: An Exploration of Love, Intimacy and Heartbreak in Africa and the African Diaspora." African Studies Program, University of Wisconsin. https://africa .wisc.edu/events-intro/events-special-events/eaten-by-the-heart/.

Edwards, Brent Hayes. "The Uses of Diaspora." *Social Text* 19, no. 1 (2001): 45–73. muse .jhu.edu/article/31891.

"Eko Atlantic City Project to Create 150,000 Jobs, Lagos Commissioner Says." *Premium Times*, April 13, 2013. https://www.premiumtimesng.com/regional/ssouth-west

/130208-eko-atlantic-city-project-to-create-150000-jobs-lagos-commissioner-says
.html.

Ellis, Nadia. *Territories of the Soul: Queered Belonging in the Black Diaspora*. Durham,
NC: Duke University Press, 2015.

Emezi, Akwaeke. *Freshwater*. New York: Grove Press, 2018.

Epprecht, Marc. "The Making of African Sexuality: Early Sources, Current Debates."
*History Compass* 8, no. 8 (August 2010): 768–79. https://doi.org/10.1111/j.1478–0542
.2010.00715.

Esekheigbe, Itohan. "6 Nigerian Women Talk About Overcoming Purity Culture."
*Zikoko*, May 6, 2021. https://www.zikoko.com/her/6-nigerian-women-talk-about
-overcoming-purity-culture/.

Ezepue, Ezinne Michaelia, and Chidera G. Nwafor. "October 1: Metaphorizing Nigeria's
Collective Trauma of Colonization." *Sage Open* 13, no. 3 (October 1, 2023). https://doi
.org/10.1177/21582440231197271.

Falola, Toyin, and Matthew Heaton. *A History of Nigeria*. Cambridge: Cambridge University Press, 2008.

Fleetwood, Nicole. *Troubling Vision*. Chicago: University of Chicago Press, 2011.

Gaines, Malik. *Black Performance on the Outskirts of the Left: A History of the Impossible*.
New York: NYU Press, 2017.

Gammel, Irene. *Confessional Politics: Women's Sexual Self-Representations in Life Writing
and Popular Media*. Carbondale: Southern Illinois University Press, 1999.

George, Jessica. *Maame*. New York: St. Martin's Press, 2023.

George-Graves, Nadine. "Diasporic Spidering: Constructing Contemporary Black
Identities." In *Black Performance Theory*, edited by Thomas F. DeFrantz and Anita
Gonzalez, 33–44. Durham, NC: Duke University Press, 2014.

Ghori, Haroon. "Review: Akata Witch by Nnedi Okorafor." *Disability in Kid Lit*, August 7, 2015. https://disabilityinkidlit.com/2015/08/07/review-akata-witch-by-nnedi
-okorafor/.

Gilroy, Paul, *The Black Atlantic: Modernity and Double Consciousness*. Cambridge, MA:
Harvard University Press, 1993.

Goodman, Nelson. *Ways of Worldmaking*. Cambridge, MA: Hackett, 1978.

Gopinath, Gayatri. "Archive, Affect, and the Everyday: Queer Diasporic Re-Visions."
In *Political Emotions: New Agendas in Communication*, edited by Janet Staiger, Ann
Cvetkovich, and Ann Reynolds, 165–92. New York: Routledge, 2010.

Gopinath, Gayatri. *Impossible Desires: Queer Diasporas and South Asian Public Cultures*.
Durham, NC: Duke University Press, 2005.

Gopinath, Gayatri. *Unruly Visions: The Aesthetic Practices of Queer Diaspora*. Durham,
NC: Duke University Press, 2018.

Gordon, Avery. *Ghostly Matters: Haunting and the Sociological Imagination*. Minneapolis: University of Minnesota Press, 2008.

Gqola, Pumla Dineo. *Female Fear Factory*. Cape Town: Melinda Ferguson, 2021.

Greslé, Yvette. "ruby onyinyechi amanze: A Story. In Parts." *Writing in Relation: Interviews, Essays and Dialogues About Art*, February 24, 2015. https://writinginrelation
.wordpress.com/2015/02/24/ruby-onyinyechi-amanze-a-story-in-parts/.

Gumbs, Alexis Pauline. "Speculative Poetics: Audre Lorde as Prologue." In *The Black Imagination: Science Fiction, Futurism and the Black Speculative*, edited by Sandra Jackson and Julie E. Moody-Freeman, 130–45. New York: Peter Lang, 2011.

Hall, Stuart. "Cultural Identity and Cinematic Representation." *Framework: The Journal of Cinema and Media* 36 (1989): 68–81.

Hall, Stuart. "Cultural Identity and Diaspora." In *Identity, Community, Culture, and Difference*, edited by Jonathan Rutherford, 222–37. London: Lawrence and Wishart, 1990.

Hartman, Saidiya. *Lose Your Mother: A Journey Along the Atlantic Slave Route*. New York: Farrar, Straus and Giroux, 2008.

Hartman, Saidiya. *Scenes of Subjection*. London: Oxford University Press, 1997.

Hartman, Saidiya. *Wayward Lives, Beautiful Experiments: Intimate Histories of Riotous Black Girls, Troublesome Women, and Queer Radical*. W. W. Norton: New York, 2019.

Hayden, Dolores. "Contested Terrain." In *The Power of Place: Urban Landscapes as Public History*. Cambridge, MA: MIT Press, 1995.

Herman, J. L. "Complex PTSD: A Syndrome in Survivors of Prolonged and Repeated Trauma." *Journal of Traumatic Stress* 5, no. 3 (1992): 377–91. https://doi.org/10.1002/jts.2490050305.

Hirsch, Marianne. *The Generation of Postmemory: Writing and Visual Culture After the Holocaust*. New York: Columbia University Press, 2012.

Hong, Grace Kyungwon, and Roderick A. Ferguson. *Strange Affinities: The Gender and Sexual Politics of Comparative Racialization*. Durham, NC: Duke University Press, 2011.

hooks, bell. *Art on My Mind: Visual Politics*. New York: New Press, 1995.

Houlberg, Marilyn Hammersley. "Notes on Egungun Masquerades Among the Oyo Yoruba." *African Arts* 11, no. 3 (1978): 51–61, 99.

Hutchison, Emma. *Affective Communities in World Politics: Collective Emotions After Trauma*. Cambridge: Cambridge University Press, 2016.

Imoagene, Onoso. *Beyond Expectations: Second-Generation Nigerians in the United States and Britain*. Oakland: University of California Press, 2017.

Jackson, Ronald L., II, and Michael A. Hogg. "Confessional Art." In *Encyclopedia of Identity*. Los Angeles: SAGE, 2010.

Jackson, Sandra, and Julie Moody-Freeman, editors. "Introduction: The Genre of Science Fiction and the Black Imagination." In *The Black Imagination: Science Fiction, Futurism and the Black Speculative*, 1–14. New York: Peter Lang, 2011.

Jackson, Zakiyyah Iman. *Becoming Human: Matter and Meaning in an Antiblack World*. New York: NYU Press, 2020.

"Jake Epelle, Founder of the Albino Foundation." *UN Human Rights*. Accessed July 21, 2024. https://albinism.ohchr.org/story-jake-epelle.html.

Jelača, Dijana. "Alien Feminisms and Cinema's Posthuman Women." *Signs: Journal of Women in Culture and Society* 43, no. 2 (2018): 379–400.

Jones, Jeremy L. C. "If It Scares You, Write It: A Conversation with Nnedi Okorafor." *Clarkesworld*, December 2009. www.clarkesworldmagazine.com/okorafor_interview/.

Jones, Joni. "Yoruba Diasporic Performance: The Case for a Spiritually and Aesthetically-Based Diaspora." *Orisa: Yoruba Gods and Spiritual Identity in Africa and the Diaspora*. edited by Toyin Falola and Ann Genova, 32–31. Trenton, NJ: Africa World Press, Inc., 2005.

Johnson, E. Patrick. *Appropriating Blackness: Performance and the Politics of Authenticity*, Durham, NC: Duke University Press, 2003.

Joseph, Miranda. *Against the Romance of Community*. Minneapolis: University of Minnesota Press, 2002.

Kazeem, Maryam. "Performances That Seek to Interrupt: Nigerian Artist Wura-Natasha Ogunji and the Craft of Spectacle." *OkayAfrica*, May 27, 2013. http://www.okayafrica.com/nigeria-art-wura-natasha-ogunji-visual-performance/.

Kebede, Kassahun. "The African Second Generation in the United States: Identity and Transnationalism: An Introduction." *African and Black Diaspora: An International Journal* 12, no. 2 (2018): 119–36. https://doi.org/10.1080/17528631.2018.1559791.

Kenyatta, Jomo. *Facing Mount Kenya: The Tribal Life of Gikuyu*. London: Secker and Warburg, 1938.

Kristeva, Julia. *Power of Horrors: An Essay on Abjection*. New York: Columbia University Press,1980.

Laenui, Poka. "Processes of Decolonization." *Reclaiming Indigenous Voice and Vision* (2000): 150–60. https://www.sjsu.edu/people/marcos.pizarro/courses/maestros/s0/Laenui.pdf.

Lærkesen, Roxanne Bagheshirin. "Wura-Natasha Ogunji: Beauty in the Streets of Lagos." *Louisiana Channel*. Accessed July 21, 2024. http://channel.louisiana.dk/video/wura-natasha-ogunji-beauty-streets-lagos.

La Pastina, Antonio C. "A Food Connection: Interview with Wura-Natasha Ogunji by Antonio C. La Pastina." *Aster(ix) Journal*, October 25, 2013. http://asterixjournal.com/a-food-connection-interview-with-wuru-natasha-ogunji-by-antonio-c-la-pastina/.

Lara, Ana-Maurine. "Wura-Natasha Ogunji, Interviewed on February 25, 2006." *The Magic Makers: A Record of the Lives of Lesbian, Gay, Bisexual, Transgendered and Two-Spirit Artists of Color*, February 27, 2008. http://themagicmakers.blogspot.com/2008/02/wura-natasha-ogunji-interviewed-on.html.

Layiwola, Peju. "Transcultural Conversations: American and Nigerian Art in Dialogue." *Nka: Journal of Contemporary African Art* 41 (November 2017): 140–52. https://doi.org/10.1215/10757163-4271696.

"Leading Contemporaries, Njideka Akunyili Crosby." *Art X Talks*, February 21, 2018. https://www.youtube.com/watch?v=K_h1i7AJCtE.

Lindow, Sandra. "Nnedi Okorafor: Exploring the Empire of Girls' Moral Development." *Journal of the Fantastic in the Arts* 28, no. 1 (2017): 46–69.

Livermon, Xavier. *Kwaito Bodies: Remastering Space and Subjectivity in Post-Apartheid South Africa*. Durham, NC: Duke University Press, 2020.

Lorde, Audre. *Sister Outsider: Essays and Speeches*. Brekely, CA: Crossing Press, 1984. http://turing.library.northwestern.edu/login?url=https://www.proquest.com/books/sister-outsider-essays-speeches/docview/2138588223/se-2.

Macharia, Keguro. "Africa: Queer: Anthropology." *New Inquiry*, July 28, 2018. https://thenewinquiry.com/blog/africa-queer-anthropology/.

Macharia, Keguro. *Frottage: Frictions of Intimacy Across the Black Diaspora*. New York: NYU Press, 2019.

Machida, Margo. *Unsettled Visions: Contemporary Asian American Artists and the Social Imaginary*. Durham, NC: Duke University Press, 2008.

Madison, D. Soyini. *Acts of Activism: Human Rights As Radical Performance*. Cambridge: Cambridge University Press, 2010. *ProQuest Ebook Central*, http://ebookcentral .proquest.com/lib/northwestern/detail.action?docID=502481. Created from north-western on 2025-03-10 20:20:54.

Madison, D Soyini. "Co-Performative Witnessing." *Cultural Studies* 21, no. 6 (November 2007): 826–31. DOI:10.1080/09502380701478174.

Marks, Laura U. *The Skin of the Film: Intercultural Cinema, Embodiment, and the Senses*. Durham, NC: Duke University Press, 2000.

McMillan, Uri. *Embodied Avatars: Genealogies of Black Feminist Art and Performance*. New York: NYU Press, 2015.

Mehta, Brinda. "Culinary Diasporas: Identity and the Language of Food in Giséle Pineau's *Un papillon dams la cité* and *L'exil selon Julia*." *International Journal of Francophone Studies* 8, no. 1 (April 2005): 23–51.

Meigh-Andrews, Chris. *A History of Video Art*, 2nd ed. New York: Bloomsbury Academic, 2014.

Miller, Ivor, and Mathew Ojong, "Ékpè 'Leopard' Society in Africa and the Americas: Influence and Values of an Ancient Tradition." *Ethnic and Racial Studies* 36, no. 2 (2013): 266–81. https://doi.org/10.1080/01419870.2012.676200.

Mohammed, Azeenarh, Chitra Nagarajan, and Rafeeat Aliyu, eds. *She Called Me Woman: Nigeria's Queer Women Speak*. Abuja: Cassava Republic Press, 2018.

Morgan, Joan. "Why We Get Off: Moving Towards a Black Feminist Politics of Pleasure." *Black Scholar* 45, no. 4 (2015): 36–46. https://doi.org/10.1080/00064246.2015.1080915.

"Multiple Black Realities: Akwaeke Emezi + ruby onyinyechi amanze on Freshwater." *Livestream*, March 6, 2018. https://livestream.com/schomburgcenter/events/8097583 /videos/171168404.

Muñoz, José. *Cruising Utopia: The Then and There of Queer Futurity*. New York: NYU Press, 2009.

Muñoz, José. *Disidentifications: Queers of Color and the Performance of Politics*. Minneapolis: University of Minnesota Press, 1999.

Murphy, Joseph M., and Mei Mei Sanford. *Osun Across the Waters: A Yoruba Goddess in Africa and the Americas*. Indianapolis: Indiana University Press, 2001.

Musser, Amber Jamilla. *Sensual Excess: Queer Femininity and Brown Jouissance*. New York: NYU Press, 2018.

"'Myth-Making, Space-Shifting': ruby onyinyechi amanze on Hybridity, 'Africanness' and Paper." *Art Africa*, March 27, 2018. https://artafricamagazine.org/myth-making-space -shifting-ruby-onyinyechi-amanze-speaks-hybridity-terminology-and-paper/.

Nalley, Yima. "Public Display of Affection? Not in Africa." *Waza Online*, May 20, 2014.

Nelson, C. J. "Origins of the Alté Movement and How It Birthed a Generation of Young Nigerians." *Teen Vogue*, October 29, 2021. https://www.teenvogue.com/story/origins -of-the-alte-movement.

Ngai, Sianne. *Ugly Feelings*. Cambridge, MA: Harvard University Press, 2009.

Nhất Hạnh, Thich. *Reconciliation: Healing the Inner Child*. Berkeley: Parallax, 2011.

Njenga, F. G. "Trauma in African Women and Children: A Study of the Kenyan Experiences as Illustration of the Phenomenon." *African Journal of Psychiatry* 10, no. 1 (2007). DOI:10.4314/ajpsy.v10i1.30230.

Nketiah, Rita. "Why Respectability Politics Is Failing African Women and Girls." *This Is Africa*, August 29, 2016. https://thisisafrica.me/respectability-politics-failing-african-women-girls/.

Nothias, Toussaint. and Rosebell Kagumire. "Digital Radical Rudeness: The Story of Stella Nyanzi," *Center on Digital Culture and Society*, January 29, 2020. https://www.asc.upenn.edu/research/centers/center-on-digital-culture-and-society/the-digital-radical/digital-radical-rudeness.

Nyong'o, Tavia. *Afro-Fabulations: The Queer Drama of Black Life*. New York: NYU Press, 2019.

Odua, Chika. "Njideka Akunyili Crosby: A Nigerian Visual Artist." *Afrocentric Confessions*. Accessed May 30, 2016. http://chikaoduahblog.com/2012/10/19/njideka-akunyili-a-nigerian-visual-artist/.

Odufunade, Bomi. "Primary Colors: Njideka Akunyili." *Huffington Post*, August 24, 2012. http://www.huffingtonpost.com/arise-magazine/harlem-studio-african-american-artists_b_1827728.html.

Ogunji, Wura-Natasha. "Beauty." Obalende Motor Park, Lagos, Nigeria, April 11, 2013. Accessed August 12, 2024. https://wuraogunji.com/artwork/4618398-beauty.html.

Ogunji, Wura-Natasha. "First Rain in Abuja." *This Road*, February 5, 2011. http://goldeniron.blogspot.com/2011/02/first-rain-in-abuja.html.

Ogunji, Wura-Natasha. "How Does That Sound Look?" *This Road*. Accessed May 30, 2016. http://goldeniron.blogspot.com/2007/11/eternal.html.

Ogunji, Wura-Natasha. "Queens." *Wura-Natasha Ogunji*. Accessed August 6, 2024. https://wuraogunji.com/artwork/4618404-Queens.html.

Ogunji, Wura-Natasha. "Sweep." *Wura-Natasha Ogunji*. Accessed March 26, 2018. http://wuraogunji.com/artwork/2233005_Sweep.html.

Ogunji, Wura-Natasha. "Videos." *Wura-Natasha Ogunji*. Accessed May 30, 2016. http://wuraogunji.com/section/231339_videos.html.

Ogunji, Wura-Natasha. "Will I still carry water when I am a dead woman?" *This Road*, April 25, 2013. http://goldeniron.blogspot.com/2013/04/will-i-still-carry-water-when-i-am-dead_25.html.

Ogunji, Wura-Natasha, and ruby onyinyechi amanze. "Paper as Body: A Conversation." *The Offing*, January 19, 2016. https://theoffingmag.com/enumerate/paper-as-body/.

Okorafor, Nnedi. *Akata Witch*. New York: Viking Books, 2011.

Okorafor, Nnedi. "Sci-Fi Stories That Imagine a Future Africa." *TED Talk*, November 22, 2017. https://www.youtube.com/watch?v=MtoPiXLvYlU&feature=emb_title.

Okpewho, Isidore, and Nkiru Nzegwu, eds. *The New African Diaspora*. Bloomington: Indiana University Press, 2009.

Oliver, Valerie Cassel. "Between Artifice and Authentic: The Black Female Body in Performance." In *Cinema Remixed and Reloaded: Black Women Artists and the Moving Image Since 1970*, edited by Andrea Barnwell Brownlee and Valerie Cassel Oliver,

36–43. Atlanta: Spelman College Museum of Fine Art/Contemporary Arts Museum of Houston, 2008.

Oluwajoba, Adeoluwa. "The Rise of Alternative Art Spaces in Lagos: The Treehouse." Accessed December 7, 2018. https://www.omenkaonline.com/rise-alternative-art -spaces-lagos-treehouse/.

Onyile, Bassey Onyile. "Embodied Morality: Ekpri Àkàtà Masquerade of Efik Society, Nigeria." *African Arts* 54, no. 4 (2021): 64–77. https://doi.org/10.1162/afar_a _00613.

Osunde, Eloghosa. *Vagabonds*. New York: Riverhead Books, 2022.

Padmanabhan, Lakshmi. "The Weather in Tsai: Slow Cinema and Slow Violence." *Cultural Critique* 123 (2024): 87–128. https://doi.org/10.1353/cul.2024.a919743.

"Persons with Albinism Suffer Most Discrimination in Public Spaces." *Vanguard*, October 17, 2019. https://www.vanguardngr.com/2019/10/persons-with-albinism-suffer -most-discrimination-in-public-spaces-%E2%80%95-survey/.

Philogynoir. "Why I'm Not a Carefree Black Girl." *Philogynoir*, June 5, 2016. https:// philogynoir.tumblr.com/post/145487408857/why-im-not-a-carefree-black-girl-see -the-way.

Quashie, Kevin. *The Sovereignty of Quiet: Beyond Resistance in Black Culture*. New Brunswick, NJ: Rutgers University Press, 2012.

Ramos, Iván A. *Unbelonging: Inauthentic Sounds in Mexican and Latinx Aesthetics*. New York: NYU Press, 2023.

Rowley, Michelle V. "'It Could Have Been Me' Really? Early Morning Meditations on Trayvon Martin's Death." *Feminist Studies* 38, no. 2 (Summer 2012): 519–29. DOI:10.1353/fem.2012.0006.

Russell, Legacy. "Digital Dualism and the Glitch Feminism Manifesto." *Cyborgology*, December 10, 2012. https://thesocietypages.org/cyborgology/2012/12/10/digital-dualism -and-the-glitch-feminism-manifesto/.

Saro-Wiwa, Zina. "The Archive on African Time: A Conversation About 'African Time' as a Nuanced Temporality That Not Only Creates but Demands New Ways of Negotiating with Archives." Conversation between Zina Saro-Wiwa and Maryam Kazeem. *CalArts*, August 5, 2020. https://vimeo.com/444808692.

Saro-Wiwa, Zina. "Did You Know We Taught Them How to Dance?" *Blaffer Museum*, 2015. https://blafferartmuseum.org/zina-saro-wiwa-did-you-know-we-taught-them -how-to-dance/.

Saro-Wiwa, Zina, dir. *Eaten by the Heart: How Do Africans Kiss?* ZSW Studio, 2013. https://vimeo.com/54346578.

Saro-Wiwa, Zina. "Sarogua Mourning (2012)." *Zina Saro-Wiwa*. https://www .zinasarowiwa.com/artworks/sarogua-mourning/.

Schneider, Hildegard. "Of the Pomegranate." *Metropolitan Museum of Art Bulletin* 4 (1945): 117–20.

Schalk, Sami. *Bodyminds Reimagined : (Dis)Ability, Race, and Gender in Black Women's Speculative Fiction*. Durham, NC: Duke University Press, 2018.

Selasi, Taiye. "Don't Ask Where I'm From, Ask Where I'm a Local," TED *Global*, October 2014,

https://www.ted.com/talks/taiye_selasi_don_t_ask_where_i_m_from_ask_where_i_m
_a_local/transcript?subtitle=en.

Shepperson, George. "The African Abroad or the African Diaspora." In *Emerging Themes of African History: Proceedings*, edited by Terence O. Ranger, 152–76. Nairobi: East African Publishing House, 1968.

Silva, Bisi. "Performing Love, Enacting Life." In *The Progress of Love*, edited by Christina Van Dyke and Bisi Silva, 113–19. Houston: Menil Collection, 2012.

Sjostrom, Jan. "Nigerian-Born Artist Explores Expatriate Identity at Norton Museum." *Palm Beach Daily News*, January 30, 2016. Accessed March 30, 2017. https://www .palmbeachdailynews.com/story/entertainment/arts/2016/09/04/nigerian-born -artist-explores-expatriate/9684074007/.

Smith, Cherise. *Enacting Others: Politics of Identity in Eleanor Antin, Nikki S. Lee, Adrian Piper, and Anna Deavere Smith*. Durham, NC: Duke University Press, 2011.

Soyini, Madison D. *Acts of Activism: Human Rights As Radical Performance*, Cambridge: Cambridge University Press, 2010. *ProQuest Ebook Central*, 112.

Stack, Carol B. *Call to Home: African Americans Reclaim the Rural South*. New York: Basic Books, 1996.

Stallings, L. H. *Funk the Erotic: Transaesthetics and Black Sexual Culture*. Chicago: University of Illinois Press, 2015.

"The Stigma of Albinism in Nigeria Explored in Research." *University of Chester*, March 11, 2020. https://www1.chester.ac.uk/news/stigma-albinism-nigeria-explored-research.

"Sub-Saharan African Immigrants in the United States." *Migrationpolicy.org*. Accessed September 5, 2024. https://www.migrationpolicy.org/article/sub-saharan-african -immigrants-united-states.

Summers, Carol. "Radical Rudeness: Ugandan Social Critiques in the 1940s." *Journal of Social History* 39, no. 3 (2006): 741–70. https://doi.org/10.1353/jsh.2006.0020.

Tan, Charles. "Nnedi Okorafor Interview on the Nebula Awards Website." *Nnedi's Wahala Zone*, January 9, 2009. http://nnedi.blogspot.com/2009/01/nnedi-okorafor -interview-on-nebula.html.

Tcheuyap, Alexie. *Postnationalist African Cinemas*. Manchester: Manchester University Press, 2011.

Thomas, Dexter. "Why Everyone's Saying 'Black Girls Are Magic.'" *Los Angeles Times*, September 9, 2015. http://www.latimes.com/nation/nationnow/la-na-nn-everyones -saying-black-girls-are-magic-20150909-htmlstory.html.

Tsing, Anna. *Friction: An Ethnography of Global Connection*. Princeton, NJ: Princeton University Press, 2005.

Udobang, Wana. "Will I Still Carry Water When I Am a Dead Woman?" *WanaWana*, Accessed March 24, 2016. http://wanawana.net/2013/04/24/will-i-still-carry-water -when-i-am-a-dead-woman/.

Uwumarogie, Victoria. "Cree Summer, Often Considered the Original Carefree Black Girl, Explains Why There's No Such Thing." *MadameNoire*, September 8, 2016. https://madamenoire.com/716416/cree-summer-carefree-black-girl-myth/.

Valentine, Victoria L. "Njideka Akunyili Crosby Painting Sells for Record 3.1 Million at Christie's, Nearly Three Times Her Previous High Mark." *Culture Type*, March 12,

2017. http://www.culturetype.com/2017/03/12/njideka-akunyili-crosby-painting-sells-for-record-3–1-million-at-christies-nearly-three-times-her-previous-high-mark/.

Van Dyke, Nancy. *Everyday Narcissism: Yours, Mine, and Ours*. Las Vegas: Central Recovery Press, 2017.

Wabuke, Hope. "Afrofuturism, Africanfuturism, and the Language of Black Speculative Literature." *Los Angeles Review of Books*, August 27, 2020. https://lareviewofbooks.org/article/afrofuturism-africanfuturism-and-the-language-of-black-speculative-literature/.

Weheliye, Alexander. "My Volk to Come: Peoplehood in Recent Diaspora Discourse and Afro-German Popular Music." In *Black Europe and the African Diaspora*, edited by Darlene Clark Hine, Trica Danielle Keaton, and Stephen Small, 161–79. Champaign: University of Illinois Press, 2009.

Wemega-Kwawu, Rikki. "The Politics of Exclusion: The Undue Fixation on Western Based African Diaspora Artists." *Stedelijk Museum Bureau Amsterdam Newsletter* 125. smba-news-no-125.pdf (xokigbo.com).

Weston, Kath. *Animate Planet: Making Visceral Sense of Living in a High-Tech Ecologically Damaged World*. Durham, NC: Duke University Press, 2017.

Wilderson, Frank B. "Grammar and Ghosts: The Performative Limits of African Freedom." *Theatre Survey* 50, no. 1 (2009): 119–25. DOI:10.1017/S004055740900009X.

Williams, Deborah. "Witches, Monsters, and Questions of Nation: Humans and Non-Humans in *Akata Witch* and *Trail of Lightning*." *International Journal of Young Adult Literature* 1, no. 1 (2020): 1–19. https://doi.org/10.24877/ijyal.33.

Williams-Forson, Psyche. "Other Women Cooked for My Husband: Negotiating Gender, Food, and Identities in an African American/Ghanaian Household." *Feminist Studies* 36, no. 2 (Summer 2010): 435–61.

Willis, John Thabiti. "Negotiating Gender, Power, and Spaces in Masquerade Performances in Nigeria." *Gender, Place, and Culture* 21, no. 3 (2013): 322–36. https://doi.org/10.1080/0966369X.2013.781013.

"Witnessing the Present, the Artist as Citizen." *Art X Talks*, January 31, 2018. https://www.youtube.com/watch?v=CCuzEsJLpyk.

Wooford, Tobias. "Africa as Muse: The Visualization of Diaspora in African American Art 1950–1980." PhD diss., University of California at Los Angeles, 2011.

Wright, Michelle. *Physics of Blackness: Beyond the Middle Passage Epistemology*. Chicago: University of Chicago Press, 2014.

Young, Harvey. *Embodying Black Experience: Stillness, Critical Memory, and the Black Body*. Ann Arbor: University of Michigan Press, 2010.

Young, Hershini Bhana. *Falling, Floating, Flickering: Disability and Differential Movement in African Diasporic Performance*. New York: NYU Press, 2023.

# Index

water in, 47; rituals in, 44–45, 62; woman-
hood in, 54, 134, 137–38; women's labor in,
28–29; writing in, 127
Nigerian Americans, 130
Nigerian culture: identity norms in, 126–27;
queer characters and, 124–25
Nigerian Independence Day, viii
Njenga, F. G., 21–22
Nketiah, Rita, 20, 151n65
"Nnedi Okorafor" (Lindow), 128
Nollywood, 21, 72–74, 78, 88–89, 91, 155n34.
See also alt-Nollywood
No Longer at Ease (Achebe), 71
nostalgia: and home, 140; Ogunji and, 32, 41;
Okorafor and, 131
Nsibidi language, 134, 160n92
Nwafor, Chidera G., 21, 22
Nwantinti (Akunyili Crosby): and Degas,
79; family photo in, 81; pop culture in, 80
Nyanzi, Stella, 152
Nzegwu, Nkiru, 12

"October 1" (Ezepue and Nwafor), 21, 22
Odili, Veronny, 52
Ogbonno Soup Is Sweeter Since Meeting You
(amanze): characters in, 114–16; queering
of home in, 116–17; 115
Ogoni deities, 85
Ogoniland, oil companies in, 88
Ogunji, Wura-Natasha: and amanze, 53,
144–47; and Atiku, 42; on belonging,
31–32; blog of, 52, 55, 58; body of work, 29;
and "community art," 57; and disbelonging,
29, 41; early life and education, 30–31; and
Fall, 48; feminism of, 58; and homeland, 30,
35–36, 152n14; impact of, 24; on invisible
labor, 28–29; Lagos and, 59; and messy
contradictions, 141–42; nostalgia in, 32, 41;
outsiderness, embracing of, 59; own body in
work, 42–44; performances of, 29, 36–59;
photography of, 36; queer/mixed identity
of, 34–36, 42; quiet in, 46–47; and theorizing, 9; threadwork of, 35; and Treehouse
space, 139; unruly return in, 23, 37–41, 58;
video works, 36–41; visual art, 32–26, 41;
and Vlado, 49, 52; as woman artist, 2. See
also individual works
Ojukwu, Chukwuemeka Odumegwu, 69

Okorafor, Nnedi: on African/black diasporic
girlhood, 23, 105–7, 125–35, 158n32; as Afri-
canfuturist/Africanjujuist, 125; and amanze,
24, 105–6, 131, 134–35; and Black Girl
Magic, 108; early life and education, 126;
impact of, 24; and messy contradictions,
141–42; on play, 131, 132; on speculative
fiction, 133; and theorizing, 9; as woman
artist, 2; young adult fiction by, 105, 159n63.
See also individual works
Okoye, Kris, 78
Okpewho, Isidore, 12
Okudzeto, Senam, 118
Okwuosa, Tobenna, 19
Olagunji, Anthony, 130
Oliver, Valerie Cassel, 36–37
"Orientations" (Ahmed), 80–81
Orimolade, Odun, 43, 139
Oshun, Yoruba deity, 35, 123
Osunde, Eloghosa, 137
outsiderness: and ada the Alien, 111, 113; and
Afropolitan, 17; and Akunyili Crosby,
62, 64, 68, 81; and amanze, 120; author's
attraction to, ix; and belonging, 41; and
black girls, 24; embracing, 59; and freedom,
7–8; Lorde on, 57–58; and Okorafor, 126,
127, 129, 130
oyinbo (foreigner) term, 42, 111, 128
Òyótúnjí African Village, 30

Padmanabhan, Lakshmi, 96
Pan-Africanism, 11
performance art, 4, 7, 29, 36–59, 139
performance studies, 8, 57
performing objecthood, 40–41
"Performing Stillness" (Campt), 56–57
Phyllis (Saro-Wiwa), 89
Philogynoir, (blogger), 109
Physics of Blackness (Wright), 30, 106, 107
play: and African/black diasporic girlhood,
105, 107; as defiance, 114; as homemaking,
105–6; liberatory potential of, 143; Okorafor on, 131, 132; as term, 109
pleasure: and African interiority, 86; vs. Christianity, 72; and cinema, 90; and intimacy,
86; for queer subjects, 114–15; scholarship
on, 65; in Saro-Wiwa, 89; and sexual
agency, 79, 143; and the West, 78

www.ingramcontent.com/pod-product-compliance
Lightning Source LLC
Chambersburg PA
CBHW041109280526
45792CB00011B/2357